FEMINISM IN WOMEN'S DETECTIVE FICTION

Names such as Sherlock Holmes, Hercule Poirot, and Sam Spade are perhaps better known than the names of the authors who created these characters. The character of the woman detective has also had worldwide appeal; yet, with the exception of Agatha Christie's Miss Marple, the names of female detectives and their authors have only recently gained wide attention through the popularity of authors such as Marcia Muller, Sue Grafton, and Sara Paretsky.

The essays in this collection grapple with a wide range of issues important to the female sleuth – the most important, perhaps, being the oft-heard challenge as to her suitability for the job. Not surprisingly, gender issues are the main focus of all the essays; indeed, in detective novels with a woman protagonist, these issues are often right at the surface.

Some of the papers see the female sleuth as an important force in popular fiction, but many also question the notion that the woman detective is a positive model for feminists. They argue that fictional female sleuths have lost the 'otherness' that a feminine approach to the genre should encourage. Collectively, the essays also reveal the differences between British and American perspectives on the woman detective.

GLENWOOD IRONS is associate professor and chair of the Department of Applied Language Studies, Brock University. He is editor of *Gender, Language, and Myth: Essays on Popular Narrative*.

Feminism in Women's Detective Fiction

edited by
GLENWOOD IRONS

UNIVERSITY OF TORONTO PRESS
Toronto Buffalo London

© University of Toronto Press Incorporated 1995
Toronto Buffalo London
Printed in Canada

ISBN 0-8020-0519-5 (cloth)
ISBN 0-8020-6954-1 (paper)

∞

Printed on acid-free paper

Canadian Cataloguing in Publication Data

Main entry under title:

Feminism in women's detective fiction

ISBN 0-8020-0519-5 (bound) ISBN 0-8020-6954-1 (pbk.)

1. Detective and mystery stories, American – History
and criticism.   2. Detective and mystery stories,
English – History and criticism.   3. Detective and
mystery stories, Canadian (English) – History and
criticism.*   4. English fiction – Women authors –
History and criticism.   5. American fiction – Women
authors – History and criticism.   6. Canadian fiction
(English) – Women authors – History and criticism.*
7. Women detectives in literature.   8. Feminism in
literature.   I. Irons, Glenwood H. (Glenwood Henry),
1951– .

PN3448.D4F4 1995   823'.0872099287   C95-931432-6

University of Toronto Press acknowledges the financial assistance to its
publishing program of the Canada Council and the Ontario Arts Council.

Contents

Acknowledgments

All writing is collaborative; editing is doubly so. In the beginning, I was encouraged by Virgil Duff of the University of Toronto Press to submit my idea for this collection. When Laura Macleod took over from Virgil, I was helped by her high hopes for the project and her interest in women detectives. Suzanne Rancourt has carried the torch since Laura moved on to other pastures. Those who wrote essays specifically for this volume were punctual as hell about deadlines. For that, I am more than grateful. Those who agreed to submit previously published work have no idea how difficult it was to track them down.

I am grateful to Detective Chief Inspector Jackie Malton of Scotland Yard, who took time from ferreting out bad guys to talk to me about her career as a London detective. I'll never forget her bullet-proof vest, with 'Malton' written on the back. It sat casually on the chair back, speaking volumes about the violence it might save its owner from.

Closer to home, I wish to thank my colleagues in the Department of Applied Language Studies at Brock University. Both Hedy McGarrell and John Sivell were more than fair in letting me use departmental facilities to finish this anthology.

Most important of all is the help from family members. Mom and Dad went above and beyond the call of parents back when I was in grade ten, forcing me to stay in high school 'for my own good'; my mom now seems to be my greatest fan in my literary pursuits. Without knowing it, my two young daughters, Nastasia and Juliette, often reminded me of the importance of 'flexing' entrenched notions of gender and genre. Last and most important is Leslie. To my best friend, my wife, and my colleague, you are my love, my life, my inspiration.

'The Detective Heroine and the Death of Her Hero: Dorothy Sayers to P.D. James' by SueEllen Campbell first appeared in *Modern Fiction Studies* 29:3 (Autumn 1983). *Modern Fiction Studies*, copyright 1983, by Purdue Research Foundation, West Lafayette, Indiana 47907. Reprinted with permission.

'Nancy Drew: The Once and Future Prom Queen' by Bobbie Ann Mason first appeared in *The Girl Sleuth* (Feminist Press, 1975). Reprinted by permission of International Creative Management, Inc. Copyright 1975 by Bobbie Ann Mason.

'Feminist Murder: Amanda Cross Reinvents Womanhood' by Jeanne Addison Roberts first appeared in *Clues: A Journal of Detection* 6:1 (1985). It is reprinted by permission and has been heavily updated in this volume.

Introduction:

Gender and Genre: The Woman Detective and the Diffusion of Generic Voices

In Oliver Stone's recent movie *Natural Born Killers*, the lyrics to a Leonard Cohen song reveal a rather grim sentiment about the world in which the protagonists live: 'I've seen the future, brother. It is murder.' Stone's movie is a satire on the violence of American society on the edge of the twenty-first century, and, as a satire, it shows a great deal of violence – the central characters manage to murder fifty-two people in less than ninety minutes. The goriness serves a satiric function, but it also goes along with what seems to be a reality: that the mass appetite for media-exploited murder shows little likelihood of abating.[1]

So popular is the presentation of death by mayhem that fictional accounts of killers often take a back seat to real-life presentations of accused murderers like the recently accused Paul Teale in Canada and O.J. Simpson in the United States. But, from the grisly Manson killings in the 1960s to the similarly grisly slayings of O.J. Simpson's wife and companion in the 1990s, the most common ingredient of the real as well as the fictional murder is the victim. Though both Manson and the killer of Simpson's estranged wife hacked apart others, the media emphasis was and continues to be on Sharon Tate and Nicole Simpson. Without doubt, the majority of the murder victims who meet their deaths between the covers of mystery fiction paperbacks, in mystery movies on the small and large screens, and even in the daily news are women.

Detectives in fiction have always seemed to be a response to what most generations feel is the uncontrollable murder and mayhem that surrounds them. Some have achieved international reputations: names like Sherlock Holmes, Hercule Poirot, and Sam Spade are still better known than those of the authors who created them. The *woman* detective has also enjoyed worldwide appeal; yet, with the exception of Agatha Christie's Miss Marple or Carolyn Keene's Nancy Drew, the names of female detectives have only recently gained wide recognition. Sharon McCone, Kinsey Millhone, and V.I. Warshawski are now well known. Their authors, Marcia Muller, Sue Grafton, and Sara Paretsky, among many other writers, have created a virtual explosion of interest in detective fiction in which a woman is the protagonist. And if, as Jean Swanson and Dean James suggest in *By a Woman's Hand*, mysteries written by women are 'reflective of the societies in which the authors themselves were raised' (13),[2] then it is clear that the fictional women detectives reflect a diversity of voices in response to the victimization of women as presented in the popular media.

Though women sleuths emerged as a separate and popular force along with their nineteenth-century male counterparts, the woman detective has seldom been perceived as having an individuality equivalent to that of the male detective. Miss Marple operates in the rigidly convention-bound, quasi-Victorian world of early twentieth-century England, and operates apart from the local police because her age and sex make her unsuitable for the job of discovering murderers. It is only recently, due in large part to the American public television series featuring her, that Miss Marple has begun to come out of the shadow cast by Poirot, Christie's 'other' detective – and the series itself emphasizes the Victorian quaintness of Jane Marple's village life far more than it focuses on her individuality. Conversely, popular male detectives like Holmes and Poirot, who also frequently operate outside the conventions of their societies, have been lionized for doing so. In fact, while they are seen to be meddlers early on in their series, they are eventually sought out by the police – a privilege rarely granted Miss Marple – because their individual quirks are respected by the largely male police forces in their fictions.

The male detectives, endlessly replayed in late-night movie versions by Humphrey Bogart and Robert Mitchum, are obviously connected to the male heroes of Westerns like Shane, and they operate outside the civilized world around them because of a mythic necessity which encourages the male hero in that lonely direction. Frequent encounters with Spade-like loners in movies, Holmes-like intellectuals on public television, and Hammer-like dicks on commercial television could create the sense that the detective *as urban hero* is, almost by definition, male. The popular representation of this male detective-as-urban-cowboy who stands out against the rottenness of society has a powerful appeal. From the outside, he restores order in the midst of the murderous chaos to which we are exposed in the popular media – all the while enjoying the undying attention of the various women whose paths he crosses – and carries the work of the Western hero into twentieth-century urban centres, stopping only long enough to change his stetson for a fedora and his Colt '45 for a Smith and Wesson.

But, essentially since the late 1960s, it can no longer be argued that such an image is the only one informing the popular imagination with respect to the detective. Even those who ignore the plethora of women detectives in popular novels cannot help but recognize the change in TV and cinema depictions of this character. In the visual media, from the mystery-writing Jessica Fletcher of *Murder She Wrote* through the central character of Disney's *V.I. Warshawski: The Movie*[3] to the gritty and powerfully realistic Jane Tennison of *Prime Suspect*, film audiences and television watchers have been witness to a wide range of women sleuths who are offering an alternative to the Holmeses, Spades, and Hammers. In fact, though Fletcher herself is loosely based on Agatha Christie's Miss Marple – *Murder She Wrote* being an obvious play on Christie's *Murder She Said* – it is clear that we no longer identify Agatha Christie's Jane Marple – the archetypal 'spinster' detective – as the *only* woman sleuth.

It will come as no surprise, then, that the publication brochure for a recently published critical dictionary entitled *Great Women Mystery Writers: Classic to Contemporary*, edited by Kathleen Gregory Klein, includes more than a hundred British and American women who have 'created, molded and altered' the detective fiction genre since the nineteenth century.[4] The advent of such a volume illustrates that women have been writing and successfully marketing detective fiction since the inception of the genre. The general ignorance of the sheer volume of detective fiction written by women may have been caused by the omnipresence of Christie, which convinced many (including academic course creators) that the 'spinster sleuth' in the person of Miss Marple was the quintessential representation of female ratiocination. Or such an ignorance may simply have suited the purposes of those who prefer to overlook the contribution women have made to both popular and literary fiction. And as if to counter any claim that women detectives and their women creators were simply an aberration of the 1970s and 1980s, Swanson and James list more than two hundred women mystery writers whose books are now in print.

Compared with reserved spinster sleuths like the early Anna Katharine Green's Amelia Butterworth and Agatha Christie's Jane Marple, the women detectives created in the past thirty years are outgoing, aggressive, and self-sufficient sleuths who have transcended generic codes and virtually rewritten the archetypal male detective from a female perspective. Beginning with Marcia Muller's Sharon McCone in the United States and P.D. James's Cordelia Gray in the United Kingdom, ratiocinative 'sisters' have created indelible changes in the genre – changes which the mass market has considerably exploited. Perhaps it was the death of Dame Agatha, considered by many the greatest mystery writer of all time, which opened the way for different types of woman detective. Some argue that the rise of the woman detective is related to the virtually coincidental publication of Betty Friedan's *The Feminine Mystique* in 1963. Others claim that the increase in reports of abuse against women is reflected in the rise of women detectives who are more than capable of defending themselves. Whatever the reason, female authors who have chosen to create a woman (and sometimes a feminist) detective have altered the male prototype to the extent that their detectives speak from a woman's perspective and address the problems which women face in modern society. In Miss Marple's Victorian sitting-room, the problems faced by women rarely entered the discussion. Miss Marple did not actually confront the problem that gave rise to the murder, she only solved the murder itself – and to that extent the murder and the murderer were essentially removed. But the newer women detectives are responding to the world in which women now live by 'detecting with a vengeance,' to borrow Tania Modleski's phrase in *Loving with a Vengeance,* and the 'mass-produced fantasies' of women speak to our collective nightmares over the marauding, bullying, Rambo-style heroes of the mass media in the 1970s and 1980s.[5] The obvious subversion of order which the woman detective represents perhaps addresses our collective desire to undercut or at least question the institutions which inform our daily lives.

This collection is a step in the rather long journey to correct a hypocrisy in the popular imagination: The male detective operates outside society's conventions because that is what male heroes do; the woman detective should not be a detective *because* she operates outside society's conventions, and that is not what female heroes should do. It is also a way of illustrating that the woman sleuth is rooted in a modern mythology which has little connection to 'accepted' literary detectives such as Dashiell Hammett's or Raymond Chandler's. The woman detective comes down to us through many voices, some of which are themselves hardly monolithic in their approach to the woman detective. This anthology illustrates the range of those voices.

Sara Paretsky, both a critical and a popular success, has perhaps the strongest voice among the new women mystery writers in the United States. Her eight novels to date exemplify some of the important shifts that occur in the hard-boiled formula when the protagonist is a woman detective. One of the shifts is manifest in the way Paretsky handles the well-known tough-guy archetype of Hammett and Chandler. Hammett and Chandler reworked the Western hero – a cynical loner whose code of behaviour frequently sets him outside the community, apart from both the outlaws and the authorities – into a tough-guy detective whose code of behaviour sets him outside the law.[6] Like an individualistic cowboy, the classic detective hero rides off into the sunset, ends up in L.A. or Chicago, buys a fedora and a trench coat, and imports the anti-Christian, anti-family, and anti-feminine morality of the Old West into the big city. Paretsky's V.I. Warshawski, by contrast, often enjoys the help of (mostly female) friends, through a consensus she builds as the novels evolve. Like other new women detectives, she has virtually *no* female antecedents – certainly not Miss Marple, for example. And rather than importing old codes and old moralities, authors like Paretsky develop new ones, based only loosely on those of the tough guys of the 1930s and 1940s.

Klein's *Great Women Mystery Writers* notes: 'Paretsky's strong interest in women's issues colors her life and her fiction. She serves as a long time member of the Chicago National Abortion Rights Action League (and has been its director since 1987). Moreover, Paretsky founded Sisters in Crime, a group dedicated to furthering "the careers of women in the mystery field and to correcting imbalances in the treatment of women"' (266). The shifts which new women writers have effected in the detective genre are generally apparent in what Klein describes as the most important theme of Paretsky's novels – the evolving and different power relations between the sexes. This is clearly not a concern of the classic detective story, since the sexual role of the male protagonist in the diegesis, or narrative, is rarely questioned. Klein completes the biographical note on Paretsky by describing how, in all her stories, the rejection of the loner model is apparent; the author chooses what 'Carol Gilligan calls an "ethic of responsibility" ... common among women ... where [the detective's] role is not simply to discover the murderer and restore order, but also to work with and develop a sense of community with and among many of the characters.'

Most critics of the genre have concluded that Warshawski is certainly not a loner and does not subscribe to the rigid loner codes which allow most male hard-boiled dicks their oft-violent, amoral *étranger* status. Though, like many of the male hardboiled detectives, she has no immediate family members to whom she can turn – both her parents have died before the series begins – Warshawski is part of a community of (mostly) women, which she has worked hard to join. Her doctor is a close friend who often acts as mother, sister, and general confidante to the detective. Her closest neighbour is a retired blue-collar worker who frequently cooks her meals, does errands, and, occasionally, reprimands her. She frequently befriends and works with female relatives and friends. For example, in *Indemnity Only*, Warshawski takes in and works with a young girl whose father has been murdered early in the story.

Another way in which Paretsky's generic voice diffuses the male-oriented hard-boiled detective formula can be found in the confrontation between the detective and the criminal. While the traditional gangsters and other criminals meet the male detective on a more or less equal (gender) footing, Paretsky's criminals – frequently upstanding members of society who represent its worst abuses of power – meet a detective whose very presence challenges their male belief that Warshawski's is an unsuitable job for a woman. The advantage often goes to Warshawski, as most of these men underestimate her *because* she is a woman, a mistake for which they inevitably pay dearly. But Warshawski's professionalism is even challenged by friends. She is frequently admonished by a male police lieutenant who was close to her father and who believes that Warshawski should leave the criminals to the police; not only is her job unsuitable, but it puts at risk the lives of the men who are forced to intervene.

Even the violence in Paretsky's novels is different from that of the early tough-guy works. We suffer through attacks and recuperation, but, unlike those of the classic private eye, many of Warshawski's injuries are long term, and memories of them often carry over into the next novel. There is no sense that she is superhuman, nor is there a sense that we can forget the fact that all her attackers are men. One might even argue (as Modleski has about Harlequin Romances) that the violence in woman detective novels is a kind of *inoculation* against the intimidation, beatings, and related violence to which women are often subjected.[7] That might explain why the violence in the novels has not proved troublesome for most readers. Moreover, as Janice Radway's *Reading the Romance* has recently illustrated, women readers of genre fiction are used to the intellectual superiority of women characters in the mass media.[8] Perhaps the woman detective offers those same readers an

opportunity to enjoy a woman protagonist who, though physically overcome by her male attackers at least once in the story, ends up physically
and intellectually superior to them.

In just about every way, Paretsky and many of her American 'sisters in
crime' have created women detectives who have forever altered the
tough-guy formula. From Marcia Muller to Barbara Wilson, they have
given us a viable alternative to the cynical loner of another age; the new
woman detective speaks from the fiction to the real world we inhabit.
She reaches out and illustrates to her readers the possibility implied in
support given and received through a community. One might even say
she detects 'with a vengeance' in order to focus on the 'evolving and different power relations between the sexes.'

While American mystery fiction by women is best known for its variations on what has often been called the 'tough-girl novel,' the British
mystery genre as created by women is inclined towards a more genteel
detective, one who seems relatively bound by convention. Taking her
cue from men of means and intellect, Miss Marple operates outside the
police force but well within the general social rules of her era. In some
popular instances, the British male detective is a gentleman of wealth –
Sherlock Holmes, Lord Peter Wimsey, and Hercule Poirot, for example;
in others, he is an employee of Scotland Yard or one of its many subsid-
iaries in the counties – Inspectors Adam Dalgliesh, Morse, and Reg Wexford, for example – and is often accompanied by another detective of
lesser rank. Until recently, leaving aside the model of convention presented by Christie, women detectives have been rare in U.K. mystery fiction, and they have usually acted as the 'other' detective accompanying
the male hero. P.D. James, for example, has a woman detective accom-
pany Dalgliesh in *A Taste for Death*. In that case, the woman detective,
accosted by the killer and used as a hostage, very nearly becomes a victim herself. She has little to do with solving the case and seems more
useful in advancing the plot – indeed, in allowing Dalgliesh to come to
her rescue. James abandoned a female partner for Dalgliesh in the subsequent novel, *Devices and Desires*, where the Commander works essentially on his own and once again attempts a daring rescue of a woman at
the end.

Although women detectives have been slow to arrive in popular narrative fiction in the United Kingdom, there are a few notable recent
examples. P.D. James's Cordelia Gray, Liza Cody's Anna Lee, Gillian
Slovo's Kate Baeier, and Sara Dunant's Hannah Wolfe come immediately
to mind. These are, however, varied voices. Cordelia Gray appears in

only two of James's detective novels, and as Nicola Nixon illustrates in this collection, she is in effect stripped of her individual resonance in the second, *The Skull beneath the Skin*. Anna Lee is perhaps the closest to an American-style tough-girl or hard-boiled character, a detective whom Cody imbues with a social conscience and a lively wit. Similarly, Slovo's and Dunant's detectives are socially conscientious, linguistically sophisticated London operatives.

In addition, the 'generic voice' of women detectives has been made known in the recent Granada television series *Prime Suspect*, *Prime Suspect 2*, and *Prime Suspect 3*, shown on the American PBS *Mystery!* program. Though perhaps only a beginning, the *Prime Suspect* series, featuring Jane Tennison, suggests a trend towards the depiction of women detectives on British television. The trend has been continued with the production of *Headcase*, written by Liza Cody, featuring Anna Lee in the unhappy role of one uncovering an incestuous father-daughter relationship. Both series examine the real-life difficulties faced by women detectives in solving crimes and in gaining the respect of their co-workers and clients. Jane Tennison is a detective chief inspector who succeeds in taking over a murder case from a male colleague, and Anna Lee is a former policewoman who has yet to prove herself to the security firm which now employs her. Both women have excellent records in their police work, yet their abilities are automatically suspect because they are women.

Prime Suspect and *Headcase* are very much a recent direction for British mystery fiction. *Prime Suspect* is based on the rise of a real woman detective, DCI Jackie Malton, who is in fact one of only four women ever to make the rank of detective chief inspector, the highest possible rank for a detective at Scotland Yard.[9] Jane Tennison, the character modelled on DCI Malton, encounters the tremendous difficulties faced by a professional woman detective who has reached the top rank in her field. Her supervisor spends many hours trying to have her removed from the sensational murder case which she has succeeded in taking over from a male colleague who died of a heart attack in the early stages of the investigation. She works hard to gain the respect and cooperation of her colleagues, who at first are suspicious; ultimately she is successful, and also keeps her superiors at bay and solves the case. But we are frequently reminded that Tennison must forego a great deal of what a male detective might take for granted. For example, her live-in boyfriend leaves her mid-way through the investigation because he feels she simply doesn't give enough time to their relationship. If Tennison were a male detective – say, Wexford in the Ruth Rendell series – it would simply be expected that her partner would put up with the strange demands of the detective's job.

While it may now be relatively commonplace to read about or see women detectives as protagonists in popular fiction and on television series, we should certainly not assume that the voice of female investigators is monolithic. Nor should we assume that the observers or critics are of one voice. Most of the detectives discussed in this collection are frequently reminded that the job is still considered by many an unsuitable job for a woman, and some observers of the genre seem to agree. In fact, many suggest that the job is unsuitable because of the impossibility of doing it without being co-opted by the male-gendered notion of law *and* order.

In a seminal essay anthologized in *From My Guy to Sci-Fi: Genre and Women's Writing in the Postmodern World*, Rosalind Coward and Linda Semple effectively overview the important role women have played in the creation and re-creation of the mystery genre both in the past and in the present revival of detective fiction.[10] But they also suggest that it is the diversity of the voices of women detectives which speaks so eloquently to the long list of issues important to women in modern society. The essays in this collection are an echo of those voices. And while all anthologies reflect the choices of those who edit them, this one has as its possible theme the seemingly contradictory place of women detectives in the order which they are working to restore.

The first group of papers deals essentially with the British woman detective. But it opens with Joan Warthling Roberts's essay on Amelia Butterworth because the essay offers a wide perspective on the problematic place of the earliest women detectives. While many modern readers assume that Jane Marple was the first woman detective, this essay reminds us of female sleuths who began their careers at about the same time as their male counterparts, but who faced far more resistance than they. Roberts paints a vivid picture of an early American woman sleuth who made a valiant attempt to escape the rigid nineteenth-century codes of behaviour for women, but who eventually was forced to succumb. Before Amelia Butterworth is happily married off at the end of the series, however, she has asked questions that imply the restoration of order is the restoration of ideology, and that demand an answer as to whether or not such a restoration is indeed in the interest of women. This is a question which every modern woman investigator, including DCI Malton, must ask. Certainly, Amelia Butterworth subverts the stereotypical representations of women of her era simply by investigating murders in the Gramercy Park of turn-of-the-century New York. But in the end the spinster sleuth such as Butterworth is a construct whose persistence allowed critics to ignore the contribution of women detectives to the mystery genre itself, just as society ignores the spinster for existing outside heterosexual convention.

SueEllen Campbell, in an essay first published in 1983, examines the heroines of Dorothy L. Sayers and P.D. James, two mystery writers who are often thought to be less concerned with women's issues than with general social problems. But Campbell maintains that Sayers and James have in fact 'explored many of the possibilities and problems raised' in the more recent detective fiction by women, particularly by giving thematic emphasis to women's concerns rather than simply following generic patterns. Sayers uses the relatively strong and independent Harriet Vane to explore questions of self-awareness and confidence, even though Harriet is eventually married off to Sayers's principal hero, Lord Peter Wimsey. James uses one of the first modern women detectives, Cordelia Gray in *An Unsuitable Job for a Woman,* to illustrate the many problems faced by a young woman who chooses to go it alone as a private detective. The novels which Campbell looks at are, as she puts it, an inquiry into the various premises underlying the woman hero's independence.

Nicola Nixon takes another point of view, by arguing that the Cordelia who appears in *An Unsuitable Job for a Woman* is very different from the detective of the same name who is the protagonist of James's *The Skull beneath the Skin.* Nixon points out that the 'residual Victorianism' brought about by the Thatcher government's support of 'family values' affects P.D. James to the extent that she renders her woman detective impotent in the later novel. *The Skull beneath the Skin* reconstructs Cordelia Gray with Victorian 'inflections' more reminiscent of *Shroud for a Nightingale* than of *An Unsuitable Job for a Woman.*

Although no one has yet accused those responsible for the *Prime Suspect* series of Victorianism, residual or otherwise, Sandra Tomc argues that DCI Jane Tennison is a rather qualified version of the truly triumphant woman detective. Like Clarice Starling in *The Silence of the Lambs* and Kay Scarpetta in *Postmortem,* Tomc suggests, Tennison has been co-opted by the male-centred Metropolitan Police Force, for which she works. Tomc in fact sees the woman detective as a victim whose status needs to be redressed at the beginning of the telefilm – an outsider in the male world of policing – but as having been brought inside and thus made less effective by the end. Tomc's central question is the degree to which certain new fictions which feature women at their centres – *Prime Suspect*, *The Silence of the Lambs*, and *Postmortem* – are committed to a 'positive evaluation of women's position within patriarchy.'

The last paper which deals with the British woman detective focuses on Liza Cody's Anna Lee. She is considered to be a more multidimensional version of James's Cordelia Gray, and like hers, Anna Lee's suitability is very much under scrutiny. But Liza Cody takes the question of suitability much further: the Anna Lee novels question the suitability of women detectives through a thematic concern with random and vicious violence against women. Such violence seems almost pervasive in modern society, and Anna herself is frequently the victim of male aggression in the novels. There are no quaint solutions, such as one would expect from Miss Marple or, indeed, such as one often gets from P.D. James. There is, rather, a powerful sense of injustice – to the detective and to the victims; readers are left with a vague sense that injustice rather than its opposite prevails.

The second group of papers examines the sub-genre from what one might call a modern American point of view. Rather than offering historical or diagetical exegesis, these essays focus on a specific element of the novels such as gender or language and discuss how that element subverts patriarchy and asserts feminine autonomy. An interest in the subversion of patriarchy and assertion of autonomy is implicit in many of the earlier papers, but it could be called the theme of the final papers in the collection.

It is strange that the Nancy Drew series has received very little critical attention – strange because of the number of books in the highly successful series, and strange because of the number of women who read the stories as teenagers. A discussion with the local librarian made it clear to me that the Nancy stories are still extremely popular, in spite of their rather dated approach to young women.[11] Perhaps the Nancy stories continue to attract teenage readers because, as Bobbie Ann Mason reminds us in an essay first published in 1975, although Nancy is everything that a girl 'free, white, and sixteen' should be – concerned about poise, clothes, and being queen of the prom – she also threatens the masculinity of the men she meets. A proto-feminist figure, Nancy Drew ultimately rejects the role expected of the teenage woman to become, for Mason at least, 'an inspiring symbol of freedom.' Perhaps Nancy is less an aberration than a thinly disguised 'final girl' who always overcomes her male adversaries, and who lends credibility to the possibility of woman as hero.[12]

Amanda Cross may be the first woman mystery writer who consciously set out to create a feminist detective. As Jeanne Addison Roberts makes clear in a paper that first appeared in 1985, the effort has as much to do with Cross's being the alter ego of the recently retired Columbia University professor of English Carolyn G. Heilbrun as it has to do with anything else in the writer's life. The academic theories of Heilbrun the critic are clearly an attempt to 'reinvent' woman; perhaps the adventures of the academic detective Kate Fansler are an attempt to 'reimagine' woman in a genre which in the popular imagination has been the domain of a large number of male heroes. And, like many of the women writers discussed in this collection, Cross's murder mysteries explore significant issues in the society in which the detective moves, not the least of which – given the number of female victims in her novels – is violence against women. Roberts here adds to her original essay a discussion of Heilbrun's most recent works featuring her detective hero, who has aged considerably, and who spends time contemplating the problems of women over fifty – once again the academic theories of the critic are linked with the fictional world created by the author.

Susan J. Leonardi investigates the similarities between the detective project and the academic project, in other words, the connection between detection and academic critique. Ultimately, though, her primary interest is in the discussion of gender which the new woman detective necessitates. Citing examples of fictional women detectives who have forced students to 'rethink their decisions and assumptions,' Leonardi likens women detectives to good professors, reminding us that both 'question rather than repair normality.'

Sue Grafton has more often than not been likened to male hard-boiled writers. Her detective, Kinsey Millhone, is a tough-gal wisecracker who might be at home in the world of Sam Spade and Philip Marlowe. Scott Christianson suggests that Millhone also challenges and subverts patriarchy, asserting feminine autonomy through talking dirty, tough, and smart. Language provides Kinsey Millhone with a way to 'sort through' her experience, and, by reduction, provides women readers with a way to sort through their experience as women in a tough, dirty world. Talking tough, dirty, and smart becomes a way of exercising power – feminine power, which asserts autonomy through voice – of playing 'hardball with the boys.'

While Amanda Cross and Nancy Drew are rather genteel versions of the American woman detective, the 'school' of hard-boiled, tough girls operate, like their tough-guy counterparts, out of the trunks of their cars

and by the wit and wisdom of the streets. And while she asserts autonomy through voice, the 'female dick,' as Ann Wilson calls her, also
causes a crisis in the normal role for male characters. This crisis is essentially characterized by a diminution of the sexual power over women
which the male character in the genre normally enjoys – to the extent
that he frequently becomes a simple bystander in the events unfolding
for the female gumshoe.

   As if by extension of the crisis, Rebecca A. Pope convincingly argues
for the presence of an 'approach/withdraw orientation towards lesbianism' in Sara Paretsky's V.I. Warshawski novels. A great deal has been
written about these novels, and the character and her author have been
treated flatteringly by critics and readers alike. It seems that the brand of
feminism which Paretsky has chosen for her protagonist is more than
palatable to the mass audience. But while the main concern of Paretsky's
books is the general breakdown of familial order – the books set family
and community relationships against power structures like the church,
the state, and the corporate world – there is an element of the V.I. Warshawski character which many readers may feel uncomfortable accept-
ing. As Pope makes clear, female friendship in Paretsky's novels –
specifically in the relationship between V.I. and her closest friend, Dr
Lotty Herschel – is 'explicitly opposed to patriarchal values.' Such
female friendship constitutes an essential difference between Warshawski and the earlier, male hard-boiled detectives.

   Kathleen Gregory Klein is perhaps the pre-eminent North American
critic of women mystery writers. Although her essay is on one of the
least known of the mystery writers discussed here, her subject – the
'deconstruction' of the construction of Woman through the insertion of a
lesbian protagonist into popular fiction – provides the most fitting end
to this collection. Taking as her model the three Barbara Wilson novels
featuring Pam Nilsen, Klein notes that detective fiction has become the
'quintessential lesbian genre,' and that Barbara Wilson has created the
quintessential subversion of the male orientation of the genre with her
lesbian detective. The narrative is structured so that 'nobody controls the
centre of discourse; discourse becomes discourses.'

   In *The Pursuit of Crime: Art and Ideology in Detective Fiction*, Dennis Porter examines male detective fiction as a 'reflector and valuable barome-
ter' of the society in which it is created (1). It is the project of this volume
to illustrate that the woman detective is a 'reflector and valuable barom-
eter' of a culture which is finally, in its popular fiction, beginning to
grapple with the aspirations and the constraints of women who, to para-

phrase Klein on Barbara Wilson, unwrite the existing idea of Woman in order to challenge it and make a brand-new game.

Glenwood Irons
September 1994

NOTES

The idea for this collection occurred when I attended the 1990 MLA convention in Chicago. Not known for its interest in popular narrative, the MLA convention for that year listed three sessions on detective fiction. That in itself was surprising; however, the fact that each of the sessions was on detective fiction written by women was virtually unprecedented. One of the sessions even employed Sara Paretsky as respondent to a number of papers written on Paretsky's hard-boiled creation, V.I. Warshawski. It seemed that the popular detective genre might make an important inroad into the humanities curriculum through the MLA, discussions of detective fiction no longer relegated to small, regional conferences or considered solely the province of the Popular Culture Association.

   Alas, the detective fiction sessions at the MLA were not to become an annual part of this formidable organization's convention. In subsequent years, there have been virtually no sessions devoted to detective fiction.

   My personal experience of detectives doesn't end with my interest in fictional sleuthing. I have *worked* with detectives on a number of police cases, ranging from an analysis of false advertising by a car dealership to analyses of poison-pen letters directed at the police. In one case, I undertook a voice analysis in a homicide, the killers having made the Hollywood-style *faux pas* of calling the police to talk about the murder. The killers were eventually apprehended and are now doing time.

1 Given the enormous popularity of the movie – look for *Return of the Natural Born Killers* to double the body count – there is more than a residual fear that the movie might *encourage* murder.
2 See Swanson and James for a clear and concise synopsis of the major works of more than two hundred women authors of mystery fiction. The authors' respective backgrounds as librarian and murder bookstore owner give them the inside track on the inclusion of many mystery writers.
3 Though the Disney production (over which Paretsky had no control) was

universally panned by the critics – it simply avoids many of the important feminist issues raised in the novels – it has been a steady success at the video stores. In fact, many women in my own course in pop fiction found the Warshawski character as played by Kathleen Turner 'easy to identify with.'

4 The book includes 117 entries which briefly describe the life and work of women mystery writers from Catharine Aird to Margaret Yorke.

5 Modleski's book is subtitled *Mass-Produced Fantasies for Women*. In a chapter entitled 'The Disappearing Act: Harlequin Romances' (35–58), she illustrates that while there is much to be said against it, the generally dismissed formula romance novel might actually empower women readers since it offers them a man who, in the end at least, has bent to the will of the central female character.

6 This reworking is certainly implied in Cawelti.

7 According to Modleski (35–58), this *inoculation* in the romance novel takes place as the central female character is exposed to the various ruses of the male and of the other female character in the romance triangle.

8 In her introduction, Radway notes that women enjoy reading romance novels because of the superior intelligence and, of course, power of the women in that genre.

9 During an interview I recently conducted with DCI Malton, she very modestly described the hideous, sexist stereotyping which she faced from her male counterparts. For example, even though she had spent twenty-two years as a stake-out cop – on 'the flying squad,' as it is called – risking her life alongside male 'squad' members, she was accused of having 'slept her way to DCI.' While DCI Malton has gained the respect of many male colleagues on the police force, it is clear that a great deal of work still needs to be done if women are to be respected for their ability.

10 Coward and Semple note the belief on the part of many readers that most of the important work in the mystery genre has been produced by men. As well, they make clear that the work done by women in the genre frequently explores concerns specific to women, concerns relating to violence and conflict that originates with men.

11 The librarian at the St Catharines Public Library – the central library in St Catharines, Ontario, a city of about 130,000 – reports that the Nancy Drew series is one of the most asked-for among teenage girls.

12 Carol Clover's seminal essay 'Her Body, Himself' makes a very strong argument for the power of what she calls the 'final girl' – the heroine who chases down the slashers, slice and dicers, and killers in lowbrow horror movies. Clover argues that this heroine of lowbrow killer movies actually percolates up into highbrow horror movies like *Sleeping with the Enemy* to become a female hero who can *credibly* fend off a male attacker.

WORKS CITED

Cawelti, John. *The Six-Gun Mystique*. Bowling Green, Ohio: Bowling Green University Popular Press, 1984.

Clover, Carol. 'Her Body, Himself: Gender in the Slasher Film.' *Gender, Language, and Myth: Essays on Popular Narrative*. Ed. Glenwood Irons. Toronto: University of Toronto Press, 1992. 252–302.

Coward, Rosalind, and Linda Semple. 'Tracking Down the Past: Women and Detective Fiction.' *From My Guy to Sci-Fi: Genre and Women's Writing in the Postmodern World*. Ed. Helen Carr. London: Pandora, 1989. 39–57.

Klein, Kathleen Gregory, ed. *Great Women Mystery Writers: Classic to Contemporary*. Westport, Conn.: Greenwood, 1994.

Modleski, Tania. *Loving with a Vengeance: Mass-Produced Fantasies for Women*. London: Methuen, 1984.

Porter, Dennis. *The Pursuit of Crime: Art and Ideology in Detective Fiction*. New Haven: Yale University Press, 1981.

Radway, Janice. *Reading the Romance*. Chapel Hill: University of North Carolina Press, 1984.

Swanson, Jean, and Dean James. *By a Woman's Hand: A Guide to Mystery Fiction by Women*. New York: Berkley, 1994.

FEMINISM IN WOMEN'S DETECTIVE FICTION

1. Amelia Butterworth: The Spinster Detective

Joan Warthling Roberts

In 1931, H. Douglas Thomson was able to say with assurance in his pioneering study of detective fiction, *Masters of Mystery*, that 'there is no future for the detective story. I mean that it is in no process of natural growth; its development has already been perfected' (274).

This kind of certainty about life and art may have been easier in the 1930s; it sounds strangely quaint in the 1990s. Few critics today would look at the many forms of detective/mystery fiction and claim that the development of the form has been perfected. 'Form' has become 'forms,' and we are cynical enough to know that perfection no longer exists. We have come to appreciate the mystery story as a microcosm of the culture and mores of the times it portrays: it changes as they change.

The essentially conservative nature of the genre (determined by its structural drive towards the restoration of order) has been frequently noted. Many commentators assume ideology to be absent or out of place in a work of fiction which is seen to be an entertainment consisting of the solution of a puzzle – as if the 'restoration of order' did not necessarily imply a certain kind of order, an ideology, which permeates the characters' lives and the narrative action. Transparent to those who accept it, it is nonetheless burdensome to those who try to work through it or against it. This problem relates to the female detective, in that changed gender roles and altered concepts of womanliness and manliness militate against the fundamental ideology that controls the detective narrative – or that *controlled* the detective narrative as imagined and put in place by male writers in the nineteenth century.

The simple presence of a female detective in fiction does not necessarily disturb the narrative order, paradoxical as that may seem. From the earliest days of the genre – the 1860s, until about 1900 – women appeared as detectives in fiction, but without disturbing the underlying ideology. They were classifiable and thus easily dismissible as fantasies or freaks, as competent human beings (that is, as honorary males), as domestic but desperate, or as lower-class contemptibles. To take an example from another genre, the fantasy/adventure mode encouraged breathtaking exploits for a female, just as it would for a male adventurer, with only an occasional nod to reality. By using a female as a pawn, the writer raised the temperature and the possibility for terror. Sensational fiction has played on that strategy for many years. These females were fantasies or freaks or pawns and thus did not disturb the essentially heroic male ideology.

Quite another story emerges when the female detective is a competent human being and in control of her situation. Two of the earliest female detectives, appearing in 1864, Mrs Gladden (created by Andrew Forrester) and Mrs Paschal (created by W. Stephens Hayward), are, as Kathleen Gregory Klein notes, essentially honorary males (Klein 18–30). They work seamlessly in a male world, occasionally adding the *frisson* of a woman in peril. 'These characters are anomalies; the novels apparently led to neither imitators nor followers. Even Forrester and Hayward abandoned their innovations after the first attempt' (Klein 29). These two women detectives are clearly honorary males.

Other early women detectives were set in a pattern which justified their unusual activity and evoked sympathy for them as women, even as it kept them within the family, firmly subsidiary to the males in their lives: they were domestic but desperate – they detected only to clear the names of a husband, lover, father, or brother who had been unjustly accused or convicted of a crime. The happy ending included a reunion with the beloved male, and *finis* written to detecting as a career or even as an activity. Also safely within her family boundaries was the woman who detected only as an assistant to a relative. Harry Rockwood's Clarice Dyke (1883) detected to assist her husband, and Mrs George Corbett's Anne Cory helped her father (1890s). Hagar Stanley, created by Fergus Hume (1899), was a spirited gypsy woman who rebelled against an arranged marriage, was given work as assistant in a pawnshop, where she solved problems that arose in the shop, and then met and married her true love. She may have been a gypsy to begin with, but her more permanent role in life as married domestic is clear by the end of the novel. Dora Myrl, conceived by M. McDonnell Bodkin in 1900, worked at detection in an adversarial relationship with a male sleuth, Paul Beck, until a 1909 novel called *The Capture of Paul Beck*.

One could make a case for Myrl's and Stanley's stories as progress – the young woman who took a job only to fill time until marriage and who chose her own mate was more emancipated than her sisters who stayed meekly at home and accepted an arranged marriage. The heroine in *Dorcas Dene Detective* was a female sleuth motivated by love of her husband. She appeared in 1897 in a collection of short stories in which the author, George R. Sims, made it clear that she was 'a brave and yet womanly woman, who, when her artist husband was stricken with blindness ... had undertaken a profession which was not only a harassing and exhausting one for a woman, but by no means free from grave personal risks' (Craig and Cadogan 23). Nevertheless, these female detectives were firmly declared to be 'womanly' because they were acting in or (almost always) ended up in the domestic context constituted by marriage to a male hero.

If the female sleuth chose this work because she needed to support herself, then her despised trade forced her to give up any position of respect in society, as did Loveday Brooke in Catherine Louisa Pirkis's stories. As Michele Slung comments in her introduction to the collection (Pirkis ix), the traditional occupations open to a woman who had to support herself were determined by her class. They ranged from that of the self-effacing, long-suffering governess, through those of the milliner, the shop girl, the laundress, and the charwoman, to those on the lowest level, those of the artists' model and the prostitute. Some of these occupations could be respectable. Like the prostitute, however, the female investigator, by her association with criminals and the lower orders, was 'cut off sharply from her former associates and her position in society' (Pirkis 2). Loveday Brooke, working as a female detective, was consigned to the category of artists' model and prostitute – lower-class contemptibles. A reader of middle-class pretension can dismiss her easily; Loveday deals only with servants and colleagues – not with anyone of quality – and she would be unable to function without the authority and position of her employer, 'Ebenezer Dyer, chief of the well-known detective agency in Lynch Court, Fleet Street' (Pirkis 1). In her stories, the fiction diverges far from reality as Loveday, a model of submission, outdoes and out-thinks her male colleagues without causing a snarl or a murmur. She is deferential to every male, offers her own ideas but does not press them, dresses and speaks unobtrusively. Her fictional persona is that of a complete facilitator in a modest woman's dress. Miss Brooke has no needs, wants, likes, or dislikes of her own.

At about the turn of the century, a stronger woman detective appeared on the mystery fiction scene, imagined by a female author. Not surprisingly, the American Amelia Butterworth, who first appeared in 1897 in Anna Katharine Green's *That Affair Next Door*, was different from many of the earlier women detectives. In the first place, she did not fit into any of the dismissible categories. Green was writing for the genteel middle class, her books published by Putnam's, a major house. Her sleuth came from a very different world than that inhabited by earlier women detectives. Miss Butterworth was unmarried, as was Loveday Brooke, but was from a distinguished colonial family. More important, she was financially secure and could do what she wanted in life, an independent woman who answered to no one but herself. Amelia Butterworth became involved in crime and detection because she was endlessly curious about her fellow human beings. Miss Butterworth was the first spinster sleuth.

The terms 'spinster' and 'sleuth' are both amusing, though they are also more than slightly mocking, and literary in their application. Together, they are a contradiction in terms that sets us up for comedy: a sharp-nosed old bag of bones, officious and self-righteous, pokes into people's business – preferably with a knitting-needle – giving us the same opportunity for snide laughter that the official male detective in the story enjoys at the woman detective's expense. Miss Butterworth set a pattern for the unmarried 'elderly busybody' (Craig and Cadogan 11) who has become a standard character, reinforced as a pop culture icon by the continued popularity of Jane Marple and by many others such as Hildegarde Withers, Maud Silver, and Miss Seeton. Michele Slung confirms that 'Green deserves credit for introducing the concept of the nosy-spinster sleuth, personified by Miss Amelia Butterworth' (134). However, in Green's Amelia Butterworth novels, a more complex geometry aims the vectors of ridicule at the age and gender perceptions of society; the spinster sleuth functions as a collector and reflector of society's obtuseness. She may be pushed aside and ignored, usually by the official male detective, but she solves the mystery at hand. She is a woman whom in the end it pays to respect.

Further, Anna Katharine Green fits Marty S. Knepper's definition of a feminist writer: 'a writer, female or male, who shows as a norm and not as freaks, women capable of intelligence, moral responsibility, competence, and independent action; who presents women as central characters, as the heroes, not just as "the other sex" (in other words, not just as the wives, mothers, sisters, daughters, lovers, and servants of men) ... who explores female consciousness and female perceptions of the world; who creates women who have psychological complexity and transcend the sexist stereotypes that are as old as Eve and as limited as the lives of most fictional spinster schoolmarms' (399).

Many male writers characterize females subconsciously and instantly into sexually interesting and not. The spinster is of course a woman who is not sexually interesting (if she were she would have married), is sexually inexperienced, and is dried up and frustrated. The spinster is thus ignored, being of no value to those active in society; she is a busybody, poking and prying into the affairs of others because she has no affairs of her own. She is expected to be censorious and moralistic, dryly envious of the lives of her neighbours. A spinster solving a mystery is on its face paradoxical. She has no experience with passion or power, so how could she ever understand the murky motives behind a passionate crime like murder?

About thirty years before Christie's Miss Marple in mechlin lace and black brocade, Amelia Butterworth was detecting in New York City in the upper-middle-class neighbourhood of Gramercy Park. She came to the assistance of the New York City police detective Ebenezer Gryce, himself a hero whom Green had created in 1878, nine years before Sherlock Holmes appeared in print. Gryce in fact was one of the earliest series detectives. He had appeared in eight novels before Miss Butterworth joined him in *That Affair Next Door* (1897). She herself became a series detective, reappearing in *Lost Man's Lane* (1898) and *The Circular Study* (1900).

In *That Affair Next Door*, on a New York City street of gaslight and horse-drawn vehicles, she comes to life: 'I am not an inquisitive woman, but when, in the middle of a certain warm night in September, I heard a carriage draw up at the adjoining house and stop, I could not resist the temptation of leaving my bed and taking a peep through the curtains of my window' (1). Amelia is the narrator in two of her three adventures, so we read of *her* reasons and rationalizations, while we piece together brief glimpses to form a picture of how she appears to the observer.

Sweetwater, a young detective who works with Ebenezer Gryce, gives us one glimpse: 'I perceived a very stately, almost severe lady descend the stairs. She was dressed for the street, and spoke to me with quite an air of command' (*Circular Study* 60). He finds her living in 'a fine brownstone front in one of our most aristocratic and retired quarters' (57) when he follows the trail of some black spangles that had been pulled away from her dress and found on the floor at the scene of a murder. Sweetwater comments on those spangles, 'They were portions of a very rich trimming which has only lately come into vogue, and which is so expensive that it is worn chiefly by women of means' (55). Despite this evidence of expensive fashion, we find that Amelia is not a slave to it: she wears an old-fashioned miniature of her father at her throat in defiance of then-current vogue (81). Perhaps as an echo of those same ties to her past and her family, Amelia is disciplined and decorous: 'Miss Butterworth had been brought up in a very strict school of manners. When she sat, she sat still; when she moved, she moved quickly, firmly, but with no unnecessary disturbance. Fidgets were unknown to her' (83).

Miss Butterworth is wealthy, fashionable, and disciplined, the product of a strict upbringing and enjoying ties to a good family. Amelia is openly independent – perhaps appropriate for an American woman. When she is sleuthing, she makes lists, orders her questions, and collects evidence. 'Having, as I thought, noticed some few facts from which conclusions might be drawn, I amused myself with jotting them down on the back of a disputed grocer's bill I happened to find in my pocket' (*That Affair* 24).

Amelia Butterworth reveals her thoughts to the reader but does not voice them out loud. 'But not being a man, and not judging it wise to irritate the one representative of that sex then present, I made no remark' (*That Affair* 11) – this, in relation to the stolid policeman first on the scene. When she and the police officer see the corpse for the first time, Amelia reacts similarly: 'At a sight so dreadful, and, in spite of all my apprehensions, so unexpected, I felt a sensation of sickness which might in another moment have ended in my fainting, if I had not realized that it would never do for me to lose my wits in the presence of a man who had none too many of his own' (7). When she is pushed aside, she says nothing: 'Such rudeness was uncalled for; but considering myself too important a witness to show feeling, I swallowed my indignation and proceeded with all my native dignity to the front door' (13). In speaking to Ebenezer Gryce, a police inspector of some note, she quails not a whit, but thinks: 'Would I have congratulated myself quite so much upon my fancied superiority if I had known he was the man who had managed the Leavenworth case? Perhaps I would; for though I have had no adventures, I feel capable of them' (21–2). This inner rumination about feeling capable of adventure has been noted by many commentators on

Green; it is revealing of Butterworth's touching sense of self-worth and her freedom from false modesty.

Amelia demonstrates her acumen many times before the story is told, and Ebenezer Gryce acknowledges it handsomely to Miss Butterworth and to his superiors when she reports her findings: 'But when I mentioned the lighted laundry and my discoveries there, his admiration burst all bounds, and he cried out, seemingly to the rose in the carpet, really to the Inspector: "See now! we ought to have thought of that laundry ourselves; but we didn't, none of us did; we were too credulous and too easily satisfied with the evidence given at the inquest. Well, I'm seventy-seven, but I'm not too old to learn. Proceed, Miss Butterworth." Gryce concluded, "a fine stroke! ... I could not have done better myself"' (*That Affair* 317).

Ebenezer Gryce has been happy to acknowledge the worth of his spinster sleuth. Still, the recognition comes from patriarchal authority and thereby clearly illustrates that women needed the backing of men in order to be effective in their societies. Nevertheless, when a respectable woman was expected to keep her skirts well away from any knowledge of evil, Amelia Butterworth was a trail-blazer. She was an insider, in class and in wealth, an unmarried female of impeccable upbringing – and she kept doing unconventional, improper things. She stepped outside, out of woman's domain, into the world, for no good reason. There was no husband or brother to save from infamy, there were no invalids or children to feed. She did not even have to work to support herself.

Green shows her awareness of the import of Butterworth's actions from the first line in *That Affair Next Door*. It is midnight, and Miss Butterworth leaves her bed, parts the curtains, and peers through her bedroom window. What she sees then, and later that same night, leads her to run out into the street the next morning to hail a passing policeman. Her interior monologue of excuses and justification for these unladylike acts creates a very human bridge between the passivity and decorum of the perfect lady, fashioned by her upbringing, and the vital curiosity and independent spirit of the new woman.

Amelia Butterworth (and later Miss Marple) emerges out of supposed sexual innocence, dependency, and passivity (all societally imposed) into activity – and in spheres where activity is not encouraged. She has not let herself sink into the pietistic, sentimental trivialities that were considered to be the proper level of emotional life for a woman of refinement. Yet most definitions of feminism make for a cranky fit in the case of Butterworth because she is able to work in the world of the capitalist, bourgeois, patriarchal, class- and wealth-dominated societal structures. She is effective by virtue of her own canniness, and of the recognition and implementation of her work by male authority figures, but this is not still another boring case of *What Every Woman Knows*. Butterworth does not work only within the sacred circle of the family. And even though she tries not to enrage any representative of the establishment who might be on the scene, she never retreats, except strategically, and never gives up when she knows she is on to something.

Amelia is not dismissible as fantasy adventurer or freak, she is not simply an honorary male, she is not domestic and desperate, and she is not a lower-class contemptible. For these reasons, Amelia Butterworth represents a step forward towards the new woman detective. What makes her interesting to the twentieth-century reader are her finicky, prying, and inquisitive qualities as a detective. She has lived long enough to have learned a great deal about human nature. She is acutely aware of 'what people will think,' but she is never so restricted by the weight of convention that she will let it stand in the way of her doing the detective work which needs to be done.

If not feminist, then perhaps Amelia might be called 'proto-feminist,' active and psychologically complex beyond the bounds of sexism, agism, or frozen respectability. The stereotype of spinster that was work-able in nineteenth- and early twentieth-century detective fiction no longer holds for the 1990s. Notwithstanding the popularity on PBS of Jane Hickson's Miss Marple, the spinster sleuth is a literary artefact whose time has come and gone. Sleuthing, as a woman's work in American fiction, has been brought in from the margin to a more central position by Marcia Muller, Sue Grafton, Sara Paretsky, and others, where it is now called investigation.

Nevertheless, Amelia Butterworth was an undoubtedly independent, psychologically complex women who had formed her own views of the world and acted on them. When Anna Katharine Green developed the effective, well-rounded, and admirable Amelia Butterworth, she paved the way for the new female detectives – the Fanslers, Grays, Millhones, and Warshawskis – of today and tomorrow.

WORKS CITED

Ball, John, ed. *The Mystery Story.* New York: Penguin, 1978.

Christie, Agatha. *Agatha Christie: An Autobiography.* New York: Dodd Mead, 1977.

– *The Clocks.* New York: Pocket Books, 1965.

– *The Tuesday Club Murders.* New York: Dell, 1982.

– *A Pocket Full of Rye.* New York: Berkley, 1991.

Craig, Patricia, and Mary Cadogan. *The Lady Investigates: Women Detectives and Spies in Fiction.* New York: St Martin's, 1981.

Gill, Gillian. *Agatha Christie: The Woman and Her Mysteries.* New York: Free Press, 1990.

Green, Anna Katharine. *The Circular Study.* New York: McClure Phillips, 1900.

– *That Affair Next Door.* New York: Putnam's, 1897.

Klein, Kathleen Gregory. *The Woman Detective: Gender and Genre.* Urbana and Chicago: University of Illinois Press, 1988.

Knepper, Marty S. 'Agatha Christie: Feminist?' *Armchair Detective* 16.4 (Winter 1983): 399.

Peterson, Audrey. *Victorian Masters of Mystery: From Wilkie Collins to Conan Doyle.* New York: Frederick Ungar, 1984.

Pirkis, Catherine Louisa. *The Experiences of Loveday Brooke, Lady Detective.* New York: Dover, 1986.

Queen, Ellery, ed. *The Female of the Species: The Great Women Detectives and Criminals.* Boston: Little Brown, 1943.

– *101 Years' Entertainment: The Great Detective Stories, 1841–1941.* Boston: Little, Brown, 1941.

Slung, Michele. 'Women in Detective Fiction.' In Ball 125–40.

Steinbrunner, Chris, and Otto Penzler. *Encyclopedia of Mystery and Detection.* New York: McGraw Hill, 1976.

Thomson, H. Douglas. *Masters of Mystery: A Study of the Detective Story.* 1931. New York: Dover, 1978.

Winn, Dilys, ed. *Murderess Ink: The Better Half of the Mystery.* New York: Workman, 1979.

Wynne, Nancy Blue. *An Agatha Christie Chronology.* New York: Ace, 1976.

2. The Detective Heroine and the Death of Her Hero: Dorothy Sayers to P.D. James

SueEllen Campbell

The beautiful finality with which the curtain rings down on the close of the investigation conceals from the reader that no part of the 'problem' has been 'solved' *except that part which was presented in problematic terms.*

Dorothy L. Sayers[1]

Despite the traditional strength of women as writers of detective fiction, detective heroines have until recently been remarkably rare. At one time, the only clear category for women in the genre was the 'little old lady' best exemplified by Agatha Christie's Miss Jane Marple. Young or middle-aged heroines – characters for whom questions of sexuality, romance, or marriage might be expected to arise – were very rare. Among major writers, Dorothy Sayers and P.D. James were thus conspicuous as early creators of such characters. In a series of books closely related both by Sayers' direct influence on James and by a shared complex of thematic concerns, these two women have explored many of the possibilities and problems raised by later protagonists of detective fiction who are young and female.

For Sayers, the exploration begins inconspicuously with *Strong Poison*, culminates in *Gaudy Night*, and closes with *Busman's Honeymoon*; for James it opens with *An Unsuitable Job for a Woman*, culminates in *Innocent Blood*, and then closes (at least for the present) with *The Skull Beneath the Skin*.[2] The central three of these books – *Gaudy Night, An Unsuitable Job for a Woman*, and *Innocent Blood* – are particularly interesting for several reasons. For one thing, all three swerve from the usual male detective story formulas: both *Gaudy Night* and *An Unsuitable Job* focus at least as much on character and theme as they do on crimes (*Gaudy Night* is notable for having no murder), and *Innocent Blood* is not really a detective story at all, although it uses many of the genre's features. It seems likely that this generic shift is at least partly a response to the presence of a heroine – a figure for whom there is no established formula and who consequently forces both characters and plots out of their usual molds. Harriet Vane, Sayers' heroine, suggests as much when she finds her own detective novel becoming distorted because she is trying to make its characters more realistic (although in this case the difficult character is male).

What distinguishes these books most emphatically from standard detective fiction is their thematic richness. Both Sayers and James are concerned with such issues as women's roles, the importance of work, the destructive power of love, and the complex relationships between men and women, parents and children. More than just a set of variations on shared themes, though, these novels reveal a pattern of gradually redefined and partially resolved problems. Each can be seen as an attempt to solve some of the problems created by the previous novel – issues that have been left unexamined or solutions which are unsatisfactory. In turn, each opens new difficulties. Such a pattern is particularly clear in two issues central to the development of a female detective: first, the age of each heroine and the quality of her independence; and second, the fate of the hero – both as the male protagonist and as the heroine's romantic interest. It is these two issues I wish to explore here; the first briefly, the second at more length.

THE HEROINE

Gaudy Night's Harriet Vane is about thirty-two years old, and her worldly independence is well established. She lives alone and makes a successful living writing detective stories. But, paradoxically it is only as her emotional self-assurance develops during the novel that she decides to marry her friend and suitor (and the hero of Sayers' other mysteries), Peter Wimsey. Sayers gradually reveals two sides of Harriet's independence: she is strong enough that she does not need to depend on anyone else, but she also fears that she is too weak to survive any emotional dependence. As she tells a friend, 'if I once gave way to Peter, I should go up like straw.'[3] In an essay about writing this book, Sayers explained how she saw *Gaudy Night* as answering a prob-

lem created by *Strong Poison*, where she had introduced Harriet, intend-
ing at the time to 'marry Peter off.' By the end of that book, however,
she had found that she 'could find no form of words in which [Har-
riet] could accept him without loss of self-respect.' In *Gaudy Night*,
then, she needed to break the impasse between her two characters: 'At
all costs, some device must be found for putting Harriet back on a footing of equality with her lover.'[4]

For Sayers' heroine, the decision to marry is identical with the discovery or development of her self-respect. But if such an identification is to
be made in good faith, of course, the heroine must already have acquired
considerable self-awareness and confidence. In *An Unsuitable Job for a
Woman*, James seems to ask through her heroine, Cordelia Gray, how a
young woman first develops the assurance that she can do her own
work and make her own happiness – the assurance that Sayers simply
assumes for Harriet. Cordelia is twenty-two; she lives alone and earns
her own living. As she investigates the death of a Cambridge student,
Mark Callender, she displays what seems to be remarkable confidence
that she can succeed as a detective – and succeed entirely on her own.
But her self-sufficiency is also a defense. Lacking Harriet's experience
with a career, she fears that personal relationships might ruin her as a
detective, so she avoids romance and resists the efforts of Mark's friends
to draw her out of her solitude into friendship.[5] This heroine is independent because she guards herself so carefully against emotional involvements. Cordelia's problem is more basic than Harriet's: she must
develop a sure sense of her own abilities.

In *Innocent Blood*, James defines the situation in terms more basic still
as she tips the balance between the positive and negative sides of the
heroine's independence even further. Philippa Palfrey has just turned
eighteen. She is about to enter Cambridge and leaves her adoptive home
to spend the summer getting to know her biological mother, who has
just finished serving time in prison for child-murder. Philippa is almost
defiantly independent, and, not surprisingly, her self-assurance is brittle.
Unlike Harriet and Cordelia, she does not live by herself, and she does
not really earn her own living. To a considerable degree, her self-sufficiency is simply adolescent defiance of her adoptive parents' control,
joined with what even she recognizes as a deeply ingrained emotional
coldness, an inability to give or accept love. The youngest and least
mature of these three heroines, she is trying in the most obvious way –
by tracking down her biological mother – to find out who she is. Before
she can be concerned with the self-respect she might find in marriage or

a career, Philippa must first learn some very fundamental things about herself.

All of these novels, then, feature a young woman of determined self-sufficiency. In turn each examines this independence, moving backward through younger heroines to ask more basic questions: how can a woman maintain her intellectual and emotional self-respect and also marry? How can she develop self-confidence through a career? How can she find her own identity as an adult? As the problems are gradually redefined, the terms are balanced differently. Thus Harriet is an orphan but makes very little of it; Cordelia is an orphan but displaces most of her feelings about her absent parents into deciphering the convoluted relationships between Mark Callender and his unloving father, his dead 'official' mother, and his unrecognized biological mother; Philippa has three living parents – two adoptive, one biological – but is obsessed with blood ties. And conversely, each novel pays less attention to the issue of a woman's work: *Gaudy Night* focuses on it; *An Unsuitable Job for a Woman* emphasizes it in its title but does not actually treat it as a problem; *Innocent Blood* practically ignores the whole matter. Read in reverse order, these books could almost tell the story of one woman's growth from adolescence to maturity. Read in the order of their writing, they are an inquiry into the premises underlying the heroine's independence.

HER HERO

Of the three heroines, only Harriet Vane has a proper hero – Lord Peter Wimsey, who is rich, amusing, sensitive, and intelligent. Harriet and Peter have known each other since he rescued her from the gallows (as Sayers says, 'in the conventional Perseus manner' [*GN* 211]) by discovering who had really murdered her lover, Philip Boyes. During the following five years, he has regularly proposed marriage to her, and she has steadily refused him, believing that 'to him she was, of course, only the creature of his making and the mirror of his own magnanimity' (p. 253). During her investigations at Oxford, though, she gradually comes to see that she loves him and to understand why he loves her. The course of their love affair is one of the main strands of the novel: little by little, Harriet and Peter reshape their friendship to include romance, and the novel ends in an embrace that signals their engagement.

But this traditional romantic framework matters less in the novel than the care with which Harriet and Peter develop a balanced relationship. Harriet tends to define problems as oppositions, and at the beginning of the novel she believes that those 'people who are cursed with both hearts and brains' have 'got to choose,' that compromise between a career and marriage can't work (p. 67). She sees Peter also as a force opposite to her. But as their relationship deepens and she learns more about him she begins to look at him differently. When he comes to Oxford to help her, she waits for him thinking, 'For good or evil, she had called in something explosive from the outside world to break up the ordered tranquillity of the place ... she had sided with London against Oxford and with the world against the cloister. But when he entered, she knew that the image had been a false one. He came into the quiet room as though he belonged there, and had never belonged to any other place' (p. 286). Symbolically, she discovers that their academic gowns are the same size: they share a belief in 'intellectual integrity as the one great permanent value in an emotionally unstable world.' As Sayers says, Harriet is Peter's 'complement' (*GN* 213, 219).

The novel represents their final union as 'counterpoint' rather than 'harmony,' as 'The repose of very delicate balance' (pp. 468, 460). As Harriet learns to replace the necessity of choice or the failure of compromise with a careful equilibrium, she can finally agree to marriage without fearing the loss of her independence. This kind of relationship is particularly necessary for her in part because it so clearly reverses the pattern of her earlier affair with Philip Boyes. In a sense, Philip is an absent and negative hero figure: the images Harriet retains from 'that hot unhappy year when she had tried to believe that there was happiness in surrender' (p. 428) are a constant, if largely unspoken, background for Peter's virtues, Harriet's self-knowledge, and the maturity of their alliance.

To a large degree, then, *Gaudy Night* succeeds in solving the imbalances between Harriet and Peter that stemmed from *Strong Poison*. Yet despite all the apparent strength of the novel's portrait of their relationship, in a few ways Sayers still gives her hero more power than her heroine. Even though Harriet has gathered almost all the necessary evidence before Peter arrives in Oxford, he solves the mystery. She cannot free herself from her emotional prejudices long enough to see the truth; he can, though he too has an emotional stake in the solution. (Sayers explains, 'I had Peter, seeing the truth from the start and perfectly conscious that he had only to leave her under her misapprehension to establish his emotional ascendency over her' [*GN* 215].) Despite the novel's explicit endorsement of the intellectual independence and ability of women, in other words, Sayers still allows the one man involved to have the final authority. She is not entirely blind to the inconsistency this involves: confronting the room full of academic women who have just listened to Peter tell them what he has discovered, the culprit, Annie Wilson, spits out, 'You can't do anything for yourselves. Even you, you silly old hags – you had to get a man to do your work for you' (p. 456).

There is a similar undercurrent of imbalance in Harriet and Peter's personal relationship – one that Sayers does not seem to have seen as problematic. In 'Gaudy Night' she writes, 'She must come to him as a free agent, if she came at all, and must realize that she was independent of him before she could *bring him her dependence as a willing gift*' (p. 216, emphasis mine). When Harriet says, 'It would be quite a relief to be ridden over rough-shod for a change,' Miss de Vine answers, 'He will never do that. That's *his* weakness. He'll never make up your mind for you. ... You needn't be afraid of losing your independence; he will always force it back on you' (p. 460). And at the end of the novel, Harriet says to Peter, 'I owe you my self-respect' (p. 465). In a novel that so clearly sees marriage as the union of two equally independent people, and whose heroine is surely responsible for her own self-respect, such statements are disturbing slips back into the kinds of traditional thinking Peter and Harriet have both been learning to surmount.[6]

In *An Unsuitable Job for a Woman*, James responds to these undercurrents and, in effect, solves the problems raised by *Gaudy Night*'s 'love interest' by leaving her heroine without a hero. Instead she splits the hero into two characters, each filling one of Peter's two main functions – one an authority figure and one a lover.

Like Sayers, James already had a well-developed male detective character whom she allows to appear in this book, even though Cordelia Gray is herself a detective. But James pushes her Chief Superintendent Adam Dalgliesh far into the background of *An Unsuitable Job for a Woman*: he appears in person only for a few pages at the very end of the book, and then only after Cordelia has solved the mystery. These two have only brief contact with each other, and so there is never any potential for an intimate relationship like Harriet and Peter's. Instead, they are antagonists. Dalgliesh confronts Cordelia in an effort to make her tell him how Sir Ronald Callender really died; she musters all her will power to keep from telling him anything, and succeeds.

But if Dalgliesh does not seem to be in a position of any real authority in this book, he still exercises considerable indirect control over Cordelia. For one thing, she learned all she knows about being a detective from her late partner Bernie Pryde, and Bernie had learned what he knew from Dalgliesh, whom he had worked under at Scotland Yard. Consequently, she goes through her investigations remembering what Bernie had told her his 'Super' always said, and at crucial moments (as when she makes Sir Ronald's murder look like suicide) she acts according to Dalgliesh's advice. Throughout the novel, then, Dalgliesh is present as a sort of transcendental authority. Furthermore, although at the end of the novel Cordelia does refuse to cooperate with him, he is nevertheless in a position of power over her. He summons her to *his* office to be interrogated; and, more important, he already knows – but does not tell her that he knows – most of the information she is keeping hidden and simply refrains from pushing the official investigation any further.[7] If she does not answer his questions directly, she surely confirms his suspicions when she bursts into 'dramatic and uncontrollable crying' at the news that Miss Leaming is dead, the news that makes her secrets safe. His relationship with her at this point is almost fatherly: he hands her a handkerchief and a glass of water and tries to comfort her. And later, when he is praising her to the Assistant Commissioner, he calls her a 'child' up to 'mischief' and credits much of her success to Bernie's (and thus his own) influence. Indirectly but unmistakably, Dalgliesh continues Peter Wimsey's role as the authority figure.[8] So James does not entirely succeed in removing male authority from this novel.

The fate of the hero as lover in *An Unsuitable Job for a Woman* is similarly ambivalent. Cordelia never develops a close relationship with a man; she deliberately turns away from the young men she meets and chooses to focus her energies on her job. Nevertheless, she does discover a romantic hero in Mark Callender, the young man whose death she is investigating. James very clearly develops a kind of love relationship between these two. Following one of Dalgliesh's precepts, Cordelia believes that she must come to know the dead person if she wants to discover why he died. So she moves into Mark's house, and as she learns more about him, she slowly becomes intimately involved with him. Early in the novel she wonders, 'Was she, Cordelia, in danger of becoming sentimentally obsessed with the dead boy?' (p. 72). And it does not take her long to recognize that 'She had identified with him, with his solitariness, his self-sufficiency, his alienation from his father, his lonely childhood. She had even – most dangerous presumption of all – come to see herself as his avenger' (p. 118). The way she takes over his belongings makes the implications of their relationship clear. Rather than put his things away to make room for hers, she spreads her sleeping bag out on top of his and puts her toothbrush next to his in his glass. She lives with him as if they were lovers.

Most important, Cordelia begins to wear Mark's clothes – clothes that help her at crucial moments as Mark himself might have helped her if he were alive. On the day when she discovers how he died, she puts on the leather belt that he had been hanged by:

She felt no repugnance as the leather tightened against her. It was impossible to believe that anything he had ever touched or owned could frighten or distress her. The strength and heaviness of the leather so close to her skin was even obscurely comforting and reassuring, as if the belt were a talisman. (p. 195)

Later the same day, when she is thrown into a well to drown, she saves herself by hanging from a ladder with the same belt.[9] And after she has escaped this danger she covers herself with one of the many thick and intricate sweaters Miss Leaming, Mark's real mother, had knit for him. The sweater warms her and protects her from harm as she is engulfed by all the violence her discoveries release. By hiding the bloody cuts on her the sweater helps keep her secrets – and Mark's – from the police.

Increasingly as well, Cordelia acts for Mark's sake more than for her own. She suppresses Sir Ronald's murder to protect Mark, even though by doing so she endangers herself:

She didn't really care if Elizabeth Leaming went to prison; she did care if Mark's mother went to prison. She cared, too, that the truth of his death should never be known ... Ronald Callender had desecrated his body after death; had planned to make him an object, at worst of contempt, at best of pity. She had set her face against Ronald Callender. (p. 237)

She does, in effect, avenge his death. Cordelia does more for Mark, sacrifices more for him, than she would for anyone alive. In his way, he does as much for her – not just because his clothing protects her but because in learning about his life and death, she learns her own strengths. And she learns from him about love – that it is not always destructive, that it takes many different forms. When she begins the case, she isn't sure 'what the word means' (p. 111); when she ends it, she cries out 'in passionate protest' to Sir Ronald, 'But what is the use of making the world more beautiful if the people who live in it can't love one another?' (p. 226). If it were not for the one fact that Mark is dead, all these things would make Cordelia's relationship with him every bit as much a love affair as Harriet's is with Peter.

In one way, then, James solves the problem *Gaudy Night* raises. She wants her heroine to be independent of men, and so she structures this novel so that neither Dalgliesh nor Mark Callender can preempt Cordelia as Peter does Harriet. Because James's romantic hero is dead, Cordelia will never have to say to him, 'I owe you my self-respect.' And no one could describe her as 'bringing her dependence as a willing gift.' But of course this independence of Cordelia's is double-edged, and not only because she shapes her actions to Mark's needs far more than she acknowledges. The hero's absence also signals her hidden insecurity, her fear of the responsibilities that loving a living man would entail. 'Thinking of her father and Bernie, Cordelia said: "Perhaps it's only when people are dead that we can safely show how much we cared about them. We know that it's too late then for them to do anything about it"' (p. 191). Only if the man she loves is dead can she keep her independence and love at the same time. Thus James leaves her heroine in an uncomfortable middle ground. She displaces the hero's functions just enough to make both Dalgliesh and Mark unable to love and to help Cordelia – neither can be her 'complement' – but not enough to free her entirely from their control.

James moves even further away from the traditional hero in *Innocent Blood*. In this novel, the kind of authority which both Harriet and Cordelia meet on at least potentially equal terms is replaced almost entirely by the authority of a father figure, and the hero's romantic function is supplanted by purely sexual attraction. These two functions meet in some of James's men, but when they do, the result is a kind of negative image of a hero. Rather than provide Philippa Palfrey with one man like Peter Wimsey or a pair like Adam Dalgliesh and Mark Callender, James here fragments, displaces, and inverts the hero's functions to create a series of male figures who are largely conspicuous for their failures.[10]

Philippa has one lover of her own age, Gabriel Lomas, who in some ways suggests the romantic hero: 'He was high on her list of objects of use and beauty which she planned to take with her to Cambridge. Having the rich and amusing Honourable Gabriel Lomas in tow would do her absolutely no harm with her contemporaries at King's' (p. 41). (Compare Sayers: Harriet 'had the rich and amusing Lord Peter Wimsey at her feet, to marry him if she chose' [p. 9].) But these two neither love nor really even like each other. Nor is there a significant sexual bond between them. Philippa remembers, 'On this bed she and Gabriel had groped and twined in that first unsuccessful attempt at making love. The phrase struck her as ridiculous. Whatever they had been making together, it hadn't been love' (p. 40). Gabriel is bisexual, and Philippa taunts him about his failure with her; by the end of the book, in petty retaliation, he betrays her and her mother to the press. Nevertheless, their sexual relationship is by far the most normal in the novel. All of Philippa's other potential lovers are primarily father figures, and their relationships with her range from near-incest to the suggestions of child-rape and perhaps even necrophilia.

The first of these men, her biological father Martin Ducton, has been dead for ten years. Philippa can't remember him at all; like Harriet's Philip Boyes and Cordelia's Mark, he is important because of his absence. He died in prison, convicted of raping a child who was much the same age as Philippa. There is never any direct evidence that he had also molested his own daughter, but the possibility persists throughout the novel as a very faint undercurrent. Philippa had been sent away to be raised by foster parents, supposedly because her mother abused her; we know, though, that Mary Ducton had known about her husband's sexual desire for children even before Julie Scase's rape, so there is an unspoken suggestion that Philippa's mother had given her up either in response to some incestuous episode or to prevent one. A second similarly indirect hint appears in one story Philippa makes up about her past: 'My uncle looked after me when I was a kid, after my dad died. He and my aunt were particular. That's why I ran away. That and my uncle trying to get into bed with me' (p. 175). When she says this, she can't remember anything that happened to her before she was eight, and she has not yet heard that she had been an abused child; James seems to be suggesting that this imagined scenario might approach the forgotten truth. What is most significant here is that these suggestions parallel the way Philippa relates to the novel's other father figures – her adoptive father Maurice Palfrey and Norman Scase, the raped and murdered child's father.

In one sense, Scase is the hero of *Innocent Blood* insofar as much of the novel focuses on his painstaking efforts to track down and to murder Mary Ducton, who had murdered his daughter. As the novel progresses, Scase develops an involved symbolic relationship with Mary and Philippa that amounts to his taking Martin Ducton's place in their nuclear family. When he first sees Mary directly, Martin feels, 'It was impossible to believe that she could be here within yards of him, yet not be struck by the shock waves from that moment of recognition. Surely not even love could so cry out for a response' (p. 127). And later, he thinks, 'He was bound to them by hate; he was bound to them, too, by envy. ... So might he have walked and smiled and been companionable with his daughter' (p. 228). More important, his first response to Philippa combines the fatherly with the sexual:

She was, he judged, some two to three years younger than Julie would have been. Julie was dead, she was alive .... He took in every detail as she passed .... The sheen of the corduroy curving over her inner thighs, the front zip which emphasized the flatness of the stomach and pointed to the gentle swelling mound beneath it, had evoked in him as she passed a small kindling of sexuality, so long dormant that the gentle disturbance released for a brief moment all the forgotten uncertainties and half-shameful excitements of adolescence. (p. 13)

For Scase, in a way, Philippa is both absent daughter and possible lover. Appropriately, the young woman he marries at the end of the novel is a kind of double for her: her name is Violet – Philippa's given name is Rose – and she was blinded at the same age Philippa lost her memory and her real parents.

Philippa, too, sees Scase sexually. When they finally meet in the room where her mother lies dead, she holds his head while he is sick in a response more erotic – and more tender – than any other we see from her: 'She supported him into the kitchen and held his head ... surprised that she could touch him without revulsion, could be so aware of the curiously silken texture of his hair, sliding over the hard skull. It seemed to her that her hand experienced simultaneously every single hair and the soft moving mass' (p. 293). (Compare Sayers' descriptions of the moments when Harriet first recognizes her love for Peter: Harriet 'noticed, with a curious little prick of anxiety, how the clear light picked out the angles of the skull on jaw and temple' [p. 235]; and 'now she saw details, magnified as it were by some glass in her own mind. The flat setting and fine scroll-word of the ear, and the height of the skull above it. The glitter of close-cropped hair where the neck-muscles lifted to meet the head ...' [p. 247].) At the same moment, Philippa looks around her at 'the teapot and two cups on the round papier mâché tray; the glistening pellets of coffee beans in their glass jar,' and she thinks 'how erotically beautiful they were' (p. 293). In her way, she does come to care for him. As Cordelia does for Mark, Philippa lies to the police to protect Scase. And the novel's last sentences suggest that she has learned from him something about loving:

If it is only through learning to love that we find identity, then he had found his. She hoped one day to find hers. She wished him well. And perhaps to be able to wish him well with all that she could recognize of her unpractised heart, to say a short, untutored prayer for him and his Violet, was in itself a small accession of grace. (p. 311)

Yet despite such signs that the symbolic love affair between these two has helped them both, their relationship remains at bottom a perverse one. Its resemblance to incest is obvious, and the structural parallel between Scase and Martin Ducton suggests the violence of rape. Even more disturbing is the murderous sexual violence revealed in one of Scase's dreams. 'One night he even had a confused nightmare in which it was the girl whom he killed. She was lying on his bed at the Casablanca, naked, and the wound in her throat was bloodless but gaping, like moistly parted lips' (p. 228).[11] This implicitly necrophilic dream not only foreshadows the bloodless cut he will put into Mary Ducton's neck after she is dead; it also tells us that subconsciously he associates Philippa with both sex and violent death. Psychologically and emotionally, Philippa and Scase are far more intimate than she and Gabriel. Yet even more than Gabriel, it is clear, Scase inverts and perverts the romantic hero's functions.

The third and most straightforward of Philippa's ambiguous father/ hero figures is her adoptive father, Maurice Palfrey. Throughout the novel, she is in rebellion against his parental authority, but there is also an unspoken sexual tension between them which becomes explicit only at the end of the book. (Remember the story she makes up about her uncle wanting to 'get into bed' with her.) After Philippa has surprised Maurice in bed with one of his students, he imagines telling her 'at least a part of the truth': 'I took her from egotism, boredom, curiosity, sexual conceit, pity, perhaps even from affection. But she's only a substitute. They're all of them substitutes. When she was in my arms I was imagining that she was you' (p. 277). When Mary Ducton is dead and Philippa and Maurice go on a trip to Italy, they do actually sleep together. Afterwards, she wonders,

What ... had it meant exactly, that gentle, tender, surprisingly uncomplicated coupling, an affirmation, a curiosity satisfied, a test successfully passed, an obstacle ceremoniously moved out of the way so that they could again take up their roles of father and daughter, the excitement of incest without its legal prohibition, without any more guilt than they carried already? That single night together ... had been necessary, inevitable, but it was no longer important. (p. 310)

To Philippa, it seems, this sexual encounter is as insignificant as the one with Gabriel; to a reader it may well seem a gratuitous, last-minute gesture toward Freud. But in light of what we have seen about Martin Ducton and Norman Scase, it is clear that the importance of this merging of father and lover is not primarily in what it says about Philippa's relationship with Maurice. Instead, it is only the most explicit instance of one of the novel's major structures. By turning this father into a lover in the last pages of the novel, James pulls together all the confusion about these roles that has shaped Philippa's dealings with men. James's language here – this 'coupling' is an 'affirmation' that will allow them to 'again take up their roles of father and daughter' – suggests that Philippa may finally have satisfied her Electra desire and may consequently now be able to move on to a more normal relationship with a man. But such an affirmation remains thoroughly suspect – in the same way that Philippa's self-awareness and self-sufficiency are suspect. Like *Gaudy Night*, *Innocent Blood* ends with an embrace; yet we have only to compare the relationship between Harriet and Peter with any of Philippa's to see how far this young woman has yet to come.

In *Gaudy Night*, Dorothy Sayers explores the possibility of a relationship that is 'a balance of opposing forces,' and the one she develops in Harriet and Peter comes close to such an ideal. But the gap which remains between their solution and the ideal is the gap James questions. She wants a heroine who can stand alone with no man to 'do her work for her.' With *Innocent Blood*, she does succeed in keeping her heroine independent of a hero. But she does so only by first making her incapable of loving, and then replacing the hero with a series of inadequate and perverse substitutes. In James's novels, all human love becomes difficult and dangerous – not just the love of a woman and a man, but also the love that joins parent with child, friend with friend, stranger with stranger. There is an innocence about Sayers' books that James has lost or given up. As Peter says in *Strong Poison* when he is defending Harriet, 'Damn it, she writes detective stories and in detective stories virtue is always triumphant. They're the purest literature we have.' But both *An Unsuitable Job* and *Innocent Blood* are cloudier: Cordelia is left trying desperately to maintain a series of lies, and Philippa has only the faintest glimpse of how she might outgrow her destructive adolescent solipsism.

In all these ways, these two writers make an almost perfect illustration of Harold Bloom's vision of the anxiety of influence in its late twentieth-century form. James 'misreads' Sayers as an 'overidealizer'; she is like our other 'belated' writers, who, as they 'swerve downward in time ... deceive themselves into believing they are tougher-minded than their precursors.' But now:

There are no longer any archetypes to displace; we have been ejected from the imperial palace whence we came, and any attempt to find a substitute for it will not be a benign displacement but only another culpable trespass, neither more nor less desperate than any Oedipal return to origins. For us, creative emulation of literary tradition leads to images of inversion, incest, sado-masochistic parody ....[12]

As we move from *Gaudy Night* through *An Unsuitable Job for a Woman* to *Innocent Blood*, we see this pattern made clear in James's 'tough-minded' but negative rewriting of her precursor. Sayers' Peter Wimsey becomes James's Norman Scase; the 'very delicate balance' of Harriet's marriage becomes the incestuous violence of Philippa's literal 'return to origins.'

If this development looks like a dead end (must the heroine's independence be negative? can the problems raised by *Innocent Blood* be solved?), James's second novel which involves Cordelia Grey suggests a possibility of a way out. On the one hand, *The Skull Beneath the Skin* is a retreat: the previous two books move away from the detective genre into regular fiction, but this one uses the most formulaic of plots – a group of people, nearly all of whom have reason to murder the victim, gathered in an isolated castle. In such a conventional situation, James has given Cordelia Gray a place less problematic than the one she filled in *An Unsuitable Job*. Most of the earlier exploration of Cordelia's character has disappeared here; she is now a much flatter figure and so a less interesting one. James seems to comment on this change through her character Ivo Whittingham, a drama critic, who thinks about a production of *The Duchess of Malfi*:

Ivo had always believed that there was only one way to direct Webster: as a highly stylized drama of manners, the characters mere ritual personifications of lust, decadence, and sexual rapacity, moving in a pavane toward the inevitable orgiastic triumph of madness and death. But DeVille, half sunk in lugubrious disgust at finding himself actually directing amateurs, was obviously aiming at some semblance of realism. (p. 81)

The Skull Beneath the Skin is a step away from realism and a step toward

revenge tragedy in the form of detective fiction, and the detective heroine and her problems consequently lose their central place.

On the other hand, Cordelia has clearly gained in maturity. She is still
without romantic entanglements, yet she approaches some kind of personal communion with most of the people around her; she does not
show the fear of emotion we saw before. She is more at ease with herself
and with her independence, as the relative strength of her position at the
end of this book demonstrates. In *An Unsuitable Job* she must hide her
lies from the police; here the police are depending on her truthfulness –
'on her sanity, her honesty, her memory, her nerve' – to make their case.

Suddenly she felt inviolate. The police would have to make their own decisions.
She had already made hers, without hesitation and without a struggle. She
would tell the truth, and she would survive. Nothing could touch her. She
hitched her bag more firmly on her shoulder and moved resolutely toward the
launch. For one sunlit moment it was as if Courcy Island and all that had happened during that fateful weekend was as unconcerned with her life, her future,
her steadily beating heart, as was the blue uncaring sea. (pp. 327, 328)

In this book, James seems to have emerged – however tentatively – from
the series of questions initiated by Sayers, perhaps just because she has
stopped asking them, but perhaps as though she had pushed her inquiries back to their origins and then come out the other side into a kind of
solution. With Cordelia's new-found strength, the detective heroine and
the possibility of a hero are at last not presented in problematic terms.

NOTES

1 Dorothy L. Sayers, *The Mind of the Maker* (Westport, CT: Greenwood Press,
   1970), p. 189.
2 There is abundant evidence that James modeled *An Unsuitable Job* on *Gaudy
   Night*. As S.L. Clark has demonstrated, James's novel follows Sayers' both in
   details and in larger structures: the parallels range from their use of the same
   quotations from Donne and Bunyan to their shared thematic concerns. See
   Clark, '*Gaudy Night*'s Legacy: P.D. James' *An Unsuitable Job for a Woman*,' *The
   Sayers Review*, 4, (September 1980), 1–12.
3 Sayers, *Gaudy Night* (New York: Harper & Row, 1936), p. 459. All further references to this book will be parenthetical.
4 Sayers, '*Gaudy Night*' in *The Art of the Mystery Story: A Collection of Critical*

Essays, ed. Howard Harcraft (New York: Simon & Schuster, 1946), pp. 211, 212. Further references to this essay will be noted parenthetically as *GN*.

5 For example, at the end of a peaceful outing on the Cam with two of Mark's friends, Cordelia suddenly realizes 'how close she had come to giving up the case. She had been suborned by the beauty of the day, by sunshine, indolence, the promise of comradeship, even friendship, into forgetting why she was here. The realization horrified her.' Later that same day, she goes to a party with the same people: 'She wasn't naturally gregarious and, alienated by the last six years from her own generation, found herself intimidated by the noise, the underlying ruthlessness and the half-understood conventions of these tribal meetings.' Avoiding conversations with the men she meets at this party, she reminds herself that she has a job to do – she uses her job as self-protection. See P.D. James, *An Unsuitable Job for a Woman* (New York: Popular Library, 1972), pp. 122, 132. All further references to this book will be parenthetical.

6 In *Busman's Honeymoon*, similarly, we learn that Harriet has insisted – against Peter's wishes – on including in her marriage vows the promise to 'obey.'

7 S.L. Clark points out, 'Where Cordelia and Miss Leaming succeed, and where Superintendent Adam Dalgliesh and the Metropolitan Police have gone wrong, is with respect to these "relations"; the authorities never know the relations between Mark and his father, his father and his real and official mothers, and his real mother and his father's assistant. As long as these "relations" are obscure, Dalgliesh will be bested by Cordelia Gray and will be compelled to take her seriously, in light of what she has been able to accomplish.' See Clark, pp. 6–7. Certainly the 'relations' Cordelia understands are important to James, but it seems to me overstating the case to say Dalgliesh is 'bested' by her; rather, I think, she just manages to hold her own, motivated partly, it is clear, by her fear. She knows that 'If she were tricked, persuaded, coerced into telling him the truth, she would go to prison. She was an accessory after the fact' (p. 278).

8 In *The Skull Beneath the Skin*, James adds a hint of romance to Cordelia's remembered encounter with Dalgliesh: 'She guarded her privacy. None of her friends and no one from the agency had ever been in the flat. Adventures occurred elsewhere. She knew that if any man shared that narrow bed, for her it would mean commitment. There was only one man she ever pictured there, and he was a commander of New Scotland Yard. She knew that he, too, lived in the City; they shared the same river. But she told herself that the brief madness was over, that at a time of stress and frightening insecurity she had only been seeking her lost father. There was this to be said for a smattering of amateur psychology: It enabled one to exorcise memories which might other-

wise be embarrassing.' *The Skull Beneath the Skin* (New York: Charles Scribner's Sons, 1982), p. 48. All further references to this book will be parenthetical.

9 Mark's belt is still a 'talisman' for Cordelia in *The Skull Beneath the Skin*, where it again (though less directly) helps save her life.

10 P.D. James, *Innocent Blood* (New York: Charles Scribner's Sons, 1980), p. 41. All further references to this book will be parenthetical. This novel also fragments, displaces, and inverts the formulaic ingredients of detective fiction. For instance, instead of the usual murder, there is one murder some ten years in the past (of the child Julie Scase), a suicide (of Julie's murderer, Philippa's mother), and an attempted murder (of Philippa's mother, by Julie's father; he cuts her throat after she is dead); Philippa tells the police she has cut her mother's throat herself because she feels (justly) responsible for the suicide. Similarly, instead of a conventional detective and a murder mystery to be solved, Philippa searches for her true parents' names and whereabouts, Martin Scase stalks his daughter's murderer, and Philippa gradually discovers the truth about her early childhood.

11 The Casablanca is the hotel where Scase lives while he is tracking Mary Ducton. The passage continues, 'He turned round, the dripping knife in his hand, appalled at his mistake, to find his mother and the murderess standing together in the doorway and clutching at each other, screaming with laughter.' This is only one of many signs that Scase's hatred for Mary Ducton is a displacement of his hatred for his own mother.

12 See Harold Bloom, *The Anxiety of Influence: A Theory of Poetry* (New York: Oxford University Press, 1973), pp. 69–70; and *A Map of Misreading* (New York: Oxford University Press, 1975), p. 31.

3. Gray Areas: P.D. James's Unsuiting of Cordelia

Nicola Nixon

In 1982, after a decade of friendly but persistent badgering from her fans, critics, and interviewers, P.D. James published *The Skull Beneath the Skin*, her second Cordelia Gray novel. Her first Cordelia Gray, *An Unsuitable Job for a Woman* (1972), had received immediate approval for James's only female detective – indeed, a resounding approval that prompted the novel's nomination for an American Edgar Award, and that seemed to grow exponentially throughout the 1970s and into the 1980s, despite the continued absence of a sequel and the publication of two more Adam Dalgliesh novels. Cordelia Gray was, after all, considered an improvement over Ngaio Marsh's Agatha Troy, a departure from Christie's Miss Marple, and a worthy successor to Dorothy L. Sayers's Harriet Vane. If the detective fiction 'buffism' displayed in Dilys Winn's *Murderess Ink* (1979) is any indication, the enormously popular Cordelia Gray achieved near cult status seven years after her only appearance in James's fiction: *An Unsuitable Job for a Woman* was well placed on Winn's '10 Most Wanted' readers' opinion poll, Amanda Cross celebrated the exciting emergence of Cordelia, and Lillian de la Torre, president of the Mystery Writers of America in 1979, extolled Cordelia's virtues at length in 'Cordelia Gray: The Thinking Man's Heroine.' Even in 1981, after discussing *Innocent Blood* (1980) for a while, Diana Cooper-Clark concluded her interview with James with the familiar, nine-year-old refrain: 'Are we going to see the girl detective, Cordelia Gray, again?' (Cooper-Clark 32).

If the relentlessly repeated question about the potential reappearance of Cordelia Gray in James's fiction reminds us a bit of Woody Allen's *Stardust Memories*, in which every fan he meets testifies to liking his films, 'especially the early funny ones,' this is no accident. Allen suggests, both self-referentially and, of course, ironically, that the fans' comments conspire to diminish the importance of his 'later, serious' films. The cultlike status of Cordelia Gray throughout the 1970s, sustained despite James's publication of *The Black Tower* (1975) and *Death of an Expert Witness* (1977) – her fifth and six Dalgliesh novels – and *Innocent Blood*, might well lead us to wonder whether Cordelia's popularity had resonances of Arthur Conan Doyle's and John Le Carré's problems with the persistent popularity of Sherlock Holmes and cold war spy thrillers, respectively. But James maintained a noncommittal silence on whether or not she would comply with public demand and resurrect Cordelia Gray. And while neither Conan Doyle nor Le Carré had any success with his historical novels, James certainly had no difficulty with the popular success of her Dalgliesh novels: both *Shroud for a Nightingale* (1971) and *The Black Tower*, written immediately before and after *An Unsuitable Job for a Woman*, won Silver Dagger Awards from the British Crime Writers' Association. In fact, the contributions to both Winn's *Murder Ink* (1977) and her *Murderess Ink* indicate that the emergence of Cordelia Gray, particularly when she was deemed a successor to Harriet Vane, inspired new interest in Dalgliesh rather than detracting from him. The romancing of Harriet had, after all, transformed Lord Peter Wimsey from a one-dimensional, pretentious, and effete aristocrat into a complex hero. According to James, her fans, presumably eager to see the same scenario enacted, asked regularly about the likelihood of Cordelia Gray's and Dalgliesh's ever joining forces.

But Cordelia Gray, in *An Unsuitable Job for a Woman*, is much more than simply a foil for Dalgliesh; she is a touchstone of early seventies feminism. Her emergence in 1972, only a year after James's *Shroud for a Nightingale*, offered a provocative and timely counterpoint to the earlier novel, and the earlier novel's representation and eventual dismissal of the antiquated gender assumptions of an anachronistic, residual Victorianism. In *Shroud for a Nightingale* James gestures, quite overtly, towards the well-established metaphoric underbelly of Victorian gender assumptions – the sexual repression, the carefully contrived exterior of propriety, the completely codified and limited expectations of women – the underbelly that had become commonplace in post-Freudian reinflections of Victorianism and formed a given for critics like Michel Foucault and for feminist revisionist historians. The nurses at James's suitably named Nightingale House, particularly the middle-aged spinsters, are cultural dinosaurs, linked firmly with their nineteenth-century professional precursor. They lament the changing times, the reluctance of the young nurses-in-training to forego marriage, embrace quasi-lesbian relations with their peers, and remain dedicated to the 'calling' of nursing; they even lament the introduction of the newfangled uniforms with their meagre lace-trimmed caps instead of the 'immense triangles of muslin' that dangle, habit-like, to the waist. By the end of the novel, James has expurgated most of the anachronistic residue: the matron, Mary Taylor, has killed the murderous ward sister, Ethel Brumfett, then has committed suicide; the lesbian Hilda Rolfe has left the clinic to teach in Central Africa; and Nightingale House itself is in the process of being reduced to rubble by the demolition wrecking-ball, making way for a new and modern school. The final line of *Shroud for a Nightingale* – 'And [Nightingale House] had never been in the least suitable as a nurse training school' (323) – suggests that the novel itself signals a metaphoric final shroud for an antiquated and rather sick system, concealed for too long but in need of exposure and, finally, demolition.

With the publication of *An Unsuitable Job for a Woman* only a year later, James implies that the culturally 'suitable' job for a woman – nursing – is suitable only superficially, that the modern woman is more than capable of doing justice to the seemingly less suitable job of private detecting. Cordelia is, quite obviously, better at her job than her former partner, the consummately unlucky Bernie Pryde, had ever been. And whenever the familiar dubbing of detective work as 'unsuitable' for women surfaces, James indicates that she is signalling some deeply entrenched but highly suspect claims that women are incapable of conducting themselves professionally as well as men.

Now this formation, with its claims to equality of talent or skill, strikes a familiar note of seventies feminism, with its explicit emphasis on the achievement of equal work opportunity and equal pay for women. So too does James's suggestion that Cordelia perceives herself as part of a larger 'sisterhood.' Cordelia's eventual act of solidarity with Elizabeth Leaming – for example, her willingness to reconstruct the murder of Ronald Callender to resemble a suicide, her usefully deployed knowledge of how the proper suicide should look, and her agreement to perjure herself at the coroner's inquest, all to protect Elizabeth from a legitimate murder charge – is clearly a gender-inflected solidarity. Despite the detection focus on the dead Mark Callender, men play a secondary role in the novel, except as obstacles for resourceful women to overcome. Elizabeth gets rid of the pernicious Ronald Callender, and Cordelia manages to trump Dalgliesh when she confounds him with the very knowledge that he had attempted to instil, quite unsuccessfully, in poor Bernie Pryde. Cordelia is triumphant in the end, over a Dalgliesh who appears only in the last few pages as a worthy, but surmountable, antagonist, and who implicitly represents yet another man who wrongly underestimates Cordelia's abilities.

Industrious, resourceful, and independent, Cordelia is, in contrast to the nurses in Nightingale House, the antithesis of a Victorian heroine; and her job, while not culturally recognized as appropriate – unlike, say, nursing – is clearly quite suitable when the novel reaches its conclusion. James's title, which is heavily emphasized throughout the novel, forms an ironic commentary on residual (pre-sixties feminist) expectations of women. Cordelia in fact represents the very means by which such anti-quated and 'chauvinist' statements can be critiqued and strenuously rejected. Replacing the Nightingale nurses with Cordelia, and offering an implicit criticism of the Victorianism endemic to Nightingale House, James inflects her genteelly British female 'private eye' with the prom-ises of the ascendent 1970s women's liberation movement.

It seems hardly surprising, then, that the single, working Cordelia Gray, as a harbinger or prototype of the seventies new woman, should sustain and indeed increase in popularity throughout a decade which saw the agitation of the women's liberation movement force such crucial parliamentary legislation as Britain's Equal Pay Act of 1970 and Sex Dis-crimination Act of 1975. The question of her potential reappearance was therefore perhaps less an expression of nostalgic fondness for a particu-lar character than an anticipation of what she might become in the con-text of specific feminist achievements. Such an anticipation did, of course, assume that the feminist promise articulated in *An Unsuitable Job for a Woman* would reach fruition in another, later novel. After ten years of encouragement, James finally responded to the question of Cordelia's return, first when she told Diana Cooper-Clark in 1981 that she was 'going to do another very straightforward mystery ... with Cordelia Gray' (Cooper-Clark 32), and then the following year, when she pub-lished *The Skull beneath the Skin*. While so eagerly anticipated, however, the second Cordelia Gray novel sank like a rock, producing scarcely a ripple in reading-public opinion. And since its appearance, critics, fans, and interviewers alike have, quite conspicuously, ceased altogether to clamour for Cordelia's return.

It would be easy to assess this critical silence as a tacit recognition that James's clever and independent heroine of the seventies simply did not translate well into the sociopolitical climate of the eighties – a recognition that seventies feminism had produced far more resourceful and independent heroines in the eighties who tended to overshadow the less remarkable or at least more genteelly demure Cordelia Gray of *An Unsuitable Job for a Woman*. We need only think of Sara Paretsky's V.I. Warshawski, Sue Grafton's Kinsey Millhone, and Marcia Muller's Sharon McCone, for example, to register the trajectory James might have traced in her eighties version of Cordelia the private detective, although, granted, the gun-toting, tough girls Warshawski, Millhone, and McCone are more distinctly modelled after the American hard-boiled private dick than Cordelia ever was. But when *Newsweek* announces that V.I. Warshawski in *Blood Shot* (1988) is the 'most engaging woman in detective fiction since Dorothy Sayers's Harriet Vane,' therein bypassing the previously vaunted Cordelia Gray altogether, that clearly has more to do with the reappearance of Cordelia Gray in 1982 than with her original appearance in 1972.

Cordelia Gray's reappearance is, in fact, curious in the context of the eighties, not because she remained static for a decade and could not be resuscitated but because she is refashioned in a manner rather inconsistent with what readers might have anticipated, given her proto-feminist promise in her first incarnation. Cordelia Gray in *The Skull beneath the Skin* represents James's conscious rewriting of her original character – and of the earlier novel itself – a rewriting that offers what seems to be James's revaluation of her earlier view of Cordelia. Because James adheres so closely and deliberately to *An Unsuitable Job for a Woman* in *The Skull beneath the Skin*, in terms of both figuration and plot trajectory, her specific revision of Cordelia surfaces minutely through the particular spin James puts on her apparent rewrites of the earlier novel. In fact, James's repetitions of the earlier novel within the later seem deployed precisely to highlight various subtle adjustments to Cordelia – adjustments, I would suggest, that are designed primarily to quash readers' enthusiasm for her as a proto-feminist who, in political terms at any rate, had proven more interesting than Dalgliesh.

James's desire to transform Cordelia Gray into a figure less satisfying to her fans is signalled for the first time five years after *An Unsuitable Job for a Woman*. In Dilys Winn's *Murder Ink*, James seized the opportunity to answer all the readers who wrote 'to enquire whether my girl detective Cordelia Gray of *An Unsuitable Job for a Woman* will marry Adam Dalgliesh' ('Ought' 68). On the one hand, this request anticipates that Cordelia, like Harriet Vane, will find her appropriate completion by being relegated to the domestic sphere; on the other hand, the actual agency assumed in the question suggests that Cordelia has the prerogative to make the decision. But James's response is curious. Titled 'Ought Adam to Marry Cordelia?,' James's answer to her fans poses a question exactly opposite to theirs, inverting the power of agency from Cordelia to Adam, and rearticulating the question not as a potential future action Cordelia 'will' take but as a future action that may or may not be advisable for Adam to take.

In keeping with her oblique reference to Cordelia and primary emphasis on Dalgliesh as the real subject of the inquiry, James discusses the possible 'imprudence' of Adam's making the decision to marry Cordelia. Then she presents the figure of a fictive 'marriage guidance counsellor' who offers to the fictive Cordelia a list of the possible disadvantages of marriage to Dalgliesh:

Here we have a widower, considerably older than you, who has obviously been unable or unwilling to commit himself permanently to any woman since the death in childbed of his wife. He is a very private person, self-sufficient, uninvolved, a professional detective dedicated to his job, totally unused to the claims, emotional and domestic, which a wife and family would make on him. Admittedly, you find him sexually very attractive, but so do a number of women more experienced, more mature and even more beautiful than yourself. Are you sure you wouldn't be jealous of his past, of his job, of his essential self-sufficiency? ... And are you sure you aren't looking for a substitute for your own inadequate father? ('Ought' 69)

Emotional and domestic claims of a wife and family? Sexual attraction? Jealousy of Dalgliesh's job? Dalgliesh as father substitute? These are odd constructions, applying much more obviously to Deborah Riscoe, Dalgliesh's sometime lover who appears first in *Cover Her Face* (1962) and briefly in *A Mind to Murder* (1963) and then drops out of the picture at the end of *Unnatural Causes* (1967) because she does not like Dalgliesh's job, is jealous of the time he spends on it, and is frustrated by his inability to make up his mind to marry her. In fact, the conclusion of *An Unsuitable Job for a Woman*, in which Cordelia meets Dalgliesh briefly during his arduous interrogation of her, suggests none of the things James mentions. Cordelia's perception of Dalgliesh is quite different: 'He was old of course, over forty at least, but not as old as she had expected' (206); he 'sounded gentle and kind, which was cunning since she knew that he was dangerous and cruel' (206); he was 'ruthless and clever' (213) and 'beat against her will with his implacable logic, his curious kindness, his courtesy, his patience' (208). There is not a whiff of sexual attraction here, nor is there the slightest indication that Cordelia is searching for a father substitute.

James's response to her fans of 1977 is ultimately a defence of Dalgliesh, not against the Cordelia in the 1972 novel but against what she perceives her enthusiastic readers to have made of Cordelia. And nowhere is this convergence more clear than in James's addressing of her comments to a second-person 'you' – simultaneously a fictive Cordelia and the implicated reader/fan. 'We,' the conflated reader/Cordelia, are dissuaded from thinking about Dalgliesh in domestic terms but encouraged, conversely, to view him as sexy. Cordelia, in turn, is reconfigured in this conflation, not as Dalgliesh's equal but as primarily focused on domesticity, emotional bonds, family, and matrimony, as dependent, potentially jealous, comparably unprofessional, and as looking for a father substitute – as, in other words, a version of the immature, inexperienced, mediocre-looking Victorian heroine rather than the private, self-sufficient, and professional heroine who actually appears in *An Unsuitable Job for a Woman*.

It is, in fact, this 1977 reconstruction of Cordelia – the reconstruction that serves to defend Dalgliesh both from the tendency of James's fans to see Cordelia as politically and fictionally more provocative and compelling than Dalgliesh, and from the machinations of a fictive (although not fictional) domestically minded husband-seeker – that James reworks in *The Skull beneath the Skin*. But this transformation is equally reworked through various models of femininity that emerged in the late seventies and early eighties, models that owed much to certain politically expedient reinflections of Victorianism and its gender constructions. The British political scene had, after all, changed rather drastically from the consensus politics and feminist advancements of the Heath, Wilson, and Callaghan administrations in the 1970s to the hard right administration of the Tory ideologue Margaret Thatcher after 1979 and throughout the 1980s. In the interest of re-establishing a Greater Britain, of putting the 'Great back into Britain,' Thatcher justified her policies, from 1979 onwards, as all part of her proclaimed mission to restore family values, to reinstate the 'Victorian values' of thrift, hard work, self-reliance, strong family life, personal responsibility, and a sense of duty, to name only the most familiar – or, from another perspective, to restore 'patriarchalism, racism and imperialist nostalgia' (Hall and Jacques 11).

If, as Julian Barnes suggests, Thatcher succeeded, among other things, in making the 'rich richer and the poor poorer until [she] had restored the gap that existed at the end of the last century' (84), this economic effect, this particular resurrection of the nineteenth century, was at least an overt aspect of Thatcherism, as opposed to, say, the resurrection of Victorian domestic values and the veneration of the home as the locus of female strength and respectability. As Lynne Segal points out, Thatcherism 'aim[ed] to protect and improve "the stability and quality of family life," and to stress the centrality of women's place in the home'; and Thatcher herself viewed 'family values as essentially women's values' (208). In other words, Thatcher did not confront feminism head-on, unlike, for example, the moral majority under President Reagan, who articulated feminism as the bane of family life; instead, she regularly celebrated feminine domesticity as the preferred formation of 'real' women.

The measure of this selective retooling of Victorianism emerges, in rather pristine form, in the historical and figural distance between *Shroud for a Nightingale* in 1971 and *The Skull beneath the Skin* in 1982. If the later novel re-envisions the seemingly maligned residual Victorianism of the earlier, making it more benign and acceptable, *The Skull beneath the Skin* equally and necessarily inflects *An Unsuitable Job for a Woman*, precisely because *An Unsuitable Job for a Woman* constitutes a representative rebellion from the unreconstructed Victorianism of *Shroud for a Nightingale*. Once the frightening Victorianism of Nightingale House is metaphorically retooled as a more tender locus of nineteenth-century family values, in other words, rebellion from that latter construction becomes more problematic. And because James articulates that rebellion in terms of gender, Cordelia is necessarily the ground on which the revision takes its shape. The transformation of Cordelia in *The Skull beneath the Skin* is not, however, immediately obvious, in part because James has clearly reread the earlier work and set out to integrate certain key moments from *An Unsuitable Job for a Woman* into *The Skull beneath the Skin*. The later novel begins, for example, with almost exactly the same narrative sequence: instead of looking at the brass name-plate that includes both Cordelia's and Bernie Pryde's names, Cordelia examines the new name-plate, identifying herself as sole proprietor of the Pryde's Detective Agency. And, as if to offer a metaphoric figure for the divergence of the second novel from the first and, indeed, set the tone for the entire novel, the name-plate bearing only Cordelia's name is skewed to one side, 'half an inch out of true' (3).

Having signalled the shift from *An Unsuitable Job for a Woman* to *The Skull beneath the Skin* with a reinscription of the first moment of the earlier novel, James offers a series of other echoes: Cordelia remembers the 'scene, garish and sharply outlined as a cinema still' (10), of her discovery of Bernie Pryde's body at the beginning of *An Unsuitable Job for a Woman*; she anticipates Sir George Ralston's question – 'Don't people ever tell you' – with a direct allusion to the title and refrain-like comment of the earlier text, 'that it's an unsuitable job for a woman?' (9). Later in the novel, Cordelia's confrontation of Ambrose Gorringe with her discovery of his guilt is almost a direct doubling of her confrontation with Ronald Callender. In *The Skull beneath the Skin*, Cordelia escapes from the Devil's Kettle, an almost exact replica of the covered well in *An Unsuitable Job for a Woman*; and during her struggle to free herself from the Devil's Kettle, she experiences the exact same memories of Sister Perpetua from her convent school. James figures Cordelia's two escapes, both courtesy of Mark Callender's belt, in exactly the same metaphors: in the earlier text, Cordelia's climb up the well is a 'parody of a difficult labour towards some desperate birth' (156), and in the later, her emergence from the water prompts her to think, 'So this was what it was like to be born: the pressure, the thrusting, the wet darkness, the terror and the warm gush of blood' (360). From the deploying of direct borrowings and allusions to the echoing of plot sequences and rhetorical figures, in other words, James constantly directs our attention back to *An Unsuitable Job for a Woman*.

And yet, for all the mirroring and parallels, Cordelia Gray in *The Skull beneath the Skin* is considerably diminished, considerably less effective. Because James seems to appropriate the earlier novel as if it were a fictional template for the later, she obfuscates the fact that the earlier novel serves merely to offer embellishments to the later, testifying to similitude while implicitly offering a difference, a falling away. And the disparity in signification between the scenes offered as parallels is telling. In *An Unsuitable Job for a Woman*, for example, Cordelia gives a 'short glance of approval' (10) at the bronze plaque because it offers proof of her equal partnership with Bernie; in *The Skull beneath the Skin*, however, she finds the plaque with only her name 'lopsided ... both pretentious and ridiculous, a fitting advertisement of irrational hope and ill-advised enterprise' (3). The first plaque invites clients like Ronald Callender, who retains her to solve suicide/murder cases, or like Mr Freeling, who hires her to investigate an adultery case; the second, 'ridiculous,' plaque invites clients like George Ralston who want their wives protected from 'nuisance,' or, more commonly, clients who want their pets found, 'clients, tearful, desperate, outraged by what they saw as the callous indifference of the local C.I.D.' (7). Dalgliesh of the CID, who met his match in Cordelia in *An Unsuitable Job for a Woman*, refuses ('callously'), in essence, to find lost pets; but Cordelia, no longer employed with cases similar to the CID's, supports the agency by doing just that.

James's refashioning of Cordelia, her detective agency, and her cases offers not simply a decline from her earlier equality with Bernie or, more to the point, Dalgliesh, but an attendant and gendered shift towards the domestic. Dalgliesh hunts murderers, whereas Cordelia, with the help of her typist Miss Maudsley – 'a gentle, sixty-two-year-old rector's sister' (*Skull* 4) equipped with 'gentility, age, incompetence and virginity' and an 'almost uncanny empathy with the feline mind' (7) – hunts house pets. As if to confirm this domestication of Cordelia, James proffers a glimpse of her home, an apartment at the 'top of a Victorian warehouse' (53). Carefully scrubbed and white if rather 'spartan,' the sitting-room contrasts with the 'extravagance' of Cordelia's bedroom, the walls, cupboard, and ceiling of which are covered in an 'expensive and exotic handprinted paper' (54); on the ledges outside the window are 'rows of pots of herbs and geraniums' (54); and the entire apartment represents 'security, comfort, her first real home' (54). Instead of the memories of sexual encounters and relationships Cordelia has in *An Unsuitable Job for a Woman*, here she has a 'narrow bed,' like a nun's; and she knows that 'if any man shared that narrow bed for her it would mean commitment' (54).

In the context of this cosy but connotatively virginal domesticity, this exemplary homeyness, James introduces a reference to Dalgliesh, a 'Commander of New Scotland Yard' and the 'one man [Cordelia] ever pictured' in her bed: 'But she told herself that the brief madness was over, that at a time of stress and frightening insecurity she had only been seeking for her lost father-figure. There was this to be said for a smattering of amateur psychology: it enabled one to exorcise memories which might otherwise be embarrassing' (*Skull* 54). Cordelia's thoughts here are decidedly divergent from her thoughts in *An Unsuitable Job for a Woman*. Unlike the other features that forge links between the earlier novel and *The Skull beneath the Skin*, the neat summary and dismissal of Cordelia's attraction to Dalgliesh, her recognition that her longing is inappropriate and 'madness,' and her 'amateur psychology' are, in fact, an echo of James herself when she produces the fictive Cordelia questioned by the equally fictive marriage counsellor: 'Admittedly, you find him sexually very attractive, but so do a number of women ... And are you sure you aren't looking for a substitute for your own inadequate father?' ('Ought' 69). Not only is Cordelia's sudden knowledge of 'amateur psychology' – what serves to 'exorcise' embarrassing memories – rather out of character, but that knowledge is, quite simply, incorrect.

Even a 'smattering' of psychology would surely suggest that daughters do not seek 'lost father-figures.' Daughters might well seek lost fathers, or seek to replace bad or lost fathers with more attractive father-figures, but they certainly don't seek lost figures. Endlessly replaceable substitutes or figures do not really get lost. The real subject of mystification here is not, however, desire, but loss itself. And James's failure either to reproduce her own, earlier construction of Cordelia's desire or to attribute a correct amateur psychology to Cordelia so that she can 'exorcise' Dalgliesh once and for all is telling, for it offers a textual moment that reflects just how high the stakes are for James to excise Cordelia's desire and replace it with loss. This textual moment of peculiar displacement inscribes Cordelia as seeking something that is neither lost nor found: and thus the real lost figure, as both the subject of a purposeless 'seeking' and of the larger text itself, is, in fact, Cordelia. With Cordelia thus reduced to the hunter of lost pets, tender of the vestal hearth, and perpetual daughter fruitlessly seeking a 'lost father-figure,' James cements this new representation with an observation guaranteed to place Cordelia firmly in the realm of the feminine ordinary: 'The most onerous part of the preparation for this new case was deciding which clothes to pack' (54).

The packing sequence, for all its ostensible similarity to an earlier inscription, clashes directly with that inscription. In *An Unsuitable Job for a Woman*, after she has meticulously checked her scene-of-crime kit, polaroid camera, maps, sleeping bag, 'copy of Professor Simpson's book on forensic medicine,' first aid kit, and fresh notebook, Cordelia at last considers what garments to pack, as if clothing were an afterthought: 'Finally, she considered her clothes' (43). The fact that James inverts this narrative sequence in *The Skull beneath the Skin*, stressing first the domestic arrangements, then the clothes, and finally the scene-of-crime kit, simultaneously accentuates the similarity of Cordelia's preparations in the two novels and subtly reworks the narrative so as to suggest an opposite order of importance; home and clothes take precedence over the job in a hierarchy that seems regressive, if not perhaps wholly anachronistic, for 1982. Not only does this subtle reworking set the stage for Cordelia's relative incompetence on the case – the only piece that she manages to unravel is Gorringe's possible motive for wanting to murder Clarissa Lisle, although he in fact has to tell her who actually committed the crime and wrote the poison-pen notes – but it equally establishes Cordelia as more suitably old-fashioned, as eminently more likely than before to traverse a trajectory from refurbished Victorian warehouse to refurbished Victorian castle.

James represents this connotatively de-modernized and refigured Cordelia within the context of an 'authentic' Victorian castle. The castle at Courcy Island is not the typically parodied 'grey-stoned, massive, crenellated sham' of the imagined Victorian 'compromise between domesticity and grandeur' (*Skull* 69); instead, the E.W. Godwin–designed 'castle of rose-red brick' has a 'slender round tower topped with a cupola, solid yet ethereal ... a lightness and repose which [Cordelia] hadn't associated with high Victorian architecture' (69). In Gorringe's castle, furnished with real Victoriana, with William Morris tapestries, stained-glass windows, and pre-Raphaelite paintings, Cordelia occupies the De Morgan room – a room 'charming' in its 'lightness and delicacy,' with 'lily-patterned chintz' curtains, bed-cover, and cushions, with De Morgan watercolours and tiles, Morris cabinet, and Ruskin paintings.

If Courcy Island presents an 'authentic' Victoriana that challenges Cordelia's preconceptions of it as heavy, stolid, and somewhat dreadful, James's revisionist reading of all that is charmingly 'light and delicate' about the nineteenth century reflects a considerably larger revisionist reading of Victorian England. In *Shroud for a Nightingale*, Nightingale House is an 'extraordinary house, an immense Victorian edifice of red brick, castellated and ornate to the point of fancy, and crowned with four immense turrets' (9), and this 'Victorian pile' has 'something forbidding, even frightening' (10) about it. In *The Black Tower*, the tower itself, which was built in 1843 by Wilfred Anstey's great-grandfather, who bricked himself in and died of starvation, scrabbling uselessly against the walls until his fingers were mangled to the bone before he finally died, is a 'symbol.' When Dennis Lerner comments that in the sunlight of summer the tower 'looks magical' but that 'underneath there's horror, pain, madness, and death' (*Black* 114), Julius Court responds, 'I don't need a phallic symbol erected by a Victorian eccentric to remind me of the skull under the skin' (114). Indeed, Nightingale House and the Black Tower seem to present the very constructions of Victorian taste and architecture that Cordelia is finding inapplicable to Courcy Island, a more benign and beautiful, more delicate and lovely Victorian model that has no phallic component, and that has only skulls interred, correctly, beneath the chapel. But then, between 1971 and 1975, when *Shroud for a Nightingale* and *The Black Tower* were published, and 1982, Victorianism had been carefully refashioned in a much more favourable light.

The proposed return to 'Victorian values' was no mere embellishment of Tory propaganda in the late seventies and early eighties. Their representation, or better, a fond, nostalgic re-envisioning of Victorian and Edwardian England, pervaded British culture, as if to offer figurative support for Thatcher's proposed project. One of the most prevalent features of eighties British culture was the rigorous attempt to recoup the benign imperial greatness of a bygone era: witness, for example, the tremendous success of Evelyn Waugh's *Brideshead Revisited* on the BBC, the anachronistic and orchestrated pomp and circumstance of the royal wedding, the televised war in the Falkland Islands – what Barnes dubs 'the last twitch of an imperial past' (88) – the enormously popular David Lean and Merchant and Ivory films that captured the sweetly romantic, touchingly fragile Edwardian England of E.M. Forster's *A Passage to India* and *A Room with a View*, and the marked success of A.S. Byatt's Booker Prize–winning *Possession: A Romance*. 'Victorianism,' in other words, gained a connotative inflection in the 1980s that was simply not present in the decades before Thatcherist propaganda refashioned the nineteenth century in a manner which could capture the British public imagination and, in turn, provide fodder for certain forms of cultural production.

In *The Skull beneath the Skin*, James signals a complementary shift in attitude. Gone are the wretched, phallic Victorian monstrosities, and gone are the critical thrusts at Victorian repression; apart from Gorringe's somewhat distasteful memento mori collection – artefacts of a Victorian fascination with death – the only real horror that lurks beneath Courcy Island is connected to the Second World War, when the island was used as an internment camp for hard-core Nazis and German nationals. But with this lighter, more delicate, and kinder view of Victorianism, comes a fonder and less inflected version of the Victorian heroine and, in turn, a considerably less secure place for the independent modern heroine who sets out to struggle against that earlier, politically demonized model. Luckily, the rewritten Cordelia fits right in at Courcy Island.

James's refashioning of Cordelia Gray as diminished, as domestically inclined, as preoccupied with clothes, make-up, and personal feelings – as, in other words, not a modern heroine struggling against residual gender assumptions – has a structural parallel in the novel as a whole. Cordelia is, in fact, little more than the heroine of a gothic romance: she rushes ineptly from room to room, discovers mutilated bodies, uncovers awful secrets in the guests' pasts, drinks a few glasses of claret with the would-be murderer Gorringe – who she thinks is Clarissa Lisle's murderer until he reveals the truth – finds herself entirely alone and without chance of rescue, manages to get trapped in a dungeon beneath Courcy Island, and finally escapes, only to be rescued by an accommodating sailor who happens to be sailing by to return her belt. Cordelia never realizes that Simon is Clarissa's murderer until Gorringe tells her, and the only useful thing she does discover is the local newspaper photograph of Gorringe at the 1977 Jubilee parade in Speymouth – the photograph that she ends up leaving for him to destroy when she rushes off to save Simon from committing suicide. At the conclusion of the novel, she has no evidence to offer the police about either Gorringe's tax evasion or his attempt on her life. And Gorringe, after apologizing that her 'first visit to Courcy Island hasn't been as happy for [her] as [he] had hoped' (370), walks off to his castle a free man.

Gorringe's personalizing of her professional visit to his island is entirely symptomatic of her failure to maintain her financially retained professionalism and of her tendency to react personally. And if this tendency is a strength in *An Unsuitable Job for a Woman*, allowing her to unmask a murderer, it is a distinct weakness in *The Skull beneath the Skin*, for she is unable to view Simon as a murderer because she likes him personally and feels sympathy for him. When Gorringe apologizes to Cordelia in such as way as to suggest that her attendance at his house party was, sadly, unsatisfactory, he relegates her to the status of a mere guest, whom the host has disappointed. And she is, finally, only a guest – or an audience-member of the meta-performance of *The Duchess of Malfi* that has played itself out in front of her – for she decides to forego charging Ralston the fee they had agreed upon for her services. In the final scene of the novel, Cordelia prepares to return to London to work on two new cases, one 'terribly urgent, a lost Siamese kitten,' and the other Mrs Sutcliffe's lost Pekinese Nanki-Poo (*Skull* 370).

It seems scarcely surprising that James's fans are no longer clamouring for Cordelia's reappearance, especially given that James basically promises, at the end of *The Skull beneath the Skin*, that Cordelia's return would have to be a narrative about her successful cases of pet-retrieval. Even the amateur teenage detectives Nancy Drew and Trixie Beldon have more exciting cases than the 'terribly urgent' finding of lost Siamese kittens. But Cordelia determines, after all, 'It was a job that needed doing, one that she was good at' (371). Presumably we are to read this without irony. James suggests, in effect, that Cordelia should leave the hard work to the professionals, to the Adam Dalglieshes. *A Taste for Death* (1986), written just after *The Skull beneath the Skin*, is, symptomatically, wholly populated with professionals, whose distinct forms of professional expertise James outlines in ample and rich detail: from Dalgliesh's elite squad of Chief Inspector John Massingham and Detective Inspector Kate Miskin, among others – an elite squad, financed, no doubt, by the post-1981 infusion of money into the police force to aid their maintenance of law and order – to the pathologist Miles Kynaston and the forensic expert Charlie Ferris. Dalgliesh's challenge, to solve the murder of his friend Sir Paul Berowne, is to surmount his personal interest in the case and, unlike Cordelia, display a consummate professional detachment and triumph over mere sensibility. Dalgliesh thus succeeds in the very area in which Cordelia fails. Dangerous and serious detective work is, obviously, an unsuitable job for her, for she is much better suited to re-establishing domestic tranquillity in households whose pets have gone missing.

If, as I have suggested, James metaphorically pulls the rug out from under Cordelia in *The Skull beneath the Skin*, she does so by carefully excising precisely what made Cordelia politically interesting in *An Unsuitable Job for a Woman*, precisely what made James's fans notice her and demand her reappearance for an entire decade. And James simultaneously mounts an implicit yet devastating defence of Dalgliesh by removing any possibility that Cordelia might represent a rival. But before we are tempted to view James's retooling of Cordelia as wholly regressive, we need to acknowledge the terms on which such regression is assessed. Appearing first in the seventies and then in the eighties, Cordelia does actually offer a representatlve touchstone for the political shift in Britain: first she eschews conventional feminine roles and works as a private detective, and then she embraces domesticity and dedicates herself to re-establishing domestic harmony. This trajectory, this transformation of the model of femininity from equal opportunity worker to upholder of domestic family values, is the very transformation that Thatcher advocated every time she spoke to the female electorate or every time she gave interviews for women's magazines. In other words, Cordelia is, both chronologically and politically – at least insofar as she adheres to ascendant Tory propaganda, at any rate – a veritable icon of postwar progress, an ideological domestic cornerstone of British (neo-Victorian) greatness. In feminist terms, however, Cordelia represents a distressing regression, a fictional testimony to or realization of the satisfied eighties woman – the woman who, Thatcher assured us, was content to tend the hearth, content, in effect, with eighties roll-backs of seventies feminist achievements.

But it is in these very pro-Thatcherite and anti-feminist terms that James rearticulates Cordelia, deliberately rejecting the very ground that encouraged all the enthusiasm of her fans in the first place. *An Unsuitable Job for a Woman* thus remains a complete anomaly, a momentary aberration, in James's fiction. And *The Skull beneath the Skin* proffers the necessary corrective, not as a monitory tale as such but as a subtle reworking that obfuscates its political trajectory as a re-establishment of a British patriarchalism that was ideologically entrenched in the nineteenth century. Indeed, James presents an object-lesson to feminists who assume that women writers express, either obliquely or directly, some manner of feminist resistance in their writing. And, we might add, Thatcher herself provided a very similar object-lesson to those who believed that a woman prime minister, as either exemplar or advocate, might further women's interests.

If James suggests that she is, like her preferred male protagonist Dalgliesh (and her prime minister, for that matter), a staunch meritocrat who refuses to 'make routine gestures to feminism, or to any other fashionable cause' (*Taste* 172), she nevertheless offers a paucity of opportunity for Cordelia to establish merit in *The Skull beneath the Skin*; or better, she determines that Cordelia's merit will be confined to the domestic sphere alone. Cordelia's recognition of her own talent – her ability to hunt for lost house pets, 'a job that needed doing, one that she was good at' (*Skull* 371) – is, ultimately, a forceful demonstration that James does not, in fact, endorse the 'fashionable cause' of feminism. But then, as *Devices and Desires* (1989) makes pristinely clear, 'fashionable causes' are invariably linked to sleazy personal politics at best and terrorism at worst; and terrorism can, of course, only be countered with an increased state power and a fetishization of law and order. Far from making any 'routine gestures to feminism,' then, James serves notice in *The Skull beneath the Skin* that proto-feminists like Cordelia in *An Unsuitable Job for a Woman* had better stay home, 'warmly cocooned' (*Skull* 54) inside their (ideologically) refurbished Victorian homes; for home is, evidently, where they belong.

WORKS CITED

Barnes, Julian. 'The Maggie Years.' *New Yorker* 69 (15 November 1993): 82–9.

Cooper-Clark, Diana. *Designs of Darkness: Interviews with Detective Novelists*. Bowling Green, Ohio: Bowling Green University Popular Press, 1983.

Hall, Stuart, and Martin Jacques, eds. *The Politics of Thatcherism*. London: Lawrence and Wishart, 1983.

James, P.D. *The Black Tower*. Harmondsworth: Penguin, 1975.

– 'Ought Adam to Marry Cordelia?' In Winn *Murder Ink* 68–9.

– *Shroud for a Nightingale*. Harmondsworth: Penguin, 1971.

– *The Skull beneath the Skin*. Harmondsworth: Penguin, 1982.

– *A Taste for Death*. Harmondsworth: Penguin, 1986.

– *An Unsuitable Job for a Woman*. London: Faber and Faber, 1972.

Segal, Lynne. 'The Heat in the Kitchen.' In Hall and Jacques 207–15.

Winn, Dilys, ed. *Murderess Ink: The Better Half of the Mystery*. New York: Workman, 1979.

– *Murder Ink: The Mystery Reader's Companion*. New York: Workman, 1977.

4. Questing Women: The Feminist Mystery after Feminism

Sandra Tomc

At one point in *Prime Suspect*, Granada Television's 1991 feminist mystery serial, Detective Chief Inspector Jane Tennison is sitting in a pub questioning two prostitutes about the brutal rape and murder of their young friend, another prostitute. Tennison's inquiries are just beginning when one of the men in the pub wanders over, slides his hand on her knee, and whispers something in her ear. Clearly, he has mistaken her for a prostitute. Informed of his error, he beats a fast retreat, leaving Tennison and the real prostitutes to have a good laugh.

For all its comic lightness, this moment is one of many in *Prime Suspect* to insist on a seemingly arbitrary analogy between the woman detective and the young women whose murders she is investigating. Immaterial to the plot – never once are we meant seriously to entertain the idea of Tennison as a potential murder victim – the analogy nevertheless adjusts our reading of the woman detective in a crucial way. For a split second as Tennison sits in that pub, with all the power and authority she commands as a police detective suspended in a misunderstanding, she and the dead girl are dangerously interchangeable. Mistaken for a hooker, Tennison can now be read as a candidate for the killer's urges. She is technically as vulnerable as any of the women he has murdered so far.

Such moments of metaphoric confusion or mistaken identity, while apparently arbitrary in this case, are typical of feminist mystery stories; they help to establish the grounds for the text's description of political options. In these stories – and by 'feminist mystery' is usually meant the novels of Sue Grafton, Marcia Muller, and Sara Paretsky – the detective embarks on a search for the criminal that ends up uncovering a network of problematic social and institutional mechanisms of which the crime itself is only one manifestation. As Maureen T. Reddy observes, the feminist detective discovers that the crimes she investigates are neither aberrant nor extraordinary; they are 'logical outgrowths of an order built on the oppression of women' (178).[1] Within the terms of this feminist polemic, *all* women are subordinated objects, a fact that is driven home precisely through the confusion of the detective – the traditional repository of knowledge and authority in the mystery narrative – with the female murder victim, the one whose knowledge has been annihilated. Frequently, the confusion is literalized as the detective herself becomes a target of the killer; she becomes the victim whose murder she is trying to redress. This collapse of identities in turn makes retrospective sense of the detective's decision to live and work alone. With any one crime only symptomatic of a systemic abuse of women and minorities, with the government, the law courts, the police, big business, even husbands and boyfriends all implicated in a 'patriarchal' orthodoxy, the detective finds her political purpose in the rejection of institutional and organized authority. As Grafton's Kinsey Millhone puts it, 'I like being by myself' (*'E' Is for Evidence* 70).

But if *Prime Suspect* adopts this model of feminist critique through its confusion of detective and murder victim, it is also part of a new breed of women's crime stories that departs substantially from what Grafton, Paretsky, and others were producing in the 1980s. *Prime Suspect* is different from detective fiction modelled after Marcia Muller because it features the woman detective not as a renegade but as an aspiring member of the very institution responsible for her victimization. While part of the telefilm, largely the first three-quarters, is concerned with elaborating the male-dominated system that traps and oppresses women, the final portions of it are governed by a compensatory effort to make sense of Tennison's heartfelt desire to be, in her own words, 'one of the lads.' How does the feminist detective's pursuit of acceptance as a police*man* mesh with her metaphoric status as a victim? It doesn't. *Prime Suspect* is one of a number of women's crime stories released or published in the early 1990s that bizarrely combine an aggressive critique of 'patriarchy' with a narrative that highlights the virtues of submission and conformity. Only nominally do these stories try to reconcile their contradictory positions. Rather, reflective of changes in feminism in the late 1980s, they tend to find their political rationale in contradiction itself, marking out a program made up simultaneously of vilification and acceptance.

That *Prime Suspect* is aggressively concerned with mapping out and critiquing its own version of an androcentred hegemony is made abundantly evident as the serial opens. A young girl has been raped and murdered and her body found in a bedsitter. And Jane Tennison, one of the first women ever to reach the rank of Detective Chief Inspector in London's Metropolitan Police Force, is passed up yet again for head officer of the murder squad for no other reason than that she's a woman. These two acts of aggression and domination, the rape/murder and Tennison's persecution at work, then function for the remainder of the serial as paradigmatic instances of what the telefilm elaborates as a world based on male privilege and power. At work, Tennison continues to suffer endless variations on the sexism we first see exhibited by her Super. Finally put in charge of the homicide investigation after the original DCI drops dead of a heart attack, Tennison is subjected to the open belligerence of the men on her team; they lie to her, trick her, hide important information from her; she is told by her Super that he won't have her 'thrusting your women's rights down my throat.' The text emphasizes that there is no refuge from this chauvinism and inequity, a point mainly made in the fact that Tennison suffers almost as much at home as at work. Her lover, Peter, while wanting her to be interested in his professional life, is jealous of hers, and eventually, when she's late cooking dinner for his friends – when she fails in the role of traditional 'wife' – he leaves her, betraying his affinity to the 'old chauvinists' on the Force.

Within this ongoing repetition of sexist acts, the murders themselves appear as mere distillations, events that recapitulate patriarchal ideology in intensified form. A series of grisly sex crimes, they, like everything else, involve the victimization of women. Their relation to the sanctioned sexism of domestic and legal institutions is made explicit by the nature of Tennison's two main suspects, both of whom are presented as pre-eminently 'normal' men. The late DCI John Shefford, Tennison's predecessor, is a pillar of the crime-fighting community, a 'crack officer.' Much of the first part of the telefilm emphasizes his status as a family man: he dies on his son's birthday; his colleagues hold a benefit to raise money for his widow and children. Tennison's other suspect, George Marlow, is featured keeping company with his common-law wife and his dear old mother; he is described by male friends as a fellow well liked by all, good-natured, and a 'bit of a lad' with the girls. But none of this normal male behaviour, the telefilm emphasizes, excludes the abuse of women. Apparently compatible with Shefford's role as a family man is his practice of getting sexual favours from the prostitutes he arrests, one of whom, perversely, affirms his paternal role by being young enough to be his 'daughter.' Similarly, Marlow, who turns out to be the killer, will not admit to doing anything wrong; his final words, 'Not guilty, your honour,' at once signify his lack of remorse and, more abstractly, imply his lack of culpability in a society that normalizes violence against women.

Finally, *Prime Suspect* emphasizes its vilification of 'patriarchy' through its presentation of Tennison herself, whose qualities as a *woman* accentuate the flaws of the male-centred system around her. Highlighted in the early stages of the investigation is Tennison's special sensitivity to the circumstances of the murdered women. Unlike her male colleagues, who barely glance at the victims before zipping them up in body bags, Tennison makes a point of *looking* at the girls: 'I want to see her face,' she says of both the first and the second. Presumably, for Tennison the girls are not, as they seem to be for the men, interchangeable objects in a routine trail of villainy. Her choice to *see* the victims, to recognize them as individuals, in turn points up the biases in the criminal system as a whole. It is Tennison who discovers that her predecessor, Shefford, has wrongly identified the first of the bodies, a woman he failed to recognize even though he occasionally slept with her.

That the men and women in *Prime Suspect* should have such disparate ways of seeing underlines how very distant, how alien, are the separate worlds they occupy. The one, the telefilm announces, is a world of misogynist jokes, boxing matches, drinks at the pub with the lads,[2] a world defined chiefly by the power and prestige of its members; the other, of course, is defined chiefly by the helplessness and anonymity of its members. The composition in the camera frames emphasizes this fact: Tennison is on an elevator with three detectives, her head tiny, barely visible between their massive shoulders; Tennison stands before a bulletin board pasted with gruesome photos of the murder victims, her straw-coloured hair almost identical to their straw-coloured hair. These shots pinpoint women's sameness to each other and their 'otherness' to men.

Prime Suspect, like other works in the feminist mystery genre, goes to some length to condemn the male-dominated world it elaborates and parodies. But in the feminist 'hard-boiled' fiction developed in the 1980s, this critique justifies the woman detective's choice to pack up and light out. Men's and women's worlds are far-flung, irreconcilable. Law enforcement agencies are repositories and progenitors of the worst kind of gender injustice. And in the absence of a rationale for putting up with this, the feminist detective just leaves. She quits the police force, as

Grafton's Kinsey Millhone does, and sets up an agency of her own; or she turns into the enemy of big business, corrupt government, conservative religion, and organized crime, like V.I. Warshawski and Sharon McCone. 'I have what I want,' V.I. says when her murdering lover (a cop) wonders why she's not like all the other women he's known, 'my independence and my privacy. You've just never understood it, have you, that all those things, all those diamonds and things just don't turn me on' (*Burn Marks* 319).[3] After shooting her lover (a lawyer) in self-defence, Kinsey Millhone announces, 'I just don't want to be a victim anymore. I'm sick of it' (*'B' Is for Burglar* 77). Following their exposure to what Sharon McCone calls 'ugly truths' – 'all the victims I'd seen during my time in the business ... All the predators I'd seen do the victimizing' (*Muller* 184, 128) – these detectives opt for an all-out rejection of structures of oppression, whether juridical, domestic, or sexual. And they do not settle merely for quitting entrenched offenders like the police or the law courts, they actively campaign against them; in McCone's words, they 'fly in the face of *the people who count*' (*Muller* 121; emphasis added).

But although *Prime Suspect* very deliberately creates the conditions for this kind of active revolt on the part of the detective, Tennison, in fact, moves in the opposite direction, *towards* the institutions that Millhone and Warshawski so vehemently reject. Nor is this unexpected rapprochement with a previously maligned institutional authority unique to *Prime Suspect*. Two other feminist mystery/suspense stories, published or released within a year of *Prime Suspect* – Patricia D. Cornwell's Edgar Award–winning novel *Postmortem* (1990), the first Kay Scarpetta mystery, and Jonathan Demme's Academy Award–winning film *The Silence of the Lambs* (1991) – make this same peculiar move. The popularity of and acclaim bestowed upon all three of these works suggest the extent to which they represent a trend. In all three, the female detective begins as a more or less persecuted member of some huge law enforcement agency (or branch thereof): the Metropolitan Police in *Prime Suspect*, the coroner's office in *Postmortem*, the FBI in *The Silence of the Lambs*. And in all three the detective follows her quest not away from the persecuting institution but into its metaphoric arms. In *Prime Suspect*, Tennison ends up finding acceptance and joy among the very men who tormented her when she first came on the case; in *Postmortem*, Kay Scarpetta becomes friends with Marino, the redneck, sexist, homophobic cop who began as a representative of everything that was wrong with male-dominated law enforcement; in *The Silence of the Lambs*, Clarice Starling seeks and achieves the approval of several initially threatening paternal figures, including her real father (a sheriff), her very fatherly FBI supervisor, and, last but not least, the perversely fatherly serial killer, Hannibal 'The Cannibal' Lecter.

In one way or another, *Postmortem* and *The Silence of the Lambs* comment as aggressively as *Prime Suspect* on male prejudice and injustice, often, indeed, making the same points: shots of Clarice Starling confronted with the gruesome photographs of the female victims, for instance, uncannily echo shots of Tennison confronted with similar photos.[4] The institutionalized, endemic character of violence against women is the central topic of *Postmortem*. Not only is there a psychopathic butcher running around loose and threatening Scarpetta personally, there is also her lover, who tries to rape her, and her chauvinist boss, who tries to discredit her professionally (which Scarpetta describes as a kind of rape [117]). That men in general are complicit in women's victimization is voiced by one of the female relatives of the victims: 'Nobody who counts gives a damn when women are raped and murdered! The same bastards who work the cases go out on the town and watch movies about women being raped, strangled, slashed. To them it's sexy. They like to look at it in magazines. They fantasize. They probably get their rocks off by looking at the scene photographs' (215). Yet all three works, along with their aggressive commentary, are driven by a kind of compensatory logic that strives, however contradictorily, to reconcile the detective to her intolerable circumstances. We should not confuse this process of reconciliation with the detective's choice of resignation or acceptance. On the contrary, unlike the fiction of Grafton, Paretsky, and Muller, these texts do not represent the possibility of choices for the detective. Rather, the detective is reconciled to her circumstances or, perhaps more accurately, shown to forgive them, by rhetorical sleight of hand, by shifts in narrative, genre, or terms of argument. The contradictions created in these turns are then allowed to stand as the seeming condition of a social order women can neither change nor escape.

In all three works, the particular nature of the crime significantly narrows whatever options the detective might entertain for herself. It has been a convention of hard-boiled fiction since Dashiell Hammett to pit the solitary private eye against criminal forces that are essentially pervasive and uncontrollable, acts that typify a larger set of conditions which the detective must confront but which he can never really defeat. Thus Robert I. Edenbaum calls detective work in these novels as much a 'metaphor for existence as war is in *The Red Badge of Courage* or *A Farewell to Arms*' (85). Describing Raymond Chandler's work, W.H. Auden remarks, 'Chandler is interested in writing, not detective stories, but serious studies of a criminal milieu, the Great Wrong Place' (151). It has been noted often enough by critics and practitioners that hard-boiled writing differs from 'classic' or Golden Age detective fiction chiefly in its refusal to present any given crime as an isolated or idiosyncratic event. Feminist mystery writers, with their emphasis on the pervasiveness of a particular gendered form of crime or abuse, are greatly indebted to this convention.[5] At one point in *'H' Is for Homicide*, Grafton (through Kinsey) draws attention to her generic sympathies: referring to her nightmarish new boss at California Fidelity, Kinsey says, 'In a world presided over by Agatha Christie, Gordon Titus might have ended up on the conference room floor with a paper spindle through his heart. In the real world [that is, Grafton's world], such matters seldom have such a satisfactory ending' (11).

Nevertheless, a 'satisfactory' ending of at least some kind is a convention that neither Hammett and Chandler nor Grafton, Paretsky, and Muller are prepared to forego entirely, although here again hard-boiled fiction has its own internal rules. Unable, as Jacques Barzun puts it, to see 'order grow out of chaos' (256), the hard-boiled detective contents himself or herself with defeating a small portion of the chaotic element, usually, in the genre's tradition of individualism, one on one. Hence the squaring off of female detective and criminal at the end of so many of these novels, a confrontation burdened, we could say, with a double function, since not only is the detective tackling certain 'chaotic' or undesirable social forces, she is, as I have already suggested, becoming the victim whose status needs to be redressed. Important here is her victory, however provisional, over the forces responsible for her victimization. No matter how endemic the crime may be, whether it's a crime of socialized passion or a fraud perpetrated by big business or organized crime, the feminist detective puts a dent in the machinery responsible for its perpetration. And in a sense her defeat of the criminal each time is what allows her to entertain options, like living and working alone, since it illustrates to her, and to us, the possibility of her altering the conditions of her victimization.[6]

But *Prime Suspect*, *Postmortem*, and *The Silence of the Lambs*, inspired as much by slasher films and sensational true crime stories as by hard-boiled detective fiction, all feature as the criminal a serial killer who targets women.[7] The crimes are unusually violent, involving sexual assault, torture, and mutilation. At the formal level, the texts linger on pictures and descriptions of the damaged bodies of the victims. We might note that rape/homicide, while surely *the* crime feared by women, is one that the older school of feminist mystery writers never deals with, very likely because it is guaranteed to highlight the female detective's helplessness over and above any victory she might manage at the end of the story. Yet pointing up the detective's vulnerability is very much on the roster of these later mystery stories. At the finale of *Postmortem*, in what is surely one of the most horrifying scenes ever to appear in a detective novel, the killer finally shows up in Kay Scarpetta's bedroom, stocking mask on his head, knife-point at her throat. She can't move, she can't scream. '"You're going to enjoy this bitch." It was a low, cold voice straight out of hell. "I've been saving the best for last." The stocking sucking in and out. "You want to know how I've been doing it. Going to show you real slow"' (312). The culmination of a series of descriptions of the killer's method, descriptions so graphic that Jean Swanson and Dean James in *By a Woman's Hand: A Guide to Mystery Fiction by Women* feel compelled to warn the 'squeamish' reader (52), this confrontation between Scarpetta and the killer has a single purpose: to dramatize the female detective's enforced passivity before a power greater than herself. In fact, Scarpetta never does defeat this killer. Marino, the sexist cop, shows up in the nick of time and guns the killer down.

The choice to feature a serial killer of women, precisely because it highlights the woman detective's vulnerability, perforce limits the terms of her independence and mobility. Witness what occurs in *The Silence of the Lambs*. Moving under the protection of the FBI and its massive apparatus for most of the film, Clarice Starling, already an object of interest for the serial killer Hannibal Lecter, is rendered suddenly all the more vulnerable when she decides to pursue a few leads on her own. If her bout of independence is responsible for her finding the killer and saving his hostage, it also provides an illustration of the dangers of autonomy. Thus the final confrontation between Clarice and the killer emphasizes her powerlessness in a particularly acute way: the lights go black; the killer has night-vision goggles (the means he uses to watch all his female victims), and we watch from his point of view as Clarice flails about, trying desperately to find her way in the dark while he stalks her. The extremity of the danger here, in turn, ensures the necessity of Clarice's return to the protective fold of the FBI. Even her relationship with Hannibal Lecter, which perversely casts her in the roles of both victim and daughter, justifies and promotes, by virtue of contrast, her membership in her 'normal' FBI family with its more 'normal' father figure.

In *The Silence of the Lambs*, then, as in *Postmortem*, the threatening, even gothic, nature of the criminal acts, together with an emphasis on the female detective's helplessness in the face of them, ensures that packing up and lighting out is never a real option. Full of stalkers, serial killers, and cannibals, the world the detective inhabits is, we are told, too dangerous for a woman working on her own. In the more devoutly realist *Prime Suspect*, the detective herself is never directly threatened, so her eventual approval of the institution responsible for her victimization is potentially more inexplicable. But *Prime Suspect* does its best to plaster over Tennison's implausible capitulation not by calling on other genres like horror but by changing the terms of its own polemic. Instead of bringing its central conflict to the expected stand-off (Tennison versus the powers of male privilege), *Prime Suspect* draws its critique to a sudden halt. The final quarter of the telefilm is concerned not with critiquing but with reclaiming the social world that the first three-quarters condemned.

That something is about to break in the telefilm's parody and vilification of 'patriarchy' is made apparent in one remarkably vivid scene: Tennison's farewell to Sergeant Otley, the biggest chauvinist in the department. Up until this point, Tennison has been the object of a generalized male aggression of which Otley was only one component, the very numbers and diversity of her antagonists indicative of the complexity and apparent seamlessness of the patriarchal order. But when in Oldham with the prostitutes, Tennison discovers that Sergeant Otley seems to be engaged in something more serious than heckling; he seems to be burying crucial information that links his friend Shefford to the murder victims, and this time when Tennison complains to the Super, he listens. Out in the parking lot, Tennison tells Otley he's off the case, slams shut the trunk of her car, and turns immediately to greet the new man on the case, Terry Amson, an old friend from her last posting. What makes this scene striking is that this is the first time in the telefilm that Tennison greets a male colleague with something other than defensiveness; indeed, as Helen Mirren plays the moment, Tennison, turning from Otley, turns into a different woman. Her smile is warm, her eyes brilliant. She presses Amson's hand with an intimacy that suggests romance. With its overtones of collegiality, affection, and friendship, their meeting suddenly topples the Manichean symmetry of the telefilm's male-female divide. But that the meeting is occasioned on a formal level by Tennison's farewell to Otley also suggests that Otley himself is possibly something isolated, idiosyncratic – something of which Tennison can readily dispose.

Accordingly, the staging of Otley's dismissal inaugurates a crucial shift in the text's polemical terms. What was earlier presented as amorphous and ubiquitous sexism is now offered as a strictly local phenomenon, with Otley (to use a term appropriate to the genre) a kind of rhetorical 'fall guy,' the solitary figure onto which a formerly 'universal' misogyny has been displaced. As if Otley alone were a carrier of gender inequity, his dismissal from the case marks a significant adjustment in the text's representation of the other men on the murder squad. Less and less often presented as petty harassers, the detectives become important for the growing respect they feel for Tennison. When the chief threatens to take Tennison off the case, every man on her team signs a petition saying he wants her to stay. When the murderer is finally indicted, the men hold a surprise party for her with cake and champagne. They sing a variation on a pub song whose lyrics – 'Why was she born so beautiful? / Why was she born at all? / She's no bloody use to anyone, / She's no bloody use at all' – are clearly part of what is now an innocuous, self-parodying sexism, less dangerous than it is funny and nostalgic.

Not surprisingly, Tennison's refurbished murder squad, with its new, politically sensitized members, responds to the discovery of the murderer in a way commensurate with the rest of these revisions. Having just examined the garage where the killer George Marlow tortured and murdered his victims, the cops at Southampton Row sit in a circle in a state of shock, expressing their horror and bewilderment. No longer are the killings represented as a matter of routine for the male detectives, which they have been till now. Still less are they offered as something intrinsic to the structures of a male-dominated world. Rather, emphasized in this scene is the *otherness* of the murders, their utter alienness to the lives of the men of Scotland Yard. 'Freak me out,' whispers one cop. 'Just give me five minutes with him,' says another as he grits his teeth and punches his hand. 'Sick bastard,' 'Sick .... sick,' they keep repeating. The implication is that, like Otley, the killer is now an aberration, a rotten apple in an otherwise decent bunch. That the men are being confronted with something 'sick' – that is, foreign – is underlined by the choice of camera shots and edits. As the men speak, the camera tracks round and round the table, pausing only briefly on any one face before pulling focus to another. In a text that generally draws no attention to its formal strategies, the vertiginousness of these shots stands out. It implies the eerie, other-worldly feeling of the men whose faces we watch; it emphasizes that the murders came from – and belong to – somewhere else.

Prime Suspect's recasting of male culture includes and supports Tennison's new position within it. Again, the scene of her farewell to Otley is key. Only the night before Otley's dismissal, Tennison has come home to find her apartment dark and empty and herself finally abandoned by Peter, her live-in lover. Coming as it does on the heels of this personal event, the scene in which Tennison greets Terry Amson so warmly suggests that the professional world he represents will now take the place of the recently lost romantic and emotional one. And effectively this is what happens, as Tennison now gets closer and closer to the men on her team, all of them embroiled in the task of finding the killer. But the subordination of the private to the professional world also signals another change: instead of positioning Tennison on the female side of a gender opposition, the text recategorizes its characters, including Tennison, along occupational lines.

Nowhere is this more disturbingly apparent than in Tennison's final interview with Moira, the killer Marlow's common-law wife. A tough, brassy ex-hooker, Moira refuses to cooperate with the investigation until she is shown pictures of the mutilated bodies of the murdered girls. At first, we think we are going to witness an instance of female solidarity. Moira asks for 'just the women' to be present; the men exit, leaving only Tennison and WPC Maureen Havers to hear what Moira has to say. And what they hear and see is harrowing: with one hand on the photo of the dead woman, an almost protective posture, Moira blurts out, 'He tried it on me once,' and then convulses and vomits into her hand. But whatever model of solidarity might be implied in this meeting of women over the issue of rape is rapidly undercut. Tennison and Havers offer no sympathy to Moira. Behind her back they exchange a smile of triumph. And what began as a gender alignment reshuffles itself along professional lines; invested primarily in the solution of the crime, the policewomen are seen to occupy a space entirely apart from that of the ex-hooker.[8]

The realignment of gender alliances into professional affiliations is justified by a larger shift in the prevailing narrative, a shift from the narrative of female victimization, which focuses on Tennison's hardships in the department, to the more conventional mystery narrative, which highlights Tennison's efforts to solve the crime and, hence, her qualities as a professional. As Tennison and her team bond around the search for the killer, a final twist in the mystery plot cements the primacy of the new professional narrative over the old gender one: Tennison has guessed wrong about John Shefford. It is in keeping with the telefilm's revised understanding of male privilege and dominance that Shefford, whose traffic with the prostitutes formerly signified the endemic nature of male violence and abuse, is found to be innocent. Nor is it entirely surprising to find him whitewashed at Tennison's expense. Like everything else that was earlier damned or praised for its part in an unjust gender economy, Tennison's womanly reading skills are refigured to conform to the new emphasis on career allegiances. Her private indictment of Shefford turns out to be a gross misreading of the evidence, an error that, significantly, puts her 'career' on the line; it jeopardizes her membership in a newly valued occupational sphere.

By all these devices, then, Tennison's implausible drift into the fold of the Metropolitan Police Force is rendered accountable. The men are no longer villains; Tennison herself is shown to value professional alliances over whatever complaints she might share with women generally; and the blame for women's oppression has been moved onto the shoulders of one or two 'sick' individuals. Yet for all these efforts to naturalize Tennison's choice of the Force, it is important to understand that *Prime Suspect* is not necessarily committed to a positive evaluation of women's position within patriarchy. One could argue that, like the choice of a serial killer, the shift in argument in *Prime Suspect*, while it seems to forgive male culture, also frees the telefilm to engage in more minute and devastating critiques of it.

We find in *Prime Suspect*, accordingly, that, much as the latter part of the telefilm draws away from a derision of male culture, the construction of Tennison as a victim of it persists. Whereas the scene of Moira's breakdown, for example, establishes the remoteness of policewoman and prostitute/victim, the final scene of the telefilm, when Marlow is arraigned, once more emphasizes their affinity: listening to the reading of the charges, Tennison exchanges righteous and compassionate glances with the two prostitutes with whom she had earlier been in the pub. Similarly, her relationship to Marlow in the latter part of the telefilm hints repeatedly of the threat he represents to her. Moments of eye contact, shots that hold on Marlow's humourless face as he gazes up at Tennison and she down at him, are featured twice following Otley's dismissal. Their final interview, when Marlow confesses, is offered as a culmination of their silent conflict throughout, with Marlow exploding in fury *at* Tennison (making her the object of his violence) before he admits to committing the murders. Even in the courtroom, Marlow glances in defiance at Tennison before announcing his 'Not guilty,' a gesture that implies his continued threat to women by implying his refusal to understand that what he has done is wrong.

While the construction of Marlow as a continued threat to Tennison and to women generally may simply underline, once again, the local or coincidental nature of violence against women, it also serves to recall the inequities associated with both the Metropolitan Police Force and the larger system of power relations of which it is a part. The ending of the telefilm especially suggests that nothing, in fact, has changed for women. The last frame freezes on a close-up of Marlow's face, his image dominating the screen as completely as men in general were shown earlier to dominate the world. It is worth noting, moreover, that *Postmortem* and *The Silence of the Lambs* present equally qualified versions of the detective's triumph. In *Postmortem*, the killer is dead and the chauvinist boss is fired, but Kay Scarpetta's lover, the date rapist, roams free, his final phone call (on the last page of the novel) hinting of the partial nature of Scarpetta's victory. A not dissimilar phone call interrupts Clarice Starling's formal inauguration into the FBI at the end of *The Silence of the Lambs*, a call from Hannibal Lecter. The serial killer Buffalo Bill has been annihilated, but Clarice's vulnerability, implied in Lecter's final invasion of her personal life, continues.[9]

But if *The Silence of the Lambs*, *Postmortem*, and *Prime Suspect* all end up insisting on the female detective's status as a victim of 'patriarchy,' is it only in order to legitimate her choice of a protected spot in one of its institutions? In one sense, it is difficult not to read what happens in these works as a rather straightforward register of changes both in feminism and in middle-class women's work situations in the late 1980s. Heavily based as it is on the real-life experiences of DCI Jackie Malton of London's Metropolitan Police Force, *Prime Suspect* especially seems concerned with the mechanics of women's entry not just into the workplace but into the professional managerial positions that became available to them during the 1980s. Indeed, the stress in all three works on corporate over independent action and occupational over gender alliances seems to chronicle and champion women's entrenchment in corporate culture. At the same time, the compensatory machinery at work in all the works – the redemption of male-dominated institutions, the localization of violence against women – seems to play out what Tania Modleski identifies as the apologetics and polemical back pedalling of 'postfeminism.' Like certain postfeminist attempts to 'relocate the struggle of feminism against patriarchy to a place entirely *within* patriarchy' (Modleski 10), *Prime Suspect*, *Postmortem*, and *The Silence of the Lambs* eradicate the adversarial space (the space outside the institution) that was so crucial to Grafton and Paretsky. They disavow the clear-cut 'essentialist' oppositions favoured by 1970s and early 1980s liberal feminism in favour of the more dispersed and accidental conflicts of its poststructuralist progeny.

And yet perhaps more interesting than the twin energies of entrenchment and dispersal that govern the direction of these later feminist mysteries is the manifest precariousness of their attempts to disown or discredit their own ostensibly outdated feminist paradigms. One of the most interesting things about all three texts, for example, is their curious preoccupation with tropes of claustrophobia and paralysis, with what might be called the dark underside of the non-adversarial space 'inside' to which their 'postfeminism' consigns them. Unlike Kinsey and V.I., who live mostly on the road, out of their purses and the trunks of their cars, Jane Tennison and Clarice Starling are most often pictured indoors, generally in small, low-ceilinged rooms. For Tennison, it's the washroom, the warren-like locker room, the kitchen; for Clarice Starling, it's a prison, a tiny bedroom, a dark, cluttered warehouse. The extreme close-ups favoured in *Prime Suspect* contribute to the viewer's perception of a lack of space. Significantly, the killer in *The Silence of the Lambs* keeps his victims prisoner in a deep, narrow pit before murdering them. In *Prime Suspect*, a dark, dungeon-like garage serves the same function. Although the killer in *Postmortem* has no such retreat, he does have a disease that makes his glands produce an overpowering sickly-sweet smell that surrounds and all but suffocates his victims. It is no accident that when Kay Scarpetta wakes to find the killer beside her, she can't move and she can't see: 'My nostrils were filled with a sick, stale sweatiness ... My body was rigid, every muscle and tendon straining, stiff and quivering with fear. It was pitch-black inside my bedroom' (308–9). Like the killer's still-pervasive gaze at the conclusion of *Prime Suspect*, such contemplations of women's paralysis and confinement point to the new feminist mystery's constant recollection of an earlier feminism's emphasis on liberation and escape.[10]

But if the new feminist mystery seems, by its insistence on women's entrapment, to lament its own curtailments, it would be inaccurate, I think, to endow this lamentation with the energies of ideological disruption or subversion. However much the new mysteries draw on anachronistic feminist models of victimization, these do not finally disturb their ameliorative 'postfeminist' strategies. Rather, the new mystery, in what is perhaps its most accurate rendering of the contradictory directions of 1990s feminism, leaves the two in unresolved suspension, the conflict between women as victims and women as winners deftly undecided.[11] It is symptomatic of their general refusal to make definitive judgments, for example, that none of these works is, properly speaking, a whodunit. George Marlow is Tennison's 'prime suspect' all along; the killer in *Postmortem* is never among the characters we know; and Buffalo Bill in *The Silence of the Lambs* is revealed to the viewer early on. All three works divert attention from the genre's traditional teleology – the 'solution' of a mystery, the discovery of a 'truth' – in order to highlight the convoluted paths of their own internal dilemmas. And I want to close now with what I think is a particularly sharp illustration of the new mystery's lack of commitment to any of its arguments: the opening of the champagne bottles at Tennison's surprise party in *Prime Suspect*. The 'lads' are laughing and singing and gathered in a circle around Tennison; their champagne bottles are aimed straight at her, streams of white foam spurting all over her ecstatic face. Ostensibly marking Tennison's final acceptance into the boy's club of the Force, this scene also conjures the ghost images of other gendered scenarios – the phallic bottles, the gang of men, the 'money shot' – and so, even while it presents Tennison's triumphant entry into male culture, it hints of her supposedly 'real' position as a woman within it. But which reading of Tennison's relationship to the police force does the telefilm itself finally endorse? We do not know. Tennison moves into her career in an all-male world; she is cornered and yet unconscious of options. She is victimized, she is a success.

NOTES

1 For similar readings, see Godard, Kaplan, and Bakerman. For an essay that questions Paretsky's commitment to feminism, see Sandels. For Paretsky's own (markedly feminist) opinion of the relationship between women writers and detective fiction, see her introduction to *A Woman's Eye*.
2 I cannot emphasize enough the heavy-handed, often clichéd, terms in which *Prime Suspect* represents male culture, from the opening moments of the telefilm, when the camera pulls focus on a patently phallic thermometer, used, we hear, to take the rectal temperature of the female victim, to the repetition of smutty jokes and misogynist comments (Otley calls Tennison a 'bitch,' a 'tart,' a 'dyke') throughout.
3 A former lawyer for the public defender, who quit because 'the set-up is pretty corrupt,' V.I. Warshawski positions herself in opposition both to conventional authority and to men: 'I have some close women friends, because I don't feel they're trying to take over my turf. But with men, it always seems,

or often seems, as though I'm having to fight to maintain who I am' (*Indemnity Only* 160).

4 Another scene in *The Silence of the Lambs* that weirdly echoes one in *Prime Suspect* occurs near the beginning of the film: Clarice Starling gets on an elevator filled with men; she is tiny, like a speck, among them.

5 For a brief discussion of this debt, see Wells 53.

6 Pykett elaborates: 'In these novels women are victims; they are hunted, they are frequently the quarry of aggressive males. However, the conventions of the detection genre also enable women, in the person of the female investigator, to become the hunter. This is not just a matter of the victim becoming the aggressor, simply by swapping roles within the existing system of power relations. Rather, the form of the detective novel is reshaped so as to deliver at least the narrative satisfaction of a transformation of existing power relations, as women refuse the role of victim by (often collectively) taking responsibility for their own lives' (27).

7 For a discussion of *The Silence of the Lambs* as 'high slasher,' see Clover 232–3.

8 Their disparity is emphasized in other ways as well, ways that place Tennison on a side with the misogynist 'lads.' At one point, Moira includes Tennison in her epithet 'You bastards' (not 'you bitch'), intended for the forces that 'never give anyone a break.' At another point, Tennison, using a phrase that would have done Otley justice, refers to Moira as 'that hard-nosed cow.'

9 That this final personal call is indeed an invasion is made clear by the warning Clarice gets from her supervisor, Crawford, at the start of the film: 'You don't want Hannibal Lecter inside your head.'

10 A similar recollection is evident in another hit women's film of 1991, *Thelma and Louise*, worth noting here if only because it was celebrated at the Academy Award presentations together with *The Silence of the Lambs* for its exemplary portrayal of women. No two films could be more disparate, of course: in *Thelma and Louise* the heroines kill the rapist, flee the cops, hit the road, and finally, in a fantasy of flight and movement, fly off the edge of a cliff into wide open sky. And yet the success of both films in the same year is no coincidence. Both works manifest, in exact mirror fashion, the same cultural upheaval, mobilizing around the topoi of women's entrapment and flight even as feminism itself ceased to imagine that women had anywhere to go.

11 The project of sustaining these contradictions is dropped in subsequent instalments in the *Prime Suspect* series. In *Prime Suspect 2* (1993) and *Prime Suspect 3* (1994), Tennison makes the choice that seems mandated by the vilification of male culture in the first *Prime Suspect*: she defies or circumvents the powers that be. She asks for a transfer, she goes to the newspapers. In

Prime Suspect 2 the last thing we see is not the murderer's face but Tennison walking out of the door of the station, moving 'outside' to a space that the first *Prime Suspect* was seemingly unable to represent. We should note, however, that the subject of these later instalments is not sexism but, respectively, racism and child abuse, two things that are much less problematic than 'men' for Tennison as a woman to reject.

WORKS CITED

Auden, W.H. 'The Guilty Vicarage.' *The Dyer's Hand and Other Essays*. By Auden. London: Faber and Faber, 1963.

Bakerman, Jane S. '"Living Openly and with Dignity" – Sara Paretsky's New-Boiled Feminist Fiction.' *Midamerica* 12 (1985): 120–35.

Barzun, Jacques. 'Detection and the Literary Art.' *The Mystery Writer's Art*. Ed. Francis M. Nevins, Jr. Bowling Green, Ohio: Bowling Green University Popular Press, 1970.

Clover, Carol J. *Men, Women, and Chainsaws: Gender in the Modern Horror Film*. Princeton: Princeton University Press, 1992.

Cornwell, Patricia D. *Postmortem*. 1990. New York: Avon, 1991.

Edenbaum, Robert I. 'The Poetics of the Private Eye: The Novels of Dashiell Hammett.' *Tough Guy Writers of the Thirties*. Ed. David Madden. Carbondale and Edwardsville: Southern Illinois University Press, 1968.

Godard, Barbara. 'Sleuthing: Feminists Re/writing the Detective Novel.' *Signature: A Journal of Theory and Canadian Literature* 1 (Summer 1989): 45–70.

Grafton, Sue. *'B' Is for Burglar*. 1985. New York: Bantam, 1986.

– *'E' Is for Evidence*. 1988. New York: Bantam, 1989.

– *'H' Is for Homicide*. New York: Fawcett Crest–Ballantine, 1991.

Kaplan, Alice Yaeger. 'Critical Fictions: Alice Yaeger Kaplan on the New Hard-Boiled Woman.' *Artforum* 28A (1990): 26–8.

Modleski, Tania. *Feminism without Women: Culture and Criticism in a 'Postfeminist' Age*. New York: Routledge, 1991.

Muller, Marcia. *Pennies on a Dead Woman's Eyes*. 1992. New York: Mysterious Press–Warner, 1993.

Paretsky, Sara. *Burn Marks*. New York: Dell, 1990.

– *Indemnity Only*. 1982. New York: Dell, 1990.

– Introduction. *A Woman's Eye*. Ed. Paretsky. New York: Dell, 1992. vi–xiv.

Prime Suspect. Teleplay by Lynda La Plante. Dir. Christopher Menaul. Prod. Granada Television. *Mystery!* WGBH Boston. 1991.

Pykett, Lyn. 'Seizing the Crime: Recent Women's Crime Fiction.' *New Welsh Review* 1 (1988): 24–7.

Reddy, Maureen T. 'The Feminist Counter-Tradition in Crime: Cross, Grafton, Paretsky, and Wilson.' *The Cunning Craft: Original Essays on Detective Fiction and Contemporary Literary Theory.* Ed. Ronald G. Walker and June M. Frazer. Macomb: Western Illinois University Press, 1990. 174–87.

Sandels, Robert. 'It Was a Man's World.' *Armchair Detective* 22 (1989): 388–96.

The Silence of the Lambs. Dir. Jonathan Demme. With Jodie Foster, Anthony Hopkins, and Scott Glenn. Prod. Strong Heart / Demme. Orion. 1991. Based on the novel by Thomas Harris.

Swanson, Jean, and Dean James. *By a Woman's Hand: A Guide to Mystery Fiction by Women.* New York: Berkley, 1994.

Wells, Linda S. 'Popular Literature and Postmodernism: Sara Paretsky's Hard-Boiled Feminist.' *Proteus* 6 (1989): 51–6.

5. From Spinster to Hipster: The 'Suitability' of Miss Marple and Anna Lee

Glenwood Irons and *Joan Warthling Roberts*

Amelia Butterworth is the prototypical spinster detective, created by Anna Katharine Green in 1897. Jane Marple, created by Agatha Christie some thirty years later, set the archetype in stone. Through mutation and reinvention, the British spinster detective has come down to us – via Harriet Vane and Cordelia Gray – in the guise of Liza Cody's modern hipster operative Anna Lee. For while the old spinster has in effect become a young hipster, many of the attitudes that surrounded the spinster remain. Just as the spinster frequently is the object of derision, so the hipster is the object of the condescension, irritation, and even scorn of her employer. And just as the spinster detective, by her very involvement in the murder mystery, undermines the structure of corporate law enforcement, so Anna, through her insistence on uncovering the violence exercised against women in her cases, subverts that structure, which, in the shape of her security firm, keeps her at the bottom of the pecking order, consigned to selling burglar alarms for the security of others.

Reflecting on the spinster who becomes hipster in British mystery fiction, we are left with a sense that, notwithstanding all the trappings of modernity which Anna enjoys, the British *woman* detective is still very much outside the mainstream – worse yet, is now more often than not the victim as well as the detector of the violent offender – and is still struggling to prove to those in authority that hers *is* a suitable job for a woman.

There are, of course, very good reasons why the *spinster* needed to prove that she had a place in the murder mystery. In *Reflecting on Miss Marple*, Marion Shaw and Sabine Vanacker describe the quintessential spinster as 'moral arbiter, curb of licence and disorder, and image of repression ... outside the normal expectations of a woman's life as it is lived in patriarchal society' (43). Obviously, the very definition of spinster implies that she has no place in the normal scheme of things – even in the abnormal scheme of things represented in a murder mystery!

The idea of a spinster involved in solving a mystery is on the surface paradoxical. Of course she pokes and pries, but then what good can come of it? What could she do with those bits and pieces of information she gets? The cliché is that the spinster is woolly-headed, has no logical methods of examining things, and worst of all, has no experience with passion or power, both of them in the domain of the young. How could she ever understand the murky motives behind a crime? But the spinster's potential lies more in her formidable intelligence and ability to connect seemingly insignificant details – indeed, in her existence outside the normal society of heterosexual couples – than in the repression which the term often implies.

And on the surface Christie seems to corroborate the stereotypically negative definition of the spinster. She gave the world Jane Marple seven or eight years after she had started writing detective fiction with Hercule Poirot as her first detective in 1920.[1] *The Murder at the Vicarage*, in 1930, is often cited as Miss Marple's début, but actually she entered the world of fiction in 'The Tuesday Night Club,' which appeared in 1928 (Wynne 208). In this first appearance, Miss Marple is about sixty-five years old, caught in the fashions and manners of the turn of the century. We see her through the eyes of her nephew, Raymond West, seated in his Aunt Jane's house: 'The room was an old one with broad black beams across the ceiling and it was furnished with good old furniture ... His Aunt Jane's house always pleased him as the right setting for her personality ... She sat erect in the big grandfather chair, wearing a black brocade dress, very much pinched in around the waist. Mechlin lace was arranged in a cascade down the front of the bodice. She had on black lace mittens; a black lace cap surmounted the piled-up masses of her snowy hair' (*Tuesday Club Murders* 2). Christie was adept at presenting her sleuth through the lens of condescending characters, in all her fuzziness (a narrative device allowing at least one male observer, someone of keener perception than most, to come to a new and startlingly revised appreciation of Miss Marple), and seen through the eyes of her fond but always condescending nephew, Jane Marple seems like a relic of a time past, functioning in the present world only as a bit of family background for her nephew's cleverness. Miss Marple never looked older and was never more of a sibyl than in that first story, seemingly 'out of time' and consulting with a host of inner voices – those of experience and memory – to find answers.

To a certain extent, the depiction of Miss Marple in such negative terms is not surprising, given Christie's failed marriage. And while Christie's spinster may, as Shaw and Vanacker make clear, 'trace her lineage back to Miss Bates in Jane Austen's *Emma*' (42), she is also connected to Green's Amelia Butterworth, a connection confirmed by Christie herself when she tells in her *Autobiography* of reading Green's mysteries as a young girl (210), and when, speaking through Hercule Poirot, she praises Green's work in *The Clocks* (116).

However, as she wrote more stories, Christie seemed to sense the too stereotypical nature of the character: Miss Marple kept getting younger, bustled about St Mary Mead in a more energetic, quotidian way, and dressed in a more country-tweedy fashion than in the earliest story. In the 1950s, for example in *A Pocket Full of Rye*, Jane Marple is a 'tall, elderly lady wearing an old-fashioned tweed coat and skirt, a couple of scarves, and a small felt hat with a bird's wing' (78). An aged but good-quality suitcase reposed by her feet. 'Aged but good quality' is the operative idea here. What does remain the same through the years is the implication of value. Jane, her house, and her belongings all embody those two shibboleths of English worth and gentility: age and fine quality. It is essential that there is absolutely nothing 'nouveau' about Miss Marple. Her quality has little to do with sexuality but a great deal to do with gender, and her experience, organized by a fine mind, makes her age an asset. She has not dried up like an unpicked apple, existing solely as a relic of fertility unused. Jane Marple has observed, thought, compared, and understood a great deal. Her interest in other human beings is natural, kindly, but never sentimentalized and fluffy, even though she finds it useful to keep a façade of fluffy knitting between herself and observers. Instead of mouthing sentimentalities, she is startlingly clear-eyed about the possibilities of human weakness and evil.

Jane Marple makes no lists but examines the evidence internally, and then brings out her observations in a flurry of apparent irrelevancies which snap together with the firmness of a steel trap. Her portrayal is the forthright and respectful portrayal of the older unmarried woman. She is still about sixty-five and is dismissed as useless and pesky by various bystanders in the novels, though the reader knows better. The pattern for the reception and recognition of Jane Marple emerges in 'The Tuesday Night Club,' where Jane is treated courteously, but where her contributions to the conversation elicit smiles and the slightest impatience. When the group is counted up, she is left out; each participant makes a case for the value of his or her insights, and the assumption is that Jane Marple has nothing to contribute. '"You have forgotten me, dear," said Miss Marple, smiling brightly. Joyce was slightly taken aback, but she concealed the fact quickly. "Miss Marple," she said, "I didn't think you would care to play." "I think it would be very interesting," said Miss Marple, "especially with so many clever gentlemen present. I am afraid I am not clever myself, but living all these years in St. Mary Mead does give one an insight into human nature"' (*The Tuesday Club Murders* 10). By the end of the story, Jane has solved the mystery, and Sir Henry Clithering – just retired as commissioner of Scotland Yard, for whom a better name might have been 'blithering' – is finally beginning to wonder about Miss Marple. After the thirteen stories in *The Tuesday Club Murders*, he is no longer wondering but has become her respectful friend and advocate, while the other participants still dismiss her in varying degrees. In *The Body in the Library*, Clithering characterizes Jane Marple as a detective so good that she is better at the job than he is. The reader has been led to see that recognition of Jane Marple's worth depends on a character's ability to perceive people clearly for what they are, and not through the fuzzy but comfortable lens of stereotype. Henry Clithering is happy to acknowledge the worth of his spinster sleuth. Still, coming as it does from a patriarchal authority, the recognition shows Miss Marple as needing the backing of men in order to be effective.

In more ways than might be obvious, the spinster character paved the way for women detectives like Cordelia Gray and Anna Lee in British mystery fiction. P.D. James effectively stripped Cordelia Gray of her power in *The Skull beneath the Skin*, but Liza Cody has revived the independent British woman detective in the six Anna Lee mystery novels, *Dupe* (1980), *Bad Company* (1982), *Stalker* (1984), *Headcase* (1985), *Under Contract* (1986), and *Backhand* (1991). Cody, however, reinvents the spinster from St Mary Mead as a young hipster from east-end London by rejecting some quintessential elements of Miss Marple and maintaining others. She rejects Miss Marple's age, her quaint Victorian surroundings, the rural location, and the cosy murder formula and maintains the protagonist's unmarried status, the questioning of her suitability for the job, and most important, the sense of victimization which seems to equate the woman detective with the murder victims themselves.

Liza Cody's first novel in the Anna Lee series, *Dupe*, was nominated for a number of awards and won the Crime Writers' Association John Creasey Award for best first crime novel of the year. The Anna Lee character first appeared in that novel and, as Swanson and James make clear in *By a Woman's Hand*, is considered by many critics in the United Kingdom to be the most important woman detective to arrive on the mystery fiction scene since Cordelia Gray (48). *Dupe* uses a device essential to all but one of the Anna Lee mysteries so far – the murder or victimization of a young woman; in this case the focus is on a suspicious car accident which kills Deirdre Jackson, the daughter of an upper-middle-class Wiltshire family.

The novel seems to be about the process of unravelling the circumstances of the car accident – the female victim is known to have been a good enough driver to have entered long-distance rallies from time to time – apparently a straightforward enough subject for a mystery novel. But like P.D. James's, to which hers is most often compared, one need only scratch the surface of Liza Cody's fiction to perceive a much more important raison d'être – a thinly veiled exploration of the random and vicious violence against women. It quickly becomes clear that Deirdre, the murdered young woman, has been the victim of male violence at various levels, but almost every woman we meet in *Dupe* is the victim of the males in her life. For example, Mrs Margolin, the wife of a nerdlike film society president, believes that her husband has been 'corrupted' by Deirdre, when in fact it is Mrs Margolin who has been victimized, by what she knows to have been a 'liaison' between the two. Anna Lee herself is the victim of a vicious attack by a male who is suspected of involvement in Deirdre's death. She is caught in the dimly lit hallway outside her flat and tries to 'protect her guts' and 'shield her head,' 'but a man with big feet can do a lot of damage in a short time' (208). She has teeth knocked out, ribs broken, and eyes blackened, injuries reminiscent of the worn and beaten victims who show up at shelters for battered women. To top it all off, Anna's boss surreptitiously keeps the reward money given to him for Anna's work – an irony not lost on the reader, who has witnessed various abuses of women throughout the novel.

Cody's novels rarely offer a tied-up-in-ribbons solution; the author wants to remind us that simple solutions are suspect. The ending of *Dupe* is no exception; we are left with a vague sense of who might have committed the murder Anna has been investigating, a vaguer sense of why Anna was beaten, and a strong feeling that the mother and father of the victim have forced themselves to come to grips with their daughter's murder in completely different ways. 'Deirdre was still an enigma, but Anna suddenly felt she should draw a line under her and get on with the next thing' (*Dupe* 245).

This modern hipster reincarnates many of the spinster qualities and reactions of Christie's Miss Marple. Anna's suitability for working on murder cases, for example, is challenged by her boss at Brierly Security. She is considered unsuitable because of her age – though rather than lacking passion because of old age, she is too passionate because of her youth. Even though Anna had been a good cop during her five years with the London Police, at Brierly Security she is best suited, it seems, to selling burglar alarms.

Cody's second and third Anna Lee mysteries, *Bad Company* and *Stalker*, introduce her readers to two very different environments. One of these, the inner circle of a motorcycle gang, is quite foreign to the average reader of mysteries, and the other, the inner circle of a town closely resembling that in which the author lives, offers a trip down memory lane. *Bad Company* continues Cody's investigation into the victimization of young women – Anna Lee and her client are held hostage by a gang of motorcycle hoodlums – but *Stalker* is unusual in that it involves the murder of a male victim. Nevertheless, the real victim in *Stalker* is Anna herself. She has extended the limits of her employment and feels no genuine satisfaction at solving the case: 'If Anna had wished for the affair to be settled by one positive action of her own, she was disappointed ... But that was the nature of her job: to paddle on the edge of other people's dramas ... Already she had taken her part in it further than her job allowed' (161).

Cody's fourth Anna Lee mystery, *Headcase* – recently made into a well-received two-hour special for ITV in the United Kingdom – is the first in a series whose theme is the treatment of women in modern England. The story introduces the tall and massive Quex, a character who challenges Anna's diffident attitude towards male/female relationships. But the mystery once again involves the victimization of a young woman – perhaps the most sordid of all, as the victim is barely into her mid-teens. Thea Hahn, the daughter of the civil servant Rodney Hahn and his wife, Valerie Hahn, has gone missing. It seems that the parents' interest in finding their daughter eleven days after she has disappeared stems mostly from a desire to protect the family image. Like many of the female victims in Cody's Anna Lee mysteries, Thea is no ordinary young woman: '"I suppose one should describe Thea as gifted," Rodney Hahn said, returning through the French windows ... "She could have begun at Cambridge last September"' (39). She is gifted in mathematics, plays expert chess, and was reading complicated philosophers like Montaigne at the age of nine.

Anna, having probed into the circumstances surrounding Thea's disappearance, discovers that she is in a hospital, and because of the young woman's mental instability Anna has her removed to Adam House, a local mental institution. We soon become aware that Thea has been the victim of a number of the men in her life, some of whom – her father, her tutor – should have been genuinely nurturing. The sad fact is that Thea's deteriorating mental condition has been occasioned by what appears to have been sexual abuse at the hands of the men to whom she was closest. And while the novel only intimates this, the television series explicitly blames Rodney Hahn for having sexually abused his daughter. The final scene in the telefilm, set in the Hahns' perfect back garden, has Anna chastising Thea's father for his sickening crime and leaves the viewer with a feeling of disgust for all men who victimize women.

Cody is not willing to let the reader find simple solutions to the familial problems outlined in *Headcase*. We are also left with an almost palpable sick feeling at the end of the novel too, less explicit though the resolution may be here. One of the men who has abused Thea is dead – his murder being the ostensible reason for the detective's quest – and Rodney Hahn is left to deal with his own not too heavy conscience. Readers, however, are left with an enormous sense of waste – the wasted life of Thea's tutor; the wasted life of Thea, at the hands of her father and her tutor; the wasted life of another woman, connected with the murder, who has had more than one unhappy extramarital affair. As in life, where there are few simple solutions, the solution of the murder in *Headcase* leaves us with a sense of emptiness since it does not explain away the victimization of the central character, Thea Hahn. In fact, the prime victimizer, Thea's father, simply believes that his daughter's mind has been 'poisoned' against him by the use of drugs.

In *Under Contract*, the fifth novel in the series, we are given insight into the strange, often violent, drug-infested world of the rock and roll singer Shona Una. A young rock star, probably modelled after Madonna in her early years, Shona is on the verge of superstardom. Unfortunately, she is being used as a chattel by just about everyone who surrounds her – the members of the rock band, which would be unknown without her; her lesbian lover and props mistress, who loves and leaves her; the manager of the band, who sees in her an important meal ticket; and finally, a rabid fan, who destroys her career at the end of the novel. Cody offers us a close-up view of a sordid world, particularly in the influence of hard drugs on Shona and her band members. But we are never allowed to forget that the rock singer's horrible fate in the penultimate chapter comes at the hands of those who have used and discarded her. 'The picture was in the evening papers next day. Somehow it looked more dreadful in black and white. "Pop Star Human Torch." Once again, Anna saw the blistered skin, the terrified eyes, blackened hair. No brows or eyelashes at all' (258). This powerful image of a life and career wasted – shortened by a vicious fan – is the picture the reader is left with in the last pages of the novel.

The most recent Anna Lee mystery, *Backhand*, gives considerable insight into the nature of Liza Cody's oeuvre, and reveals a great deal about the evolution of women detectives in the United Kingdom since the advent of Cordelia Gray. Anna Lee is a single woman who works for Brierly Security. She has been assigned the relatively uninteresting job of consulting with potential clients and installing burglar alarms. Anna's boss and the firm's secretary have more than occasional doubts about her competence, though her colleagues share her frequent contempt for both. In *Backhand*, Anna links up with a client, Lara Crowther, who is trying to help a friend, Penny Garden, salvage a fashion design business which seems to have gone bankrupt under mysterious circumstances. The client is also interested in finding both the friend's teenage daughter, Cynthia, who, it appears, has been taken against her will by Garden's husband, Hugh Fellows, and a great deal of the bankrupt company's merchandise.

Lara Crowther requires Anna to travel to Florida to trace Penny Garden's husband and daughter. In the United States, Anna takes on some of the characteristics of Sara Paretsky's V.I. Warshawski. She becomes exercise conscious and is beaten up and nearly killed in a hail of bullets while attempting to save the missing daughter. It emerges that Hugh Fellows is involved with the Mafia, and that Lara Crowther has neither been giving Anna the full story nor been telling the truth. Like V.I., Anna becomes mired in a problem – drug running – which seems out of all proportion to the case for which she was originally engaged.

Not surprisingly, most of the victims in *Backhand* are women, and many of them seem to be victims of their own unhappy circumstances. Moreover, while the finale to this mystery is a reunion of sorts, the restoration of order expected by readers of mystery fiction is not necessarily achieved. As in the earlier novels in the series, Cody avoids the relatively straightforward solutions of the Cordelia Gray novels, preferring to leave Anna with a sense of emptiness at the desperate future faced by her clients and even by herself. This kind of ending is indeed a Cody trade mark. In *Headcase*, for example, Anna discovers the murderer but also some unsavoury sexual facts about a teenage girl and one of her relatives. In *Under Contract*, Anna visits the destroyed rock star in her hospital bed, leaving readers with a feeling of waste and devastation at the loneliness of the once powerful singer, now deserted by almost everyone in her former entourage.

In fact, unlike the cosy murder mysteries featuring Amelia Butterworth and Jane Marple, Cody's stories never leave us with a sense of orderliness, either in Anna's life or in the lives of the characters around her at the end of the novels. But while the themes of the victimization of women and of familial breakdown seem to differentiate the Anna Lee series from other series with spinster detectives, by their very nature they also create a powerful link with the Miss Marple stories. Yes, we are anxious to see justice done and the killer apprehended, but we are always aware that uncovering the killer of a woman or the destroyer of a family may also uncover startling and troublesome facts about the lives of those close to the killer, about the lives of readers, and, of course, about the 'suitability' of the detective herself.

NOTES

1 The Miss Marple stories have never stopped coming off the presses, and the books are still hot items in used book stores. Recent BBC productions feature Joan Hickson as the redoubtable Jane. Forty years ago Christie observed Joan Hickson playing a young maid in a film starring Margaret Rutherford as Jane Marple. The author said at that time that she would like to see Joan Hickson play Miss Marple when she was old enough to do so. And, in a strange irony, so she does today.

WORKS CITED

Christie, Agatha. *Agatha Christie: An Autobiography.* New York: Dodd Mead, 1977.
– *The Body in the Library.* New York: Pocket Books, 1946.
– *The Clocks.* New York: Pocket Books, 1965.
– *A Pocket Full of Rye.* New York: Berkley, 1991.
– *The Tuesday Club Murders.* New York: Dell, 1982.
Cody, Liza. *Backhand.* 1991. Toronto: Seal, 1992.
– *Bad Company.* New York: Charles Scribner's Sons, 1982.
– *Dupe.* London: Arrow, 1980.
– *Headcase.* New York: Charles Scribner's Sons, 1985.

– *Stalker*. New York: Charles Scribner's Sons, 1984.

– *Under Contract*. New York: Charles Scribner's Sons, 1986.

Shaw, Marion, and Sabine Vanacker. *Reflecting on Miss Marple*. New York: Routledge, 1991.

Swanson, Jean, and Dean James. *By a Woman's Hand: A Guide to Mystery Fiction by Women*. New York: Berkley, 1994.

Wynne, Nancy Blue. *An Agatha Christie Chronology*. New York: Ace, 1976.

6. Nancy Drew: The Once and Future Prom Queen

Bobbie Ann Mason

On the secret shelf in my study stand all my girlhood books: the green Bobbsey books with Pennsylvania Dutch hexes on their covers; the brown Hardy Boys (I did have a few); the blue-gray Beverly Grays and Vicki Barrs; the red Judy Boltons and Cherry Ameses; and the most impressive looking of them all, the royal blue Nancy Drews.

It occurs to me now that Nancy's color is blue, and that this may be an important tip-off to the mystery of the girl in blue. Blue, after all, is our culture's chromatic emblem of boyhood. Blue is the color of baby boy bunting, of toy airplanes and motorcycles, of the vast skies and seas that Tom Swift and the Hardy Boys and all their rambunctious cohorts busily conquer. And blue is also a classy expression of reserved, WASPish 'good taste.' It's a perfect complement to Nancy's blond hair. And it's patriotic. Not only are the books blue, but Nancy's eyes are blue, and her sporty roadster is blue as well. In fact, my abiding image of Nancy is of her in a blue suit serenely driving her very own blue auto.

Nancy wears her blue primly, of course, and the reader of a Nancy book is never allowed to forget that our heroine – gunning down crooks – is a sweet young lady who dresses nicely and enjoys having tea with little cakes. But, as if authorized by a blue uniform, she is more boyishly daring than your average female adventurer. Nancy manages the impossible feat of being wholesomely 'feminine' – glamorous, gracious, stylish, tactful – while also proving herself strong, resourceful, and bold, the most independent of the girl sleuths. Nancy is a paradox, and she is also the most popular girl detective in the whole world.

There had been nothing in children's books like the success of Nancy Drew. She solved her first mystery in 1929, serenely ignoring the world crashing all around. By 1933 Macy's in New York was selling 6,000 Nancy Drews (ten titles by then), 3,750 of Bomba, the Jungle Boy, the most popular boys' series.[1] Edward Stratemeyer wrote (or plotted) the first three Nancy mysteries under the name 'Carolyn Keene,' but he did not live to see the spectacular rise of the new type of heroine he had helped fashion. His daughter, Harriet S. Adams, took over the series, pseudonym and all, and has written a volume nearly every year since 1930. She estimates that sixty million copies of Nancy Drew books have been sold. Nancy has managed to solve more than fifty mysteries (plus two or three versions of those which have been updated from time to time), most of them in the summer of her eighteenth year.

Much of Nancy's popularity, like that of the Bobbseys, comes from the appeal of her high-class advantages. She has everything a girl could want – a mere given for the privilege of sleuthing, Nancy style. She lives, with her understanding and trusting Dad, in a comfortable, tree-shaded colonial brick home with a circular drive – the affluent American version of fairy-land. Her lovely home is located in elusive River Heights, a city which is variously Eastern and MidWestern. Nancy has an endless wardrobe (with numerous 'sports dresses,' whatever those are), a dependable and worshipful boyfriend, and her own car. She gets to go anywhere in the world she wishes and she doesn't have to go to school. And for all her privileges, she is utterly unspoiled and charming. She is independent, brilliant, poised, courageous, kind, attractive, gracious, well-to-do – i.e., free, white, and sixteen.

Nancy is sixteen at the beginning of the series, then advances to eighteen, but she always behaves as if she is about thirty. She hasn't a shred of childishness in her. She is as immaculate and self-possessed as a Miss America on tour. She is as cool as Mata Hari and as sweet as Betty Crocker. She plays parent to frightened children and victims of misfortune, allaying fears and inspiring rapturous confidence instantly with her soothing, reasonable voice. The reason given for her astonishing self-possession is that her experience has matured her:

Since the death of her mother many years before, Nancy had managed the household. On the whole she had engineered everything so skillfully that her father little dreamed of the heavy responsibility which rested upon her shoulders.

The Mystery at Lilac Inn, p. 12

In short, there's no nagging mamma around to needle Nancy. Most other sleuths have mothers, but the degree to which the mothers interfere is the measure of how much fun the sleuth is allowed to have. The Hardy Boys have a mother, but she is hidden so successfully that the reader never suspects she has any power. Nancy has a housekeeper, Mrs. Hannah Gruen, a jackie-of-all-chores who plays the maternal role (worrywart and cook), but Nancy is mistress of the household, and her power extends beyond the home. She gets instant service from policemen, even in a strange town. She calls up, identifies herself and says,

'Please send a plainclothes detective at once. I'll meet him in the lobby here and explain everything to him when he arrives. How will I know him?'
    'He'll pretend to be lame.'

The Clue in the Crumbling Wall, p. 123

No questions asked.

Nancy is the type of person who leaves calling cards, another indication of her maturity and authority. She doesn't have to resort to any humiliating wheedling, whims, or fits, like most kids, to get what she wants. She doesn't have to beg to go on an impossible trip to Florida, as I once did. When she needs to follow up a clue, she says simply (but cunningly), 'Dad, do you suppose you could manage a Florida vacation next week?' (*The Clue of the Black Keys*, p. 126) Obliging Dad lets her make the trip without him. And, once there, Nancy finds it necessary to pursue the mystery to Mexico, a trip she makes with ease. (I still haven't been to Florida, and I've abandoned all hope of ever seeing Mexico.) Readers respect Nancy's seriousness. She is usually too busy solving a mystery to engage in frivolity. Only in rare instances does she lose her cool, and then only momentarily. Even when she is locked in a room full of spiders, she doesn't get the creeps, as any real girl would. Instead, she proceeds logically, calmly, to find an exit. At all times Nancy possesses infinite courage, calm, and modesty:

Bess was concerned. 'Why, Nancy, you might have slipped off that roof and been killed!'
    Nancy grinned. 'I guess I'm just a tough old sleuth,' she answered.

The Clue of the Broken Locket (rev. ed.), p. 74

'As for Nancy and her exploits, girls have thrilled vicariously to their heroine's unusual ability. How all of us, in our childhood, aspired to the heroic!' comments Andrew E. Svenson of Stratemeyer Syndicate.

Nancy's abilities certainly left me limp with longing. I couldn't even answer roll call in the schoolroom without blushing, so my adulation of Nancy was understandable. I wonder how many little girls – especially shy ones – secretly imagine themselves as circus performers or movie stars. I did, certainly. Nancy acts out those fantasies. She is a bareback ballerina in a circus, a dancer, an actress. When a leading lady is taken ill, Nancy replaces her after rehearsing only once. (Once! I feel as if I have rehearsed my whole life.) Even when she has to fall back on purely feminine arts, she is applauded: her flowers win first prize in the flower show. Nancy is so accomplished that she can lie bound and gagged in a dank basement or snowed-in cabin for as much as twenty-four hours without freezing to death or wetting her pants. And she is knowledgeable about any convenient subject. She always has, at tongue's tip, virtually any information needed on a case. She once did an overnight cram course in archaeology and passed a college test with a brilliant score. The ease of her achievements is inspiring to every bandy-legged or pimply little girl who follows her adventures. In one book Nancy discovers an injured man who has a shell fragment in his forehead. When the doctor arrives, her friends respectfully leave. 'Nancy alone remained to assist the man of medicine.'

'Have you a steady nerve?' he questioned her.

'I think so,' Nancy answered quietly.

The operation was not a pleasant thing to witness, but at last it was finished, and the doctor declared that the patient had an excellent chance to recover.

'Have you ever studied nursing?' he asked Nancy abruptly.

'Oh, no, I've had only training in first aid.'

'You seem to have missed your calling,' the doctor told her with a smile. 'You appear to have a natural bent for nursing.'

Nancy flushed at the praise.

The Haunted Bridge, p. 121

If girls cannot aspire to important careers in medicine and law and business, they can be rewarded for assisting men, and Nancy dares the limits of the female nursemaid-secretary role. Her father, a lawyer, admires her talents so much that he makes her his special assistant, and she frequently shows him up.

Not only is Nancy perfect, but she possesses the ideal qualities of each age and sex: child, girl, teenager, boy, and adult. She has made a daring stride into adulthood, and she also trespasses into male territory without giving up female advantages. Nancy's adolescent readers may not know whether to shave their legs and giggle to attract the boys they are discovering, or to join the boys' games and emulate them to win their approval, but Nancy does both; although, being pure, she gives no thought at all to romance – or, flush, sex. Nancy's two sidekicks, squeamish Bess and tomboy George, emphasize this ambivalence. Bess Marvin is 'dainty' and 'feminine,' and George Fayne, her cousin, is boyish and says 'Hypers' a lot. George wears her hair short and scoffs at Bess's romantic ideas.

'Old lace is valuable,' declared Bess.... 'Oh,' she sighed, 'we girls should wear more lace. In olden times ladies appreciated its lure! The great ladies of the Court knew its power!'

'Yes,' said George with a grimace. 'You know who first thought of lace, don't you? Fishermen. The first lace was a fish net, made to lure food from the sea!'

'George, you're disgustingly unromantic,' said her cousin.

The Secret in the Old Attic, p. 136

When Nancy and her friends tour Pleasant Hedges, a run-down estate where Nancy is working on a case, they inspect the old slave quarters.

'What a story this place could tell,' sighed Bess. 'Old mammies crooning, little pickaninnies dancing—'

'You certainly have a good imagination,' said George practically. 'Without a piece of furniture or a rug or a picture in the place, how can you think of such things?'

The Secret in the Old Attic, p. 17

Bess is the most passive, squeaky-feminine character in girls' mysteries. She is gullible and giggly. She buys a perfume which her friends suspect is a cheap imitation. When a swindler plays on her sympathies, she is sucked into giving money to a nonexistent orphan Indian. In the presence of a handsome male, she flirts selfconsciously. ('Bess daintily disciplined her hair with her finger tips.' *The Clue of the Black Keys*, p. 20) She is plump because she eats too much, always lapsing into mindless sensuality when fudge sundaes are around. She embodies the stereotype of passive female consumerism. Bess can't keep secrets, or whistle, and most of her thoughts are about boys, fun, and food. She watches the picnic supplies carefully when the girls are traveling, for fear they will starve to death.

Nancy sleuths virtually unaided. George and Bess spend most of their time hanging around, wringing their hands, window shopping or drinking tea, while Nancy figures and figures. They are recognizable only by their loyalty and as mirrors of Nancy's two halves, demonstrating the extreme options open to young females – tomboy and fluff-head. The two roles are clumsy, short-sighted examples of the females we are taught to loathe as we become more and more alienated from our selves. When I played at solving mysteries with a girlfriend in 1951, both of us had to contend with all the conflicting impulses to be girls, boys, tomboys, ladies. Nancy serenely pulls all the impulses into one role. George, for all her muscles and ability to climb and row, and her habit of 'galloping' into the room, doesn't have the poise and grace which enables Nancy to maneuver slickly through tight situations, and Bess couldn't even begin to try.

The plots of Nancy Drew mysteries are like sonnets – endless variations on an inflexible form. A plot may contain any or all of these elements: the pursuit of at least two separate mysteries which turn out to be astonishingly intertwined; a warning to get off the case; a trip to a quaint or exotic place (with tourist bureau description supplied); the befriending of an innocent victim (a gentle foreign girl, a kindly businessman, a helpless little old lady) who faces ruin if the mystery isn't solved; a romantic story about a tradition or secret in a prominent family; the appearance of twins or doubles; sinister encounters with the villains (burglaries and sabotages, kidnappings and chases); any number of mishaps (including frequent, but not serious, injury to Nancy); and imprisonment of either Nancy or the innocent victim. The ending is usually a crescendo of swift events: catastrophe just as Nancy is about to break the case, rescue by police/friends/family, an easy roundup of the crooks (who can't have gone far in the time it takes for Nancy's loyal protectors to find her), the immediate and crestfallen confession, discovery of the treasure or secret, and celebration and praise of the girl sleuth. Nancy tries to point out that there would have been no victory without the superb aid of her friends, but everyone gives her the credit for solving the mystery.

Nancy Drew plots are based on coincidence. In one book Nancy witnesses a pickpocket performing his art at least a dozen times, and she happens to be snacking at the very hamburger heaven where he is finally arrested. In *The Password to Larkspur Lane*, Nancy happens to be picking larkspurs in her garden when a plane flies over and drops a message which leads her into the mystery. The message, of course, is the password to Larkspur Lane. The workings of mysteries depend on convenient coincidences – mysteries celebrate coincidence. And for readers the longing to solve a mystery is also a desire for a real coincidence. Indeed, it would have been some coincidence if my parents had okayed that trip to Florida. And little girls depend on coincidence. They learn to be passive, and wait for the day when they will coincidentally be in the same room with a handsome man who will coincidentally fall in love with them.

The settings a girl sleuth like Nancy has to work within are all feminine, domestic, aristocratic, slightly Gothic – quaint reminders of a traditional, Victorian, idealized world. They are 'enchanting,' fascinating and intricate, like enlarged dollhouses. In *The Clue in the Crumbling Wall*, Nancy and her friends explore the grounds of Heath Castle, a replica of an old English castle, which has decayed into a jungle of neglect.

At the end of the oak-lined avenue the girls came to a weather-stained loggia of stone. Its four handsomely carved pillars rose to support a balcony over which vines trailed. Steps led to the upper part.

Mounting to the balcony, Nancy and her friends obtained a fine view of the near-by gardens. They had been laid out in formal sections, each one bounded by a stone wall or a hedge. Here and there were small circular pools, now heavy with lichens and moss, and fountains with leaf-filled basins.

The Clue in the Crumbling Wall, pp. 30–31

They cross a 'rustic bridge which spanned a stream so clogged with water lilies that there scarcely was any space between them.' A slippery, moss-grown path labeled 'Haunted Walk' spooks Bess. They find themselves in 'a vine-tangled, fern-matted bower. Two handsome stone vases lay on their sides, cracked from having filled with water which had frozen during the winter.' (p. 30) Such rich description is reserved for quaint settings in the Nancy books, for usually the language is formal and sparse. Here, romantic ruin evokes nostalgia for a past order, and it whips up the tidying impulse. A girl sleuth is a kind of gardener for tragic victims. When she enters the case she already envisions the hedges trimmed, the flowers blooming, the grass mowed. The unscrupulous lawyer responsible for the upkeep of Heath Castle has ignored it, as men whose wives are away (in a conventional world) will let the sink pile up with dirty dishes.

The wronged woman in that book, Miss Flower, is also a dedicated gardener, and when her property is recovered she turns the estate into showplace perfection, with a velvety smooth lawn and masses of blooms, before you can say Jack Sprat. The fact that she is crippled and has suffered ten years of woe is irrelevant. The recovery of property rights is like a dose from the fountain of youth.

All mansions in the Nancy books are haunted – not by ghosts but by swindlers seeking secrets. They haunt hidden passages and secret attics in their search for concealed treasure. Scenes about Nancy's discovery of hidden compartments go something like this:

'I can feel something with my fingers!' Nancy said in an excited voice. 'A little bump in the wood!'

'Probably it's a knothole,' George contributed skeptically.

'It's a tiny knob!' corrected Nancy. 'Girls, I've found a secret compartment!'

The Secret in the Old Attic, p. 138

(With hilarious clarity, I see here the girls' mysteries as a celebration of masturbation!) Nancy is called away for five pages and when she returns Bess and George are still tugging at the knob, but as soon as Nancy renews her grip, the panel opens. 'Nancy gave the knob a quick jerk sideways. A little door pulled up, revealing a recess below.' (p. 143)

Sometimes the mystery revolves around an intricate object which is a miniaturized version of the mansion: a carved brass chest filled with jewelry, an ancient map, a will hidden in an old clock, an ivory charm, an old family album, a broken locket. Two of the most splendid objects appear in *The Clue in the Jewel Box*.

One piece completely captured the girl's interest. It was a pink enamel Easter egg which stood on a tiny gold pedestal. Its rounded cover was encrusted with delicate gold work. (p. 6)

Inside, rising from a nest of velvet, was a tiny tree set with emeralds. Upon a jeweled branch was perched a delicately fashioned nightingale. (p. 30)

This Fabergé-inspired nightingale sings out the clue in the jewel box – yet another splendid object. The allure of these objects and settings derives from the books' essential conservatism. Femininity is safely enthroned in charming Victorian manses: this is the tea-party world.

As the girls sipped their tea and ate delicious, frosted cakes, their hostess spoke rather sadly of present daily life in her native land so changed from the past.

The Clue in the Jewel Box, pp. 27–28

The most appealing elements of these daredevil girl sleuth adventure books are (secretly) of this kind: tea and fancy cakes, romantic settings, food eaten in quaint places (never a Ho-Jo's), delicious pauses that refresh, old-fashioned picnics in the woods, precious jewels and heirlooms. These things are, subtly, more appealing than the car chases, kidnappings, and burglaries. The word 'dainty' is a subversive affirmation of a feminized universe. It sneaks in and out of the books like a delicate gold thread, offsetting the pell-mell action of the plot. Nancy wears dainty dresses to dainty tea dances where she nibbles on dainty sandwiches. The stories seem to satisfy two standards – adventure and domesticity. But adventure is the superstructure, domesticity the bedrock. The Nancy books give it to the readers from both sides, and never once betray a suspicion that they are contradictory. Nancy's daring exploits release readers from the abyss of sorority teas and sewing bees while at the same time congratulating that tea-party and sewing-basket world.

The girl sleuth's quest, then, is not really for the unknown, but for the known, for the familiar. No thugs and smugglers can dwell in their grungy hideouts on canned beans for long when a girl sleuth is around. Solving a mystery, in girls' books, is actually the fictional equivalent of baking a cake, piecing together a quilt or jigsaw puzzle, sewing a fine seam, or spring cleaning.

In her defense of the cozy tea-party scene, Nancy uses traditional feminine wiles, relying on her instincts, intuition, and charm. A sleuth, that is to say, is a sneak. In *The Secret in the Old Attic* Nancy's father assigns her to get information from the secret laboratory of a factory, which may be using a stolen formula. Nancy gets into the factory by cultivating the friendship of the director's daughter, Diane, a conceited girl she dislikes. Nancy arranges to meet Diane 'accidentally,' and then cajoles the girl into taking her on a tour of the factory. Nancy wears her best party things to arouse Diane's interest and envy. She accomplishes her goal, reaching the secret inner sanctum, where, to divert attention from her real mission, she feigns illness. A workman helps her.

'Are you sick?' he asked in a coarse, heavy voice.

Nancy did not want to answer questions. To avoid them she pretended to faint. The act was well timed, for the man, frightened, immediately rushed into the hall for help. The young detective smiled.

The Secret in the Old Attic, p. 67

While he is gone, she gleefully snoops, and afterward beguiles a brusque businessman. Her father 'could not hide a smile when he heard of her ruse.' (p. 69)

Nancy is generally above the low habit of eavesdropping, but when she 'accidentally' overhears something, she always tunes in at the critical moment. No sooner does she hear voices than they say something like 'That Drew girl is on our trail!' And Nancy won't snoop around people's private papers without good reason – but there generally is one. Once she is lecturing a young professor on detecting: he hasn't learned to notice things like people's mail and telephone messages. '"I'm afraid a good detective has to snoop," Nancy said.' (*The Clue of the Black Keys*, p. 92)

To the extent that a girl sleuth is a sneak, some of her wiliest sleuthing involves deceiving her boyfriends or leading them on a merry chase. Nancy won't go out with a creep even if it means missing the dance of the year – until she finds out, of course, that she might pursue some clues there. In *The Haunted Bridge*, Nancy is plagued by the attentions of Mortimer Bartescue, one of the slick, conceited characters Nancy instantly dislikes (her judgment of character is flawless and instantaneous). He is not a criminal, just a 'cheap boaster.' Nancy, however modest and generous she is, has no room in her heart for people who are uppity and shallow-minded. Mortimer Bartescue is an unpleasant flirt with:

sleek black hair plastered back from an angular, hard face.... Obviously he was a braggart, and she rather distrusted his claim that he came from an excellent family.

The Haunted Bridge, pp. 6–7

However, she accepts an invitation to a dance because she needs to do some sleuthing.

Although Nancy admires her steady boyfriend, Ned Nickerson, she is not gaga about him and she doesn't treat him much better than she does Mortimer. Ned is a college football star who is as bland as Nancy is blonde and he has nothing on his mind except football and sex. Every time Ned gets Nancy alone a mystery intervenes.

'Are you willing to help me?' Nancy asked eagerly.

'Of course. I thought you didn't need any assistance.'

'Oh, Ned, it was just that I couldn't explain everything, and I'm afraid I can't even now.'

'That doesn't matter, Nancy. You tell me what to do and I'll obey orders with no questions asked.'

'It may mean ruining your evening, Ned. Are you willing to substitute sleuthing for dancing?'

'We can dance when we get back to River Heights.'

'That's the way I feel about it,' Nancy agreed in satisfaction. 'It may be that I am too hopeful, but I honestly believe matters will come to a climax tonight.'

The Haunted Bridge, pp. 170–171

Nancy has Ned under her thumb, and she must keep him there if she is to protect her purity. The series is purposely mum about sex, as any girl's premarital life is supposed to be. But as it is in anything that interests adolescents, sex is subtly present. Mysteries are a substitute for sex, since sex is the greatest mystery of all for adolescents. The Nancy Drew books cleverly (and no doubt unintentionally) conceal sexual fascination, especially since Nancy is frequently embarrassed by Ned's attentions. Once Nancy and Ned go to a carnival and get stuck at the top of a ferris wheel. And up there on top of the world Nancy gives way to one of her rare giggles. Pity for Ned that they weren't stuck in the Tunnel of Love.

Ned longs for a moment alone with Nancy, but she diverts his attention toward sleuthing. At the climax of *The Secret of the Golden Pavilion,* Ned unearths the treasure, a long, colored cape of bird feathers.

'Why, this is one of those ceremonial capes made from the extinct o-o bird!' Nancy exclaimed softly. 'A museum piece!'

The Secret of the Golden Pavilion, p. 168

Nancy is a scholar, and a scholar is a version of a sleuth, but Ned has only the male's territorial rights in mind. He puts on the cape and struts around proudly like a peacock parading its plumage. Again the mystery intrudes: the thugs come, whisk away Ned's feathers, and imprison the couple in a dungeon. There they are, together at last in the dark, but Nancy urges escape. They find a secret door which won't budge, so Ned throws himself against it.

Ned, down on one knee like a football lineman about to charge his opponents, lunged. His shoulder thudded against the masonry.

'Oh, Ned,' Nancy whispered. 'You'll break a bone.'

The Secret of the Golden Pavilion, p. 172

They escape and Nancy is eager to find their captors and the cape. 'This is our chance to do a little sleuthing,' she says. Ned reluctantly follows. First, Nancy has to find her shoes and stockings, which she had earlier removed in order to impersonate a white-robed ghost in the moonlight, hoping to frighten the crooks. Poor Ned Nickerson! They could have stayed blissfully in their prison till morning with no questions asked. Nancy had even shed some clothing.

Nancy and her girlfriends are shockingly independent, but a strong moral code guards them. They travel and stay at motels by themselves, and even meet their boyfriends at motels – where they stay in carefully assigned separate rooms. The girls stay only at places with a 'charming and homelike atmosphere.' A hilarious slip occurs in *The Mystery of the Tolling Bell* when Ned and Nancy have a car accident and have to hitch a ride on a truck to Nancy's boarding-house.

Then, at Mrs. Chantrey's insistence, Ned accepted an invitation to stay over-night, and everyone wearily went off to his room for a much-needed sleep.

The Mystery of the Tolling Bell, p. 154

It is difficult to imagine Ned with everyone sleeping in *his* room! The formal, correct style of the Nancy books tripped over itself in this unconsciously sexist phrase.

Ned and Nancy are 'friends' in the early books, and Nancy greets him 'cordially' on the phone. Ned strains to win Nancy's approval, but she notices him most when she needs his muscles. On one occasion Ned is eager for their date, while Nancy is preoccupied with her current case.

'How do you like my new suit?'

'You look handsome in it,' Nancy praised, without noting in detail what he wore.

The Haunted Bridge, pp. 168–169

The books affirm a double standard for female sexuality: attention to beauty and clamps on virginity. Nancy has all the glamour of a starlet, but the entrances to her emotions and physical desires are closed up tight. Nancy driving her convertible looks like the come-on car ads, but she resists this passive, seductive image. She is no leisure-lily lolling on tiger upholstery. Her foot is on the accelerator. But indignant male chauvinists are always puncturing her tires or shoving her into a ditch. A girl isn't supposed to drive! She's supposed to be an accessory to a car, like a vinyl steering wheel cozy. Men threaten Nancy because she threatens their masculinity. Crooks and cops alike want to stifle Nancy's energy, but she is smugly superior.

'I guess those two younger men were pretty annoyed with me!' Nancy thought as she left the police station. 'Afraid I'll take some glory from them!'

The Clue in the Jewel Box, pp. 147–148

The evil-eyed desperados on Nancy's trail (because she knows too much) are actually insecure old geezers with funny names who draw attention to their basic weaknesses by resorting to clumsy, melodramatic ploys. They use mysterious haunting devices (ghostly bells, phantoms, weird noises) to frighten Nancy away from their hideouts. As soon as Nancy gets a whiff of a mystery, the crooks start hurling rocks through her window, sending crude messages ('Keep off the case or else!)', sabotaging her car, kidnapping right and left – all sorts of ill-tempered tricks. But their underhanded efforts only get Nancy's dander up. She knows instinctively that they are cowards. She keeps her wits and hits them with the weapon they fear most – truth. They can't stand to have such a nosy know-it-all trip them up. In fact, they are usually so deeply humiliated when Nancy catches up with them that they spew out confessions without any urging, taking pride in having eluded her for as long as they did. Lee Zacharias, author of an unpublished paper on Nancy Drew, notes that Nancy is vain, revengeful, and competitive in her pursuit of justice, and that she wants to humiliate her enemies. 'Nancy is no mere detective. She has a compulsion to reduce her villains to broken old men. The attractive young sleuth is a ballbuster!'[2]

No girl sleuth is so frequently injured as Nancy. Nasty mean men are continually bopping her over the head with phallic objects, but they never get her down. She manages to dance an inspiring ballet in spite of her sprained ankle and she wins a golf tournament after spraining her hand when she topples into a flowerbed, trying to avoid slimy Mortimer Bartescue. Thus, Nancy busily fends off sexual advances, including 'evil' desires in her own trusted Ned, who is always trying to get her alone in the moonlight. She runs from sex but literally chases substitute forms of 'evil' – threats against property and law and order. Nancy thinks nothing of racing after a shadowy figure.

'Dad, that man stole a purse!' Nancy whispered excitedly. 'I'm going after him!'

Before Mr. Drew could recover from his surprise, she had scrambled past him and was hurrying up the aisle after the thief.

The Clue in the Old Album, p. 2

It would never occur to her that he might shoot or rape her. This restraint on realistic violence has the effect of exaggerating Nancy's power. And it underscores the contradiction: Nancy both pursues sex and runs from it.

The evil embodied in the purse-snatching, kidnapping jewel-thief gangs Nancy chases is a vaguely defined lurking force. This was precisely my understanding of evil, too, in 1951. It was always some Humbert Humbert version of a bogeyman who might hide behind bushes, or in the hayloft, or in the impenetrable darkness of the night air itself. Little girls are taught to look for evil everywhere, and to be on guard (that accounts for the contradiction, the eager defensiveness). Whenever it occurs to Nancy to look for footprints she always finds them 'freshly made,' like cookies, in the 'soft earth.' I looked for footprints until I was blue in the face. They are a lot harder to locate than one might suppose.

Nancy is out looking for evil because there are treasures to be protected. We follow clues toward something hidden, precious, and beautiful which must be defended from the greedy, disreputable tricksters. This, one supposes, is a neat Freudian analogy to the precious jewel of a girl's virginity (wonder why I didn't pick up on that in 1951? Or did I?). Often the treasure in the story is something priceless – information about a long-lost relative, an irreplaceable heirloom, or a chest of jewels. The villains are symbolic rapists who want to violate the treasure, men who haven't the proper credentials (refinement, family, education, property) to claim it. They are pushy, grabby, crude, rough, illiterate.

They are found in an assortment of Gypsies, tramps and thieves – rootless crooks and carnival clowns who have strayed from maternal and institutional influence, who want to snatch at the upper echelons of the good life. Evil is not only sexy in Nancy's universe, it's disgustingly lower class. And the men aren't just evil, they're strange. Their names tell that: Rudy Raspin, Tom Tozzle, Tom Stripe, Mr. Warte, Bushy Trott, Grumper, Alonzo Rugby, and Red Buzby. They are all good-for-nothings who want to upset the elitist WASP order. They are tricksters and hucksters who sneer at the authorities – the paternal benevolence of the businesses, institutions, and laws of the reigning upper classes.

Appearances are never deceptive in Nancy's Ivory-pure life. Good and evil are strictly white and black terms. Criminals are dark-hued and poor. One crook is 'dark, with a mottled complexion and piercing black eyes.' (*The Clue in the Old Album*, p. 4) This typical comic-strip crook shows up book after book:

The brim of his battered felt hat was pulled low over his forehead and the turned-up collar of his topcoat concealed his mouth and chin. But Nancy could see a pair of piercing black eyes.

The Clue of the Leaning Chimney, p. 3

Piercing dark eyes are the most common characteristic of Nancy's foes. Their greedy eyes are piercing because they are disrespectful, gazing threateningly beyond their station, perhaps seeing through the facades of the gentry whose power they crave. All the virtues of refinement, taste, intelligence, and beauty belong to Nancy's class, while everyone else is vulgar, greedy, ill-tempered, insolent. Most of them are braggarts and boasters who use aliases and bad grammar and wear wicked facial expressions. Their evil permeates the slums, which are dangerous dens of cut-throats, thugs, and thieves. When Nancy drives by, the dirty kids on the street force her to slow down, and when she is sleuthing along the waterfront, disreputable persons stare at her.

There is an even lower class in Nancy's universe, but its members rarely cross the boundaries. Nancy's housekeeper, Mrs. Gruen, is portrayed in the early books as an elderly charwoman; in later books she is Nancy's motherly confidante, but she is still a servant. Nancy feels that 'To be mistaken for a housemaid was not at all flattering' (*The Clue of the Tapping Heels*, p. 146), but in *The Whispering Statue* she impersonates a maid in order to snoop in someone's room. In the first eighteen books there are seventeen Blacks – all servants.[3] They speak, grinning, in *Gone with the Wind* language, and they are often unpleasant. In *The Mystery at Lilac Inn*, Nancy interviews a servant sent from an employment agency. In despair she learns the only one they have left is 'a colored woman.'

... a more unlikely housekeeper Nancy had never seen. She was dirty and slovenly in appearance and had an unpleasant way of shuffling her feet when she walked.

The Mystery at Lilac Inn, p. 16

Blacks are rarely villains, however. I suppose the specter of a black man organizing a gang of jewel thieves would have been thought by the white upper classes to be much too unsettling and threatening for a blonde white girl sleuth series. One of the few characters who unnerves Nancy during her detecting career is an odd 'freckled-faced colored man who sways when he walks.'

'Oh, you startled me!' Nancy laughed, whirling around. 'I half expected to see a colored man leering at me.'

'Well, that's complimentary, I must say,' the youth returned with a grin. 'I'm pretty sunburned but I didn't know I looked as dark as that.'

Nancy told him about the missing tools and her theory that they had been taken by a colored person who had visited the house the previous day.

'Why, I met a darky on the street yesterday!' Ned exclaimed.

The Clue of the Tapping Heels, pp. 78–79

When Nancy travels to the South, she *is* waited on by cheerful black servants in colonial mansions. In *The Hidden Window Mystery* (1956) lovable old Beulah serves squabs, sweet potatoes, corn pudding, piping hot biscuits, and strawberry shortcake.

When the maid left the room, Susan smiled and whispered to the girls, 'I try to make things easier for Beulah but she insists upon working and serving everything the old-fashioned way. I must confess, though, that I love it.'

Cliff's eyes twinkled. 'Beulah's a rare person,' he said. 'She sort of lives in the past, and is very much like her mother, who worked for my mother. She imitates her in everything.'

The Hidden Window Mystery, p. 64

In the 1930s and 1940s the series treated badly a number of other minority groups, especially Italians (swarthy gangsters) and Jews (scheming snobs). The police always had Irish names and they were blockheads, except for Nancy's kindly Chief McGinnis. Gypsies get the familiar Bobbsey treatment in Nancy Drew books, but because Gypsies are so exotic – with much romance about child-brides and mysterious violinists – Nancy is careful to distinguish between good and bad Gypsies. Gypsies embody everything any all-American straight-A girl sleuth would like to wipe off the face of the earth; but because they wear nice costumes and make beautiful music they are treated like a tourist attraction. In the original version of *The Clue in the Old Album,* which is still in print, Nancy solves a mystery for Mrs. Struthers, a fine old soul whose daughter eloped with a Gypsy. The daughter had died (retribution for her sin) and left a half-wild child for Mrs. Struthers to bring up. Nancy restores the child to her exiled father, a brilliant Gypsy violinist. Family reconciliation banishes all wildness, and Mrs. Struthers accepts the man.

Foreigners in the Nancy Drew series are either shifty-eyed sneaks or benevolent aristocrats. The shifty ones have dark, piercing eyes and are from southern Europe, while the Nordics are more beautiful and aristocratic. At the beginning of one mystery Nancy aids 'an aristocratic elderly lady' who is ill and asks Nancy to take her home.

Nancy hesitated, not because she was unwilling to help, but because for an instant she wondered if she might become the victim of a hoax. Although the stranger used perfect English, she spoke with a slight accent.

The Clue in the Jewel Box, p. 3

Girl sleuths can't be too careful, especially with foreigners. But this lady's noble heart shows in her face. 'The smile with which she was rewarded immediately erased any doubt in the girl's mind that this person intended to bring any harm to her.' (p. 3)

That story illustrates perfectly what Nancy Drew is all about. In *The Clue in the Jewel Box* Madame Alexandra (the foreigner with the smile) is an elegant, exiled ex-queen, the epitome of the endangered aristocratic tradition Nancy supports. Nancy reunites Madame Alexandra with her long-lost grandson, who has grown up under the name Francis Baum, without knowing he was a prince. Baum turns out to be a bum; he is ill-educated and has horrible manners. Ignoring Nancy's explicit instructions to wear evening clothes, he wears sports togs to the elegantly formal eight-course dinner which Madame Alexandra has arranged to celebrate his return. Soon Nancy begins to regret having solved this mystery, because it is obvious that Francis Baum is siphoning off the old lady's treasures. Actually, of course, he is an impostor, but there are no proofs of this yet, except his boorishness. Mrs. Gruen indignantly picks up this sure clue one day when she is feeding him lunch:

'If that man is a lost prince, then I am a queen! Did you see the way he gobbled his food? A few bites, indeed! He ate enough for six men!' (p. 62)

Nancy concurs. Mr. Drew, who is for giving the 'prince' the benefit of the doubt, chides Nancy for her harsh judgment; 'No doubt he has had to shift for himself for a long time.' But Nancy isn't fooled. She knows in her heart that a real prince has innate refinement. She ultimately exposes the impostor and finds the real prince, who turns out to be a Mr. Ellington, who lives right there in River Heights. In fact, Nancy has already admired him (Mr. Ellington is SO elegant) and secretly wondered if he is perhaps the lost prince, since he has such beautiful manners. Miraculously, it turns out to be so. His identity is proven by the clue in the jewel box – the same clue that is the downfall of Francis Baum.

Thus, the original Nancy Drew series – the first thirty-five or so volumes which accumulated throughout the 1930s, 1940s, and 1950s – portrays a fading aristocracy, threatened by the restless lower classes. These are the themes which informed my childhood, when I aspired toward the delicious snobbery of Nancy's privileged life. When minorities know their place, Nancy treats them graciously. She is generous to truck drivers and cabbies and maids. But woe betide the upstarts, the dishonest social climbers who want to grab at the top.

Nancy's job is to preserve the class lines, and for her the defense of property and station are inextricably linked with purity and reputation. She defends beautiful objects, places, and treasures from violence – the sexual violence of nasty men who want to stifle her energy. There is a 'proper' male authority which Nancy accepts. Almost inevitably she needs Dad or Ned to step in at the climax of the mystery to help save the treasure and rescue her from kidnappers' clutches. ('"Oh Dad. I thought you'd never come!" she said, snuggling to his neck.' *The Clue in the Old Album*, pp. 209–210) A girl's purity and reputation are preserved, apparently, when she accedes to the protective role of the proper male authority figures. Nancy's father will protect her from sexual evil and at the right time will transfer her to the protective arms of a husband. When the good men in her life appear, the mystery is solved and all ends happily – like a wedding scene (that most respectable cover for sexual 'evil') making all a girl's dreams come true.

It is a contradictory situation, of course, since the girl sleuth is in pursuit of the very world – the happy ending, the mystery solved, the symbolic wedding – she seeks to escape. According to the series' values, if Nancy were to marry she would become Mrs. Bobbsey. She already has some of Mrs. Bobbsey's dread traits: both exercise grace, charm, and cool control; the smile is their main tool; they aren't overly squeamish or weak; they are tolerant and good-humored; they laugh 'good-naturedly'; they always speak words of wisdom and sympathy; they never play tricks or cavort gleefully or stomp their feet and toss their heads childishly, mussing their hair (Honey Bunch is their conscience). Mrs. Bobbsey is perfect, and to become so she has cut herself off from the action and transferred to her children the right to fun and adventure.

But Nancy Drew, as girl detective, gets to be adult without sacrificing that right to adventure. Nancy transcends the ordinary alternatives – silly Bess, ludicrous George, dull Mrs. Bobbsey. In the role of girl sleuth, Nancy, always eighteen, escapes time and enjoys the best of all worlds. She doesn't have to confront feminist anxieties. If she is as indomitable and determined as the books, then I suspect in real life she could not become a Mrs. Bobbsey. In real life lame-brain Ned Nickerson would marry bubbly Bess, and Nancy would be a familiar feminist – frustrated and too clever to stay at home, perhaps brilliantly successful. Or maybe she would marry Ned and be sorry the next day. Ned Nickerson could never hold her down.

Cool Nancy Drew figures it is better to be locked in the timeless role of girl sleuth – forever young, forever tops, above sex, above marriage – an inspiring symbol of freedom. But was she? Once I dreamed I was a prostitute in a cream-puff shop, an old-fashioned soda shop/tea room straight out of the Nancy Drew books I had been reading. The point of the dream is not clear, since many women would argue that prostitutes are free. But I think the dream is suggestive of the ambivalence in Nancy Drew. She always has it both ways – protected and free. She is an eternal girl, a stage which is a false ideal for women in our time. Nancy's adventures take place outside time and space. Her task is to restore a crumbling place to a past and perfect order.

NOTES

1 'For It Was Indeed He,' *Fortune*, April 1934.
2 Lee Zacharias, 'Nancy Drew, Ballbuster,' unpublished paper, p. 40.
3 Professor James P. Jones made this observation in 'Nancy Drew, WASP Super Girl of the 1930's,' *Journal of Popular Culture*, Spring, 1973.

MYSTERIES IN THE NANCY DREW SERIES CITED BY BOBBIE ANN MASON

4   *The Mystery at Lilac Inn*
10 *The Password to Larkspur Lane*
11 *The Clue of the Broken Locket*
14 *The Whispering Statue*
15 *The Haunted Bridge*
16 *The Clue of the Tapping Heels*
20 *The Clue in the Jewel Box*

21 *The Secret in the Old Attic*
22 *The Clue in the Crumbling Wall*
23 *The Mystery of the Tolling Bell*
24 *The Clue in the Old Album*
26 *The Clue of the Leaning Chimney*
28 *The Clue of the Black Keys*
34 *The Hidden Window Mystery*
36 *The Secret of the Golden Pavilion*

7. Feminist Murder: Amanda Cross Reinvents Womanhood

Jeanne Addison Roberts

In the works of Carolyn Heilbrun we have a rare and fascinating opportunity to observe both the formulation of feminist theory and the embodiment of theory in fictional creation. The publication of the fictions began before that of the theoretical works, and the reader can trace an evolution of ideas which seem enriched by the interaction of the two. Heilbrun's mystery stories, published under the pseudonym Amanda Cross, began in 1964. Her early feminist theories are articulated in two pioneering feminist books, *Toward a Recognition of Androgyny*, 1973 and *Reinventing Womanhood*, 1979.[1] One can speculate that the genesis of the detective stories may have been an effort to imagine a female detective operating in modes and situations comparable to those of the traditional male – an effort spurred on by the hope of altering the image of the female in our culture. The attractions of the detective story as an innocuous-seeming forum for re-education are obvious. Its conventions offer suspense of plot, well-established categories of stock characters, and ample opportunities for enlightening digression. It appeals to a large popular audience already hooked on the form.

But the genre presents built-in difficulties for communicating a feminist message. In its nineteenth-century origins it is conservative. Its plots predictably and repeatedly affirm the belief that justice prevails. The classical detective is an agent of God – or at least of an anthropomorphic image of a God who protects the established values of a given society. The solver of crimes is an embodiment of Freud's 'male' principles of rationality and justice, and his body is, of course, traditionally masculine. Even female detective story writers, many of them acknowledged masters of the form, have overwhelmingly chosen to write about male heroes.[2] The classical detective's infallibility reinforces faith in an orderly universe. One female addict confesses that she reads detective stories because she is 'lonely and frightened and needs the consolation that comes from believing that everything comes right in the end.'[3] And David Grossvogel has described the structure of the detective story as 'optimistic and self-destructing,' presenting a 'mechanistic detective' and 'an antiseptic corpse' in 'a garden of delightfully fulfilled expectations' where nothing worse than murder transpires.[4] As this description suggests, the setting of the classical detective story, typically a country house or a small town, is as conservative as the plot: the chief interest is in a reconstruction of a past often felt to be more real than the trivial-seeming present;[5] and at the end of the story, with disruptive forces banished, the social ritual, typically an upper-middle-class ritual, is quietly resumed. It is because this conservative faith in tradition no longer fits our collective world view that many critics have predicted the demise of the classical detective story.[6]

And yet the form has demonstrated some ability to evolve.[7] American writers like Ross Macdonald have given us detective fiction in less traditional settings than the older British versions, and a world of gray values where stumbling human effort, because of its persistence, succeeds at great cost in discovering ambiguous truths and achieving some shadowed justice.

While Carolyn Heilbrun has presented us with other possibilities, the tradition is clearly present. Kate Fansler, her detective, modeled perhaps on Lord Peter Wimsey, is rich, aristocratic, and slightly eccentric without flagrantly violating convention. She is comfortingly rational and competent. Heilbrun's academic settings permit the pleasures of nostalgia, the aura of permanence, and ample opportunity for instructive digressions on female friendship, sexism at Oxford and Harvard, and the delights and uses of literature. The solutions to her murder mysteries offer the promise of return to order. But Heilbrun's innovations are striking and extensive. It is a sign of her extraordinary skill that she has introduced change without losing the large popular audience which the genre attracts, and has established herself as an important practitioner of the art. Indeed her novels satisfy the first time and they richly repay rereading.[8]

Heilbrun's most obvious evolution in the tradition is her female detective, Kate Fansler. I will return to this important feature after considering a few less conspicuous characteristics of the works. Unlike the creator of the classical detective story, Heilbrun has deliberately paralleled her murder plots with significant social and political issues – so much so that the present is often much more gripping than the past. Most notably she relates death in *Poetic Justice* to the academic disturbances of the 60's, in *The Theban Mysteries* to the Vietnam war, and in *The Question of Max* to the Nixon era and Watergate. In using these parallels she maintains a delicate balance between the conservative traditions of the conventional detective story and the feminist insistence on change. These parallels give vigor and relevance to the narratives, emphasizing enduring values even as they point up the ambiguities and complexities of their current applications. The emphasis on the present and on growth as well as continuity prevents the easy optimism of conventional detective endings and points up the possibilities of evolutionary progress as well as conservation. For women the implication is that social mores, though essentially patriarchal, need not be fixed and unalterable.

Heilbrun's victims are of especial interest. She has, with increasing clarity, conceived of the detective story as a vehicle for demonstrating some of the ways in which society murders and maims women. Accordingly, all but one of her victims are women, and all but one of her murderers, actual and metaphoric, are male.[9] Two of the victims, those in *In the Last Analysis* and *The Question of Max*, are promising young professional women innocently enmeshed in male chicanery and brutally and cold-bloodedly sacrificed to male ambition. The cases of the three other female victims are more complicated.

In *Reinventing Womanhood* Heilbrun has insisted on the need for establishing new female prototypes. She offers (pp. 152–63) a reinterpretation, for women, of *The Oresteia*, suggesting that women must identify with Orestes and see the story as a myth of the killing off of traditional concepts of motherhood in Orestes' murder of Clytemnestra. In the same vein, in *The James Joyce Murder*, *The Theban Mysteries*, and *Death in a Tenured Position*, she has killed off women who represent for her antiquated modes of female behavior, particularly those characterized by the submerged anger and neurotic need for revenge engendered by enforced dependency in a patriarchal society. The figure of Mrs. Bradford in *The James Joyce Murder* is the recipient of totally unmitigated vituperation from all sides. In addition to being a mother and housewife, she is a gossip, a nag, and a termagant. She is self-centered and self-righteous. In another sort of novel she would be comic – a satiric portrait of the cursed wife. But here she is painted as villainous. Her murder is described as 'an act of sanitation' (p. 75). Similarly the corpse in *The Theban Mysteries*, never seen alive, but sufficiently described to be a presence, is an hysterical and neurotic mother, dismissed by Kate as being 'absolutely better off dead' (p. 168). In *Death in a Tenured Position* the victim is not a mother but an achieving academic woman who has rejected feminine sisterhood because she believes she has risen to her status as the first tenured woman in the Harvard English department entirely through her own efforts. Only very marginally sympathetic, she too is generally agreed to be happily eliminated; she is to be succeeded we are promised by a woman who will tell her male colleagues 'what for' instead of bursting into tears (p. 155).

In theory, the eradication of negative prototypes of femininity may be valid, but when one is dealing with fictional embodiments – even the most one-dimensional types – it causes real problems. It is true that in the classical detective story the disposal of the corpse is usually cleansing, but to a feminist reader the violent eradication of any woman is disturbing. Surely no one can *rejoice* at the murder of Clytemnestra. In my experience, reader identification is typically stronger with her than with Orestes – she, after all, is the one who has dared to assert herself against male conventions. And the violence of the hatred directed at Mrs. Bradford seems totally out of proportion to her actual behavior. As a theory she needs to be rejected; but, as a character who emerges with some individuality as a human being, she certainly does not deserve to be shot. The final irony is that she is replaced as housewife and mother by a sweet, beautiful young girl whose chief distinction is that she bakes cakes from butter, eggs, and flour rather than from packaged mixes (*JJM* 141). It is very hard indeed to rejoice, as we seem meant to do, at such female 'progress.'[10] Janet Mandelbaum, the tenured Harvard professor, is enough of a personage that we are prevented from feeling at her death the conventional pleasure in the purging of evil that we feel in other detective stories. Indeed one senses a streak of anti-feminine rage in these three superficially feminist murders, a rage directed specifically and unforgivingly at the failures of the older generation of women. We might hope that, even while rejecting their life-styles, the author might show tolerance, reconciliation, and compassion.[11] Among the older women there are some appealing characters but no totally acceptable models: Kate's friends, Phyllis and Nicola, are intelligent but impotent housewives; Sylvia, her confidante at Harvard, is a government consultant, powerful and comfortably married, but we have no idea how she got that way – except that we know she is rich and well-connected. Heilbrun's most attractive older woman, Grace Knole, a famous professor, has achieved her status only through the sacrifice of sex and progeny.

The younger generation of women do not fare much better. Two of its most appealing members are killed off. One of Kate's nieces is as fool-ishly conventional as her parents; another, a Greek major at Harvard for whom there seems to be some hope, is never developed as an active force; Lina, a budding 25-year old scholar is encumbered almost fatally with her own virginity; and Luellen May, an embittered Lesbian, is no more lovable than the murdered Janet – and considerably less so than an attendant dog, enigmatically christened 'Jocasta.' Only in *The Theban Mysteries* do we have young women, the members of Kate's seminar on *Antigone*, developed enough to be interesting; and we leave them in a formative and inconclusive stage.

The scarcity of female role models in Heilbrun's fiction may be an intentional commentary on society, an involuntary reflection of literary conventions, or a sign of the author's inability to construct in her fic-tional imagination a community of women. In *Reinventing Womanhood*, Heilbrun laments 'the failure of imagination' which has so far rendered female writers incapable of creating autonomous women characters, even when the writer herself has achieved such status. She says,

The failure of women writers to imagine female selves is a ... profound failure.... Thus Simone de Beauvoir explains that her novel *The Mandarins* was to contain 'all of myself.' Yet even in this novel she cannot, she knows, create a positive her-oine. 'Anna,' she writes, 'hasn't the autonomy that has been bestowed upon me by a profession which means so much to me.' Anna 'lives the relative life of a secondary being: Henri resembles me more than Anna does.' (p. 72)

Surely Heilbrun's female detective was conceived in part as an effort to portray an autonomous woman character. To a large extent the portrait is successful. Kate Fansler, no longer young, is a tenured professor at a major university. She is blessed with an independent income which enables her to come and go as she pleases. Like the classical detective, she is in some respects comfortably conservative – manners are impor-tant to her, and she loathes the promiscuous use of first names and bad grammar. She is tall and lean, with hair drawn back in a French twist. She dresses elegantly in ultra-suede suits and flat but fashionable shoes. She shaves her legs and wears gold jewelry. She dresses, Heilbrun has her say, 'for the patriarchy,' and she is frequently described as *soignée*.

Like the classical detective, Kate has eccentricities. However, they are fairly minor, and they are copied in most cases from male models.[12] She demands time alone; she smokes; she drinks, usually martinis; and on at least one occasion she attempts to imitate W.H. Auden by downing a pitcher of martinis, and a bottle of champagne followed by a bottle of Cherry Heering – although she fails to finish off the liqueur (*PJ* 41). The imitation of male models is undoubtedly conscious and deliberate. In *Reinventing Womanhood* Heilbrun says that she saw her father as 'the only possible role model' (52), and she specifically urges women that 'the male role model for autonomy and achievement is ... the one they must follow' (31). The principle, questionable in theory, seems even less satisfactory in fiction. A feminist reader must hope for some more distinctive and uniquely feminine model than one which simply recapitulates the male. But the vision of precisely what this model might include continues elusive. As an autonomous woman Kate writes books, succeeds at her job, and cherishes her independence. When we first see her (in *LA*) she has elected not to marry; and she exhibits no maternal yearnings, although she agrees to board a recalcitrant nephew for the summer (*JJM*). She aspires, she says, to be one of an unpublicized group of women who require and enjoy the love of men and scorn the role of homemaker (*JJM* 117). She has had a number of lovers, at least one of them a casual, one-night stand (*PJ* 29). Her long-time friendship with Assistant District Attorney Reed Amhearst has been notably marked by an occasion in the past when through bad judgment he landed in a 'most magnificent muddle' and was rescued by Kate 'on the brink of disaster' (*LA* 36). But we do not see this happen, and the details are not revealed. There is a curious emptiness at the heart of these outlines of character and career. Kate becomes most vivid in her literary digressions and in her long conversations with female friends – both of which are peripheral to power and to plot.

In the early novels there is a conscious emphasis on androgyny. Reed is frequently characterized as sensitive, thoughtful, and lacking in macho qualities, while Kate is forceful and assertive in managing her own life. In *Poetic Justice* there is the fullest development of the concept of androgyny in the portrait of Peter Packer Pollinger, whose academic passion for a male writer with a female alter ego is both amusing and illuminating.[13] But the idea of androgyny does not ultimately prove very helpful in imagining an autonomous woman. Although it may have served a transitional purpose, the concept has now been abandoned by most feminine theorists as one which continues to allow male to precede female and to draw its strength from definitions rooted in a male-female polarity of little use in discovering the uniquely female.

Kate Fansler is androgynous and frequently autonomous. Her autonomy meshes well with the autonomy of the classical detective. And yet there are lapses which are very difficult to account for. In almost every case where Kate needs help she calls on a man – a nephew, a prospective in-law, a lawyer, her friend Reed. In two cases Reed actually solves the mystery, and in a third he provides a vital segment of the solution. Although female autonomy does not rule out a certain amount of emotional and social dependence, such dependence should not, in the detective genre, cause the central figure to abdicate her crucial role as problem solver. Dependency may humanize Kate, but it vitiates her efficacy both as detective and female role model. She is often strangely passive, and occasionally really stupid – for example, she permits her nephew to engage in rifle practice, aiming a supposedly unloaded gun at a living target. She explains lamely that she is intimidated by the fear of being 'spinsterish and antimasculine' if she denies him the use of a phallic symbol (*JJM* 39–40). This occurs in *The James Joyce Murder*, from a feminist point of view Heilbrun's worst book. In it Kate suffers an automobile breakdown, is arrested for lacking a driving permit and registration card, waits docilely in a police station for Reed to rescue her, and nearly confesses guiltily to the police that he is her lover. Reed masterfully takes over the investigation and identifies the criminal.

Poetic Justice is a novel conceived in part, I think, as Heilbrun's revenge on Lionel Trilling, who was her favorite professor at Columbia, despite his callous treatment of women, and described movingly in *Reinventing Womanhood* (125–37). In the novel, a very Trilling-like professor proves to be the murderer. But here again Reed and not Kate solves the mystery. In *The Question of Max*, a novel with fascinating accounts of the lives of three dead academic women, Kate's leadership is sustained to the very end, at which point she lapses, to use the words of one of her characters, into 'one of those dumb broads in stories who are always getting trapped by the villain in deserted houses' (*DTP* 112). Like any heroine of romance, she is rescued by heroic and quick-thinking males.

Perhaps most unaccountably of all, in *Poetic Justice* Kate agrees for the flimsiest of reasons to marry Reed, having frequently earlier refused him in the confusions of the 60's. She now says that 'being a woman alone doesn't seem as easy as it has been.' She needs, she adds, 'the confidence of having a man.' She admittedly does not love him as he loves her, but she accedes to his insistence on marriage rather than co-habitation (50–51). In all these cases one cannot but feel that the medium has overpowered the message – that the conventions of masculine mystery stories and of romance have obscured Heilbrun's goal of depicting the autonomous woman. In the case of the marriage, there may be a conflict between detective story conventions and the desire to depict a satisfactory male-female relationship which would involve mutual dependence as well as autonomy. But the motives of the marriage are insufficiently developed; and the result is a violation of the tradition of the classical detective who, although himself often androgynous, almost never deviates into dependency or romantic attachment.[14] These human frailties are relegated to the ingenues of the subplot. The detective may have assistants but not equals. He must be a model of autonomy if he is not to jeopardize his role in the reassuring ritual of crime and punishment carried out with 'divine' sanction. When the detective is a woman, the risk is even greater that romance and dependency will undercut her already precarious authority. God, especially if she is female, does not need a spouse.

The marriage of Kate and Reed seems comfortable enough, and Kate does not merely dwindle into a wife. She continues to eschew domesticity and to maintain an independent career and a private country retreat. But the reader feels that the author is searching for rather than fully achieving her ideal. Kate's very vacillation between autonomy and dependence speaks eloquently of the difficulty of imagining a female hero. There is some progress. From a feminist perspective, Heilbrun's strongest novel is *Death in a Tenured Position*. In it the female victim is most clearly 'murdered' by social prejudices; and in it we have Heilbrun's most successful development of female community. Kate has interesting encounters with female undergraduates, relies on her friend Sylvia to smooth her investigative paths, and succours a Lesbian commune which has become innocently enmeshed in murder. She also solves the mystery herself. And yet even here there are signs of a fumbling search for a feminine ideal rather than a full realization of it. The search seems to me hampered by imitation of male models. Perhaps feeling cramped by the restrictions marriage has imposed on her heroine, the author has dispatched Reed to Africa, evoking his presence only as an epistolary murmur. In his absence, Fansler rather casually resumes an affair with an old lover. Now adultery certainly suggests freedom, but it is difficult to reconcile this freedom with Kate's earlier acquiescence in matrimony, or with the conservative patterns of the detective story. We sense that Kate, in the security of her fictional framework, is exploring avenues open to women rather than defining goals. Appropriately we last hear of her giving a public lecture on 'the new forms possible to women in making fictions on female destiny.'

It is clear that Carolyn Heilbrun herself continues to grow in making fictions of female destiny. Her evolving use of detective fiction helps us, like all literature, to see problems and imagine solutions. If it is discouraging to find so skilful an artist occasionally lapsing into clichés or outmoded conventions, both literary and social, and failing to imagine completely an autonomous woman, her successes greatly outweigh her failures. The female struggle to imagine and achieve a balance between autonomy and dependence goes on. In both her theory and her fiction Heilbrun has advanced the collective feminist effort to reinvent womanhood.

The extraordinary development and proliferation of mystery novels with female detectives which has occurred in the seven years since my initial discussion of Amanda Cross has dramatically changed the genre. The pioneer work of Marcia Muller, now newly reprinted and appreciated, and the growing lists of popular works by Sue Grafton and Sara Paretsky among others have made the classic British detective story begin to seem more than old-fashioned. In these American works by women, the aristocratic hero and upper-class country house have been replaced by lower- or middle-class women braving the mean streets of San Francisco and Chicago and the sterile wastelands of suburban California. And yet the academic novels and the mysteries modeled on the classic British prototypes have not lost their appeal. P.M. Carlson's Maggie Ryan, for example, continues to explore the groves of academe, although she is younger and more footloose and fancy free than Dorothy Sayers's Harriet Vane or Amanda Cross's Kate Fansler.

Since 1985, there appears to be a change in direction for Heilbrun. She has produced four more Kate Fansler books: *Sweet Death, Kind Death, No Word from Winifred, A Trap for Fools*, and *The Players Come Again*. She has also published a new consideration of female biography and autobiography entitled *Writing a Woman's Life* (1989).[15] The interplay between her theory and her practice continues to be intriguing and instructive, focusing perhaps more strongly on the problems of imagining a positive view of an autonomous woman who is over 50.

It is clear that Heilbrun has been concerned in recent years with female biography, and her conclusions are outlined in *Writing a Woman's Life*. She seems thoroughly aware of the difficulties of conceiving a 'new plot' for women's lives. Of Virginia Woolf, who specifically called for such a new plot, Heilbrun writes, 'She wrote one with her life, but never with her fiction: nor did George Eliot, or Beatrice Webb – nor has anyone' (89).

Heilbrun delineates recurring characteristics of traditional female biography and autobiography. She sees in them muffled and inchoate narratives, which deny 'both accomplishment and suffering.' Their subjects shrink from admitting that they sought responsibility or 'were in any way ambitious,' but take full responsibility for their failures (23). They insist that their work has discovered and pursued them, not that they have initiated it (25). These stories display a nostalgia for childhood (which, Heilbrun says, is 'likely to be a mask for unrecognized anger' [15]).

Such biographies are notable for an absence of mothers, an essential powerlessness in their protagonists, and a failure to achieve recognition in the public sphere (24–25). Heilbrun quotes Myra Jehlen as concluding that even visions of female autonomy are deceptive because the effort to demonstrate it reveals 'not actual independence but action despite dependence – not a self-defined female culture either, but a sub-culture born out of oppression and either stunted or victorious only at often-fatal cost' (17). Heilbrun concludes of marriage that it 'has suited the man, and appeared to suit the woman because she was satisfied with the rewards offered in place of her own self determination,' and that these 'rewards' constitute consolations supporting 'the most persistent of myths imprisoning women, and misleading those who write of women's lives' (76–77).

In this work, Heilbrun also discusses love and friendship between women, the patriarchal structure of myths, and the importance of what she calls (after Stanley Cavell) 'remarriage' at some stage of conventional marriage, a phenomenon which occurs as a result of woman's awakening to new possibilities after 50. She regards this change as 'uniquely female' (124), suggesting that 'It is perhaps only in old age, certainly past fifty, that women can stop being female impersonators, can grasp the opportunity to reverse their most cherished principles of "femininity"' (126). She notes the corpulence of older women like Dorothy Sayers, Elizabeth Cady Stanton, and Margaret Mead, asking, 'Can it be doubted that for a woman to grow fat in middle age is to dissociate her personhood from her feminine appeal?' (54–55). The context is laudatory, but the tone seems to me ambivalent. The vagueness of 'femininity' and 'feminine appeal' leaves a troubling uncertainty as to what it is that is being abandoned.

The author devotes a chapter to her detective novels and to her hero,

Kate Fansler. She records her initial conviction that she began to write these books because 'she had run out of English detective novels' and 'felt an enormous need to enter the world of [their] fiction' (113). She acknowledges that Kate Fansler was a fantasy figure – unmarried, childless, rich, beautiful, successful at a career in the public sphere. She argues, however, that Fansler is no longer just a fantasy, 'but an aging woman who battles despair and, one hopes with a degree of wit and humour, finds in the constant analysis of our ancient patriarchal ways, and in sheer effrontery, a reason to endure' (122).

Turning from theory to the novels, one finds that there have indeed been some changes. But the element of fantasy clearly survives. Kate Fansler is still slim and *soignée*, although we now hear less about her clothes; and she has added Laphroig Scotch to her alcoholic repertory, in spite of the fact that 'people have been telling her that she drinks too much' (*SD* 10). She is a connoisseur of restaurants, nineteenth-century novels, and ladies' rooms. Her husband calls her 'wonderful you' and manages to be less active than formerly in helping solve her cases. Indeed he is often out of town, though he may return when a crisis looms. The people she meets almost invariably compliment her, as does Bertie in *Sweet Death, Kind Death*: 'You are quite elegant, and slim, and were obviously born knowing how to look elegant' (48). The good guys also regularly comment on her cleverness, her sympathy, and her ability to listen. She is not, in fact, particularly witty, and she does not seem to be battling despair. She is still without financial worries and travels nationally and internationally with ease. And her speech continues to be characterized by name-dropping and literary allusions, presumably flattering to the reader who 'gets' them.[16]

Although she obviously doesn't mean to be writing biography in them, Heilbrun's detective novels deal intriguingly with many of the issues in the theoretical work. She is clearly deeply concerned with the problems of aging women, and perhaps the most striking development in these later novels is the increasing presence of women over 50 – at least eight are developed in some detail.

In this regard, the author is once again a pioneer. What we are told of these women's lives recapitulates many of the observations of *Writing a Woman's Life*. Patrice Umphelby (although christened Patricia, she 'had since girlhood delighted in the French form of Patrick' [31]) of *Sweet Death, Kind Death* is 58 (approximately the age of the author when the novel was published). Her husband was violently killed when she was 49, and since then her life has profoundly changed. She says she was 'born again' (24). She has begun to write fiction instead of history, and she keeps a journal in which she abjures the usual search of the past and its childhood beginnings in favor of the present. She also admits that she has never met an old person she enjoyed for more than a minute (22). Patrice has abandoned fashion and is oblivious to the effect of her straggly haircut and dowdy shoes. She has also 'fallen in love with death' (the epigraph and title of the book are from Stevie Smith) and is resolved, like Charlotte Perkins Gilman, to end her life before old age closes in. She is an interesting contradiction, embracing her age on the one hand but determined to limit her life on the other. As it turns out, she is 'done in' prematurely by jealous colleagues (a male professor and his sour housewife spouse); and so in a sense the story recapitulates the theme of the earlier novels, which concentrate on women destroyed by patriarchal society. In the later works, interest in the lives of these women prevails over the drive to show what kills them off.

No Word from Winifred features the 80-year old Sinjun (her given name has been dropped early on), whom neither Fansler nor we ever actually meet but about whom we hear in letters.[17] She is described as 'fat, with great dewlaps of flesh, [great fat legs], and next to no hair on her head' (80). But she is a distinguished Tudor historian. Again revulsion seems to war with respect. Penelope Constable (nicknamed PC, another androgynous appellation) is a 65-year old novelist introduced in *A Trap for Fools*, the weakest of these four mysteries – its weakness is compounded by rather meaningless epigraphs from Kipling's 'If.' PC's role is incidental, but her presence is somewhat developed. She has black hair, probably dyed, an 'air of being entirely herself.' Best of all she is 'essentially youthful' and not, apparently, fat (86–89). Edna Hoskins is an older woman administrator with a 'comfortable shape' and a 'lack of sexual competition.' She claims to be attractive to Kate because of her 'motherliness,' which provides the 'comfort' looked for by the world from God and Jesus (117); but ironically this motherly figure proves corrupt.

Heilbrun's most recent and most interesting work is *The Players Come Again*, in which the focus is most clearly on older women. It is also the work in which the author seems most concerned with variations on writing women's lives. Kate's goal through most of this novel is quite literally to write a woman's life – the biography of Gabrielle Foxx. Journals and letters are used extensively to fill in childhoods and set plots in motion. (In *No Word from Winifred*, Winifred suggests that 'women keep diaries and journals in the hope of giving some shape to their inchoate

lives' [35].) Through the journals and letters, we have glimpses of Gabrielle as a young wife exploited by a husband who uses her to construct a
novel of bogus female life. We see her later as a woman of 66 disposing
of her effects. In this later incarnation, she lives in one room; her hair is
'mottled gray and white, cut off at her ears.' She wears a long, formless
dress and an old cardigan, thick stockings and men's slippers; but she
has vitality – 'the vigor that is not an imitation of youth' (67–69). However, she refers to herself as doomed by her disastrous marriage. She is
author of a revolutionary novel never published in her own lifetime.
Eleanor is an insecure young housewife in a rich home, who finally by
age 82 has found serenity and is actually 'elegantly dressed' (115). Most
interesting of all are three women about the age of Heilbrun herself, 65
years old. They are Anne, Nellie, and Dorinda (finally no more androgynous names), who have maintained a friendship from childhood. Aware
that they have been hampered by patriarchal expectations, they nonetheless now find their lives adventurous and rewarding. All three work
outside their homes; only one married young; and only one has children.
All three say they want to forget their own childhoods and 'think forward together' (228).

It is clear in these four novels that Heilbrun is endeavoring to write
women's lives and has broadened her horizon to include more women –
her niece, Leighton, becomes an incidental Watson to Kate's Sherlock,
and female friendships are emphasized. However, curious anomalies
remain, perhaps introduced deliberately, which reveal how very difficult
the project of recording and changing female experience is. In *No Word
from Winifred*, Charlotte Stanton is an Oxford don who writes novels
about Greek mythology, but she writes from the perspective of the traditional patriarchy. The men are the heroes and Ariadne, for example, is
'the worst sort of monster of male imagination' (128–29). The three
women of *The Players Come Again* want to forget their childhood, yet a
large part of the book has been devoted to sketching it in some detail. A
huge gap separates their lives at 18 from their lives at 65. Winifred, in *No
Word from Winifred*, shares Kate Fansler's scorn for passive housewives.
She says of a friend's mother – an Oxford wife – 'I blamed her for being a
fool, [and] forgave [her husband] for finding her a bore' (52). A woman
of great independence and determination who has yearned to be a boy,
and whom we first see as a part-time farmworker by choice, she nonetheless leaves the country as the result of an affair with a married man,
and the rest of her life becomes a blank. Emmanuel Foxx rewrites Ariadne's story but, by enforcing his wife's collaboration, produces a dis-

torted picture of her life. His wife, Gabrielle, again rewrites this myth to make Ariadne heroic and an authentic woman. We are told that she translates the story into modern terms, but we do not see how. Fansler ends up defeated in her biographical project and settles for editing the novel.

Perhaps the most puzzling anomaly is Kate Fansler herself. She actually has remarkably little character. If she has aged at all, it is glacially. Other women may grow gray and fat and dowdy, but Kate remains slim and elegant. (Heilbrun points out that this is 'unlike her creator' [*WWL* 23]). Throughout the novels, fat seems to be the antithesis of elegant – a sign of dowdiness and, by extension, of rejected sexuality. When menopause is mentioned, Kate, who seems to be about 45 (*PCA* 101), declares rather smugly that she does not anticipate it for years (*NWW* 182). She repeatedly flaunts her dislike of children. This dislike is often echoed by her 'good' characters such as Gabrielle and Anne. She seems contemptuous of women's colleges (*SD* 146 and passim) and continues scornful of housewives and mothers, declaring in *Sweet Death, Kind Death* that it was not easy to have a mother one despised and scorned as she had hers 'because although rich enough to have done anything,' she was 'stupid enough to have done nothing' (84). Such 'honesty' about mothers and children is bracing but residually disturbing. What hope does it leave for the future? Heilbrun makes the point in *Writing a Woman's Life* that she herself had three children and that she had, in fact, great affection for her parents (119). I do not mean to suggest that Heilbrun and Fansler are identical, but rather that there is an intriguing dialogue between them, as if between a real person and her ego ideal.

The question of mothers is, of course, tricky. In *Writing a Woman's Life*, the author argues that mothers cannot free their daughters; but surely some do, and surely some sort of reconciliation between daughters and mothers who can't be liberating is necessary. Heilbrun concedes that some other female mentor or figure often operates 'to inspire awakening' (64–65). Gabrielle does this for Nellie in *The Players Come Again*, but Kate's only specifically 'maternal' figure, Edna Hoskins, betrays her. Problems are set out, but not solutions.

As we have seen, in *Writing a Woman's Life* Heilbrun has pointed out that in traditional biographies the script deemphasizes women's initiative, insisting that their work discovers them and that they have not sought it. Amazingly we find Kate acknowledging such a belief in 'destiny, providence, the wisdom of chance' and asking about herself, 'Had she ever sought a case in her life? No, she had not. They had come to her, and she had pursued them because when you are called, you must answer' (*PCA* 16). This might well be a line from what Heilbrun has rejected as 'the old genre of female biography' (*WWL* 16). Perhaps because she was conceived as already an autonomous woman, it is hard to see how Kate can achieve in her life or her marriage the kinds of 'rebirth' and 'remarriage' which are celebrated and add interest to other lives. What effect have these changes, developments, and dilemmas had on these works as detective fiction?

It seems to me that they are eroding the traditional conventions of the genre. In the best two of the four books there is, in effect, no murder. In *No Word from Winifred*, Winifred disappears, but we do not so much feel that society has eliminated her as that she has escaped to uncharted territory. In *The Players Come Again*, a very incidental and very long-past murder of a man by his son is introduced five pages from the end. In the other two books, murders are committed. *Sweet Death, Kind Death* tells of the murder of the 58-year old Patrice in a manner contrived to copy the suicide of Virginia Woolf, but Patrice's life is more interesting than her death. *A Trap for Fools*, the most conventional of the four, begins with the murder of an obnoxious man and includes that of an attractive young black woman. She is a victim sacrificed to male greed, not because she is black or female but because she knows too much. The real target is the corruption of university administration.[18]

Heilbrun has never been strong on plots, perhaps because they are not her primary interest; but in the two murder novels, the propositions which we are expected to accept approach the preposterous.

In *Sweet Death, Kind Death*, we must believe that in a small college community a lake-side householder has, unobserved, installed a pipe from the lake to his swimming pool in order to drown a colleague because her research data disagrees with his own, and because he and his wife hated her. We must also believe that a female ex-nurse has broken into the office of a doctor on vacation and convinced Patrice that she is his replacement. (The real point is that she is an older woman, and that people don't pay much attention to her.) In *A Trap for Fools*, the reader feels that the author herself must be bored with the plot. We are asked to accept the idea that a young black woman who is attempting benevolent blackmail willingly accompanies her intended victim, who she knows is a murderer, to her own apartment while he, a white man, is in blackface! (Were they rehearsing for a minstrel show?) Fortunately the solution goes by quickly.

In the two non-murder stories, the mysteries are rather inconsequential – usually involving the identification of parents. They are clearly subordinated to the points the author wants to make about character – about female friendship, female autonomy, life stages and their obstacles, and androgyny. Kate becomes a less central presence in these stories. The pleasures come, as always, from transcontinental peregrinations, eating and drinking, and conversations, increasingly between women. It is perhaps something of a joke that Kate finds the plastic name-badge holder from a convention of the Modern Language Association and doesn't know what it is (*NWW* 101) – Heilbrun is a former president of the MLA; but we are eventually treated to an MLA meeting and to the usual academic insider gossip.

In *The Players Come Again*, a truly remarkable novel because of its array of aging women, Fansler is quite overshadowed. The idea of rewriting a patriarchal myth for modern women is powerful. But the plot of the book is sustained toward the end by the feeble device of the necessity of putting the pages of Gabrielle's novel into their proper order, copying them, and properly deploying the copies. The message overpowers the medium – the author is showing us that even at this advanced stage it is difficult to bring order to the inchoate lives of women. Although we see the difficulty, we still have only a vague sense of what that order might reveal.

If Heilbrun's interest in examining lives has superseded her interest in examining deaths, readers may expect from her a new kind of murderless mystery story. In exploring the problems of writing a woman's life, these four novels continue to be searches rather than solutions. They reveal both barriers and possibilities. In her most recent work, Heilbrun is closest to finding the new plot called for by Virginia Woolf. There are glimpses of autonomous women and fragments of their lives. But we must still wait for Gabrielle's unpublished novel to be written, and for someone like the modern Ariadne, who holds the clue to the labyrinth, to put the pages in order. To do a complete job Kate Fansler may have to admit to aging, let her hair go gray, grow fat, kill off her husband, forgive her mother, give up the pleasures of Laphroig and martinis, and perhaps adopt a daughter. Altogether a rather gloomy prospect for those who admire her.

NOTES

1 Carolyn G. Heilbrun, *Toward a Recognition of Androgyny* (New York: Knopf, 1973); *Reinventing Womanhood* (New York: Norton, 1979). I have used paper-

back editions of the first five Amanda Cross mysteries. Original publication dates and abbreviations follow titles: *In the Last Analysis* (New York: Avon, 1966), 1964, *LA*; *The James Joyce Murder* (New York: Ballantine, 1982), 1967, *JJM*; *Poetic Justice* (New York: Avon, 1979), 1970, *PJ*; *The Theban Mysteries* (New York: Avon, 1979), 1971, *TM*; *The Question of Max* (New York: Avon, 1977), 1976, *QM*; *Death in a Tenured Position* (New York: Dutton, 1981), *DTP*.

2 There are, of course, exceptions, and the female detective has become more common in recent years. The most notable exception in the early years of this century is Agatha Christie's Miss Marple. But Christie seems to prefer Hercule Poirot. Her mystery story writer, Ariadne Oliver, who dabbles in crime solving, appears to be a parody of Christie herself.

3 Mary Cantwell, 'Go to Bed with a Mystery,' *Vogue*, January 1983, p. 42.

4 David I. Grossvogel, *Mystery and Its Fictions* (Baltimore: Johns Hopkins Univ. Press, 1979), pp. 15, 41. Grossvogel also discusses the function of nostalgia and ritual, see especially pp. 41, 52, and the importance of the detective's infallibility, p. 49.

5 See Tzvetan Todorov, 'The Typology of Detective Fiction' in *The Poetics of Prose*. Tr. Richard Howard (Ithaca: Cornell Univ. Press, 1977), p. 44.

6 For an extended definition and discussion of the genre, see John G. Cawelti, 'The Art of the Classical Detective Story' in *Adventure, Mystery, and Romance* (Chicago: Univ. of Chicago Press, 1976), Ch. 5.

7 Todorov insists that masterpieces of popular literature must conform to the rules of the genre. To develop these norms is to disappoint them and to move from the popular to the literary. (p. 43). Christie's Ariadne Oliver boasts 'I've written thirty-two books by now – and of course they're all exactly the same really....' in *Cards on the Table* (New York: Dell, 1977), p. 55.

8 See her 'Who Did It? Michael Gilbert and P.D. James,' *New York Times Book Review*, September 12, 1982, pp. 9, 24.

9 The victim in *Poetic Justice* is male; the person accidentally responsible for the death in *The Theban Mysteries* is female.

10 One would like to suppose that Heilbrun is commenting here with deliberate irony on the monotonously repetitive patterns of female entrapment; but if this were so, Kate Fansler would surely express some awareness of the irony, and she does not. She seems delighted with the new wife.

11 My colleague, Laura Tracy, has suggested that psychoanalytically this murderous rage reflects the author's unresolved conflict with her own mother, which in turn reflects her mother's conflict with her mother. There is some support for this idea in *Reinventing Womanhood* (52, 57–59, 68–69). Such a theory would help to account for Heilbrun's difficulty in developing models of successful female community.

12 In modern adaptations of the genre, particularly in America, the male detective may not be completely infallible; but he regularly solves the mysteries himself.

13 For a fuller analysis of Pollinger as a playful and serious study of androgyny, see Steven R. Carter, 'Amanda Cross,' in *10 Women of Mystery.* Ed. Earl F. Bargainnier (Bowling Green State Univ. Popular Press, 1981), p. 277.

14 In the case of the most notable exception, Lord Peter Wimsey, the novel in which he marries, *Busman's Honeymoon*, is arguably the weakest of the Dorothy Sayers canon. There are a few other married male detectives, but the wife does not assume a major role in solving mysteries. Frequently, of course, the male detective has a subordinate side-kick or assistant of the same sex.

15 I have used paperback editions of these works. All were published in New York by Ballantine Books: *Sweet Death, Kind Death*, 1985, *SD*; *No Word from Winifred*, 1989, *NWW*; *Writing a Woman's Life*, 1989, *WWL*; *A Trap for Fools*, 1990, *TF*; *The Players Come Again*, 1991, *PCA*.

16 The literary allusions are often curiously off-center even when one gets their drift. Discussing an unwelcome invitation, Kate says it's 'as though Caesar had asked Brutus to brunch' (*NWW* 3) – in fact such an invitation would have been neither unlikely nor unwelcome – though Caesar's ghost might have felt differently. In a domestic living room, in conversation with a merry widow, Kate suddenly grows silent, then decides to 'stop being a green thought in a green shade' (*TF* 45) although there's no green in sight. A woman says that 'like Jaques' she has played many roles, although Jaques enumerates roles in *As You Like It* but doesn't play them. And Kate, speaking of a 92-year old woman, says, 'She must be old, as Master Shallow said to Falstaff' (*NWW* 143, 112).

17 Heilbrun's names are always interesting. The first three novels favor male or androgynous names for women. Charlotte Lucas, appropriately named for a practical woman in Jane Austen, prefers to be called Charlie. Harriet St. John Merriweather quickly becomes Sinjun. Charlotte Stanton evokes both Charlotte Perkins Gilman and Elizabeth Cady Stanton. Winifred may be named for the independent Winifred Holtby, discussed at some length in *Writing a Woman's Life*. Penelope Constable is PC. Only in the last novel are the women permitted female names. Dorinda is named for a character in an Ellen Glasgow novel; Nellie is Eleanor rewritten; Gabrielle is something of an angel (although Emmanuel Foxx is anything but a savior).

18 Heilbrun has recently taken early retirement (at 66) from her professorship at Columbia University because she says she felt frozen out by the Old Boy network running the hierarchically structured English department (Judy Mann, 'Heilbrun vs. the Hierarchy,' *Washington Post*, Friday, June 26, 1991, E3).

8. Murders Academic: Women Professors and the Crimes of Gender

Susan J. Leonardi

'The whole point about mysteries,' one of the characters in Amanda Cross's *The James Joyce Murder* says, 'is that it is so nice to read about other people's doing things without having to do that sort of thing one-self' (96). She refers here to the adventures of the detective, but one might easily extend the 'thing' to include the violent acts of the offender. That is, we are all at times tempted to resort to violence. And this per-haps explains partially what so attracts academics to detective fiction. As members of academic institutions, we long to poison, stab, shoot, or strangle presidents, deans, department chairs, colleagues, and students. But as creatures of the mind we content ourselves – usually – with read-ing about such crimes, with, that is, murders academic. A few academics – most of them, I suspect, English professors – go one step further (per-haps feeling the urge to violence more strongly) and *write* about them, which has the almost inevitable result of said professors reproducing themselves. It is not surprising then that most of the new women aca-demic detectives are English professors[1] – Anna Clarke's Paula Glen-ning, Susan Kenney's Roz Howard, Theodora Wender's Gladiola Gold, Joan Smith's Loretta Lawson, Valerie Miner's Nan Weaver, and Edith Skom's Beth Austin are among the many colleagues of the most familiar of them all, Amanda Cross's (pen-name of former Columbia English professor Carolyn G. Heilbrun) Kate Fansler.

As a distinct subset of the amateur female sleuth novel (itself a subset of the woman detective novel), the academic-woman-as-detective novel falls more easily into the British than into the hard-boiled tradition, pre-dictably enough, since these heroines are by profession more inclined to research and deduction than to chases, break-ins, and more than one brush with death per novel. One characteristic that almost all these professorial fictions share is their consciousness of the similarity between the academic and the detective enterprises. Research skills make good sleuths, they suggest. 'Aren't all scholars really detectives?' (223) asks one of the characters in the Kate Fansler mystery *The Players Come Again*. In *The James Joyce Murder*, Kate sorts out the papers of James Joyce's publisher as she tries to sort out the murder of a rural busybody. Professor Hilary Tamar in Sarah Caudwell's *The Shortest Way to Hades* announces: 'I am a scholar. Few mysteries are impenetrable to the trained mind' (177). In the first of that series, *Thus Was Adonis Murdered*, one of the characters congratulates Hilary on a good guess, and the professor replies, 'The careful process of reasoning by which the Scholar (capital S) advances from established premise to ineluctable conclusion is hardly to be described as guess work' (201).

English professor Beth Austin in Edith Skom's *The Mark Twain Murders* tracks down a plagiarized paper while an FBI agent looks for a thief and killer. Both, the text points out, spend their time 'tracking down answers' (28).[2] Lois Marchino points out the similarity between 'the phrases describing the process of scholarly research and crime detection' – for example, 'following leads, examining the evidence, evaluating sources, tracing and searching, etc.' (92). And the blurb of Carol Clemeau's *The Ariadne Clue* tells readers that 'sleuth' Antonia Nielson, Associate Professor of Classics, adapts 'her academic research techniques to the *real* world of detection' [emphasis added]; Nielson solves the crime with her 'nimble' literary imagination that, a colleague taunts, 'accounts for those critical papers you're so good at' (157).

Analogies of language and method between detection and research, however, do not exhaust the similarities explored in these texts. For instance, Cross and others use the writing of biography, a prototypical academic project, to parallel, explore, and critique the detecting enterprise – and vice versa. Both undertakings are fraught with long-standing secrets, complicated and mysterious relationships, false identities. In *The Mystery Lady* by Anna Clarke, English professor Paula Glenning uncovers murder and fraud in the process of writing a biography of author Rosie O'Grady. In Cross's *Sweet Death, Kind Death*, the mystery is also of a piece with the writing of a biography. The novel opens, in fact, with a journal announcement: 'For a life of the writer and teacher Patrice Umphelby, we would appreciate hearing from anyone who has letters from her or personal knowledge of her' (1). The mystery of Umphelby's death, soon discovered by Kate Fansler and the biographers to have been not a suicide but murder, is solved, in part, by recourse to excerpts from Umphelby's journal, the journal being, of course, a staple of biography as a genre.

Kate proceeds in her investigation as though she too were writing a biography. 'Tell me about her,' she says to one of Umphelby's friends, 'What did she look like ... what was her physical presence like?' (143). Kate herself comments on the similarity between her detecting and writing itself: 'We never know it all; we only make up stories about it ... And if we call ourselves biographers, we call the stories and the characters we have invented biography' (96).

The clear relationship between biography as a genre and the work of a detective appears in several other Cross novels.[3] In *The Question of Max*, for example, the eponymous villain is working on the papers – with a view to writing a biography – of the writer Cecily Hutchins. Among the papers is an 'autobiographical fragment.' He forges letters, creating a false biography – of himself, of Cecily Hutchins, and of her circle of writing friends (based loosely on the Somerville novelists). Kate must produce the right biography, the right narrative, to bring about justice. Autobiographical fragments and biography figure importantly in *No Word from Winifred* as well. Kate and her niece Leighton learn to know and love Winifred from her journal excerpts as well as from their more formal investigation of her disappearance. And one of Kate's friends brings biography and detection together when he tells her: 'All Charlie's life she has wanted to write a biography of Charlotte Stanton ... Good biographers are good detectives, as Charlie says' (21). The most thorough development of the relationship between biography and detection, however, appears in *The Players Come Again*, in which Kate herself is asked to write a biography of Gabrielle Foxx, the wife of a famous modernist writer. Here the entire mystery seems coextensive with the biographical project itself, no mention of murder, in fact, until the final three pages of the book.

The publisher who is trying to convince Kate to undertake the biography gives her a diary of a woman who knew Gabrielle; the diary reveals that Gabrielle wrote, under duress, letters to order for her husband, letters that later became the basis for his best-known work. Like a good biographer, like a good detective, the author of the diary wonders about the authenticity of the letters. There's no question, that is, that Gabrielle Foxx wrote them, but were 'those words forced from her ... indeed her words, or, like the words of masochistic women in pornographic novels, men's fantasy, really, women saying what men wanted them to say' (73)?

Thus another literary layer is added to this already very literary mystery. And lurking under the surface of the diarist's question is another, more disturbing, question: Can women, inscribed as they are in men's language and/or world, ever write their own stories? Kate this time calls into question, during her investigations, the previously clear relationship between biographer and detective: 'Detectives are not biographers ... In fact, as she thought about it, the point of le Carre's excellent books was precisely that the more you knew people, the less you know them' (15). But when Kate says cynically to her husband, Reed, that she's 'going to invent the story of Gabrielle's life,' she immediately qualifies – somewhat – the cynicism: 'But like a good biographer, I shall search for the evidence to substantiate my interpretations.' Reed adds the obvious: 'Like a detective, too' (82). Thus, while this novel conflates almost entirely the biographical enterprise with the detective enterprise, it seems uneasy with the conflation, perhaps because of the plethora of voices that the biography must take into account. That is, the biographical project becomes more complicated than mere murder – the reason, one suspects, that the murder itself, that almost unvarying staple of the detective novel, is here practically a footnote. More important is the question of women's voices: Kate tries to hear as clearly as she can all the voices in the case/biography – Anne's, Dorinda's, Nellie's, Gabrielle's. And it is perhaps in this 'diffusion' of 'not only the single voice of the narrator but also the single image of the heroic detective' in the later Cross novels that we can, as Kathleen Gregory Klein suggests, hear the 'heteroglossia' of the novels (in a genre so frequently mono- rather than dialogic) and see the novels themselves break the conservative trap of the detective fiction genre (Klein 229). I will return to this point shortly.

Besides extensive exploration of the relationship between research and detection, another characteristic (and a characteristic this sub-genre shares with much women's detective fiction) is a significant change in the protagonist, sometimes over the course of the novel, as with Nan Weaver in Valerie Miner's *Murder in the English Department*, sometimes over the course of the series. Protagonists change, perhaps, as their authors change, as Heilbrun has suggested in *Writing a Woman's Life* of her own Kate: 'She ... held a few opinions I now consider retrograde ... but she has changed with time, she's learned, and that's all one can ask of anybody' (116).[4] The Kate of the 1960s could say, for example (in *The James Joyce Murder*), only half-jokingly, 'Emmet, are you suggesting that I have not only exposed my nephew to murder but have placed him in a camp filled with queers?' (105), and the 1960s Reed – Kate's then lover, afterwards husband – joked about wife-beating (80). Reed, in fact, rather than Kate, solved some of those early mysteries (*The James Joyce Murder* and *Poetic Justice*).

More germane to the genre itself, the Kate of *In the Last Analysis* (1964) wants, she says, nothing more than to restore the universe of Thomas Carlyle (118). She attempts heroically to save the language, order, and manners of the past – except, of course, that she wants equality for women. This traditionalist is in many ways quite different from the Kate of *A Trap for Fools* (1989), who says of a murder: 'Then let it go unsolved. I understand about communities and the finding of the guilty individual to return innocence to the rest of the community. But we have moved beyond those halcyon, or Agatha Christie, days. We are all guilty' (13). The later Kate knows that one cannot simply inject equality for women into 'the universe' of the Victorians or into detective fiction universes, which find and found their order in inequalities of various sorts, including gender inequality.

One could argue – and it is argued – that the very idea of the detective upholds this order, whether the detective is male or female, misogynist or feminist, that in fact the feminist detective might be the greatest promoter of patriarchy in that she seduces the female reader into complicity with an order based on her subjugation.[5] Much the same argument can of course be made, at other levels, for the novel in general, for women's studies in the academy, and so on. Kate Fansler in *The Players Come Again* says she is going to begin her biography of Gabrielle Foxx with a quote from Luce Irigaray: 'Virgin means one as yet unmarked by men ... not yet imprinted by their sex, their language.' Reed responds by suggesting that Kate is 'setting out to prove Gabrielle was all her life a virgin' and asks, 'Are you one too?' Kate's answer reflects her understanding of some of the issues at stake here: 'Of course I'm not. No member of an English department faculty is a virgin. Not yet, anyhow' (84). That is, women in English departments (and, I suspect, anywhere in the academy, the government, the literary establishment, the media) are always already imprinted by 'their' sex and 'their' language. No simple insertion of women chairs, women writers, women lawyers, women editors will change this, just as no simple insertion of a woman detective will transform the detective genre.[6]

While the danger of overestimating the revolution in detective fiction occasioned by the proliferation of women detectives seems clear, I would like to suggest that underestimating it is equally simplistic and does not take into account some of the subversions of which the woman detective genre is capable. I want to discuss two examples, both of which occur in mainstream popular mysteries (that is, I'm not treating here the more formally subversive postmodern fiction like M.F. Beal's *Angel Dance* or Mary Wings's *She Came* novels, which deserve their own analysis).[7] One is the ubiquitous reflection on gender in these works, reflection almost necessitated by the woman detective, who so clearly revises the detective role. Often this reflection is central to the novel's plot, as in Amanda Cross's *Death in a Tenured Position*, in which the victim is the first tenured woman at Harvard, hounded, it turns out, to suicide by the old boys. Less obvious but nonetheless central is the search for the truth about Patrice Umphelby in Cross's *Sweet Death, Kind Death*, in which Patrice's very feminine/feminist being threatens a fellow professor, who kills her. Other gender reflections are more peripheral, such as Kate's comment in *The Question of Max*: 'It strikes me as odd ... Here we sit, in a women's club, discussing a woman writer whose work is certainly getting more attention because of the women's movement, and you have sold her papers to a stuffy male club that admits women only on occasional evenings and by special invitation' (63). Or further in the same novel: 'A woman professor I know, very important, cancelled all her courses for the rest of the semester because her husband had a heart attack. Well, it was damn worrying and I sympathized. But one little part of me kept asking: would he have cancelled his courses if she had had a heart attack...? no. He would have ... used old notes ... But the woman professor was worried about how heartless she would look if she went about business as usual' (86).

While Kate's observations are hardly themselves radical, they do, by questioning its very order, at least *disturb* the detective fiction universe. In fact, I would argue that the presence of the feminist detective, working on her own, can't help but subvert to some extent the patriarchal order.[8] And I don't think we can glibly underestimate this. In a course I taught two years ago on biographies of women by women, we read *Sweet Death, Kind Death*. None of the theory I introduced, none of the more academic reflections on writing women's lives had nearly the effect of that book. The students, 90 per cent of them women, wanted only to talk about the amazing Kate, who says angry and feminist things, who takes off on her own and leaves a husband behind – without even asking him if it is okay. Two young women in the class who were engaged to be married said they had been forced by the book to rethink their decisions and assumptions. I was completely taken aback by this response, thinking that this gentle, fairly traditional, and generally conservative novel offered little by way of revolution. Many critics have in fact criticized Cross for not being feminist enough. Maureen T. Reddy, for example, notes her male-centred world: 'She seems able to connect most closely with dead or otherwise-absent women' (65). Anne Cranny-Francis objects to Kate's casting Janet Mandelbaum's problem (in *Death in a Tenured Position*) as 'not a social, but a personal one'; Cross, she argues, displaces 'social injustice and social irresponsibility into personal incapacity' (74). And I think that Cross's novels' odd and oddly ambivalent attitudes towards lesbianism need to be explored. But my students' responses suggest that Heilbrun may be right when she opines that 'detective fiction, often called formula fiction, has almost alone and with astonishing success challenged the oldest formulas of all' ('Gender' 7).[9]

My second example of subversion occurs in a series which seems in its stricter adherence to the British school to be even more traditional than the Amanda Cross novels, but which, it seems to me, questions our gender ideology at its roots, the Professor Hilary Tamar series by Sarah Caudwell. The success of a good mystery depends in part, of course, on fooling the reader, on offering real clues but also red herrings. Sarah Caudwell's texts intensify and take advantage of this tension between text and reader by teasing, evading, and thwarting readers' expectations on several levels. The most dramatic – and disconcerting – is the complete absence of gender markings for the narrator and chief detective, Professor Hilary Tamar.[10] Tamar is a law professor (Sarah Caudwell, by the way, is a lawyer – more evidence for my reproduction theory) who as one 'versed in the art ... of textual criticism' has learned 'to distrust the reading which seems at first sight to be the most obvious' (*The Sirens Sang of Murder* 173).[11] Since Professor Tamar is a senior Oxford don, the most obvious reading of the professor is as a male. And many of the readers and reviewers of the first novel made that assumption. In fact, Caudwell said in a talk at MysteryBooks in Washington, D.C., a couple of years ago that when one reviewer referred to Professor Tamar as a new woman detective, her own editor called her up, horrified at the 'mistake.' 'Mistake,' Caudwell said. 'Was it?'[12]

The trained reader of mysteries looks for clues. Very early in the first novel, *Thus Was Adonis Murdered*, Professor Tamar describes the group of barristers who will become familiar to readers over the course of the series. The narrator's attention to Cantrip's startling and attractive black eyes and Ragwort's 'demure autumnal colouring' (10) suggests a possible erotic attraction to the two young men. But is the attraction hetero- or homoerotic? Professor Tamar's initial description of Julia seems at first to offer a gender hint: 'Poor Julia's inability to understand what is happening, or why, in the world about her, her incompetence to learn even the simplest of practical skills required for survival – these must have made it evident, even in childhood, that she would never be able to cope unaided with the full responsibility of adult life' (10). A man being patronizing, a reader easily concludes. When Julia appears, however, in all her charming awkwardness, one revises the judgment. Perhaps Professor Tamar is only, like Julia's colleague Selena, feeling protective towards another woman.

While Professor Tamar's ambiguous gender is the most puzzling of the gender subversions in the novels, it is by no means the only one. When Julia appears, for example, we discover that she is just as incompetent in practical matters as Professor Tamar describes but is by no means that feminine stereotype the airhead. She is, on the contrary, a brilliant tax lawyer much admired by her colleagues and by Professor Tamar her/himself. And she is besides quite aggressive – both in tax law and in her sex life. Her colleague Selena must remind and caution her 'that young men like to think one is interested in them as people: if one discovers too early the true nature of one's interest [that is, sexual pleasure], they are apt to be offended and get all hoity-toity' (*Thus Was Adonis Murdered* 17).

Julia falls frequently for young men with classic profiles and describes herself as the sentimental type.[13] When one of her clients, however, whom she has advised to marry a penniless man for tax purposes, accuses her of being cynical, Julia defends herself: 'I am by no means cynical, being on the contrary sentimental to a fault; but if people are going to let sentiment interfere with their tax planning, there is no helping them' (*Thus* 56). Of men, she says, 'They are blown like feathers this way and that in every changing breeze of mood and fancy, so that it is quite impossible to predict, on any rational basis, what they will do next' (*Thus* 127). And though some of her best friends are men, she isn't sure she'd want her daughter to marry one (96). This opinion of men's irrationality is shared by Selena[14] and could suggest, in a wonderfully perverse way, that the ever rational Hilary Tamar must be – by virtue of that rationality – a woman.

While our question about Professor Tamar's gender may seem straightforward – Is he/she male or female? – it is, as I suggested before, rather more complicated. A heterosexual or homosexual male? A heterosexual or homosexual female? Some combination of the above? These questions hover around the other characters as well. One of Julia's male colleagues, for example, resents 'the jolly attractive girls' (*Thus* 56) who find themselves drawn to Julia. Selena, another of the barristers, is Julia's chief admirer and defender, and Julia returns the admiration, for, she says, 'to know Selena and not to admire her is a thing impossible' (*The Shortest Way to Hades* 50). Their loyal and vocal friendship frequently leads others to the conclusion that they are lovers, a conclusion they do nothing to refute – sometimes, in fact, using it to their advantage. The spectre of lesbianism holds no threat for either. In *The Shortest Way to Hades*, Ragwood, the moralist of the group, describes a women's bar as having 'a most unsavory reputation. I have heard it spoken of as a place frequented by females of unnatural propensity, seeking companions in disgraceful conduct.' Selena counters: 'I have heard it spoken of as an agreeable little establishment where single women may enjoy one another's company in relaxed and convivial surroundings' (97). Both she and Julia enjoy themselves there and do, in fact, pose as lovers. In *Thus Was Adonis Murdered*, Julia, in a state of undress, physically comforts Marylou (whom she has previously kissed, quite oblivious to the mocking observers); when Marylou's husband walks in, he 'misreads' the scene – as readers are invited to do.

One of the most amusing passages in the first novel concerns Julia's infatuation with a young man who is travelling with a male companion. Julia writes to her colleagues that she has discovered something horrible about him which she cannot reconcile with his physical beauty: 'The monstrous cannot disguise itself in an angelic mask. Reason and nature prohibit it. The deformity of mind would necessarily distort the perfection of the profile' (*Thus* 39). The words depravity, deformity, monstrous, reason, and nature slyly suggest the right-wing and religious rhetoric against homosexuality, but the monstrous deformity she discovers turns out to be the young man's employment by the Department of Inland Revenue. He's a tax man and Julia, the tax lawyer, loathes the profession. She does, however, seduce him, after convincing herself by a specious but impressive logical argument that she will not hurt his male companion by so doing. If Cora Kaplan and David Glover are correct in their guess that 'for some heterosexual readers a world which excludes the positive possibility of same-sex love [which most mainstream detective novel worlds do] is somehow a "safer" space for fantasy' (228), then Caudwell's seemingly traditional, 'cosy' British world has become profoundly and unexpectedly unsafe.

The instability of both gender and sexual orientation, then, is the subject of constant play in Caudwell's texts. Such play effectively calls into question all our assumptions about gender and sexuality and makes concrete, in a comic way, their constructedness. They do, besides, goad the reader, in good detective fashion, into constant vigilance. And it is of course our very obsession with gender and sexual orientation that fuels the vigilance. In spite of Caudwell's adamant refusal to name Hilary Tamar's gender, for example, the audience at MysteryBooks returned anxiously and obsessively to the question 'But *really,* is Hilary a man or a woman?' And thus does the text take advantage of the vigilance of readers of detective fiction to remind us that we are, in fact, obsessed – to remind us, that is, of the alarming extent of our own unhappiness and anxiety in the face of ambiguity about sex and gender.

In *The Players Come Again*, Kate Fansler laments that 'what had begun as a biography was, before her eyes, transforming itself into something else, as yet vague and troubling' (147). She might have said of the novel itself that what had begun as detective fiction was, before her eyes, transforming itself into something else, as yet vague and troubling. What I have been suggesting here, more generally, is that what has begun as detective fiction – that genre whose 'inherent conservatism upholds power and privilege in the name of law and justice as it validates readers' visions of a safe and ordered world' (Klein 1) – is, before our eyes, transforming itself into something else, destabilizing and troubling. While I do not want to claim too much for the subversiveness of these fictions, I do think, with Rosalind Coward and Linda Semple, that 'the boundaries of the detective fiction genre ... are relatively fluid and do not necessarily have conservative implications' (45).

In *The Novel and the Police*, D.A. Miller claims that 'whether the investigation is conducted by police or private detectives, its sheer intrusiveness posits a world whose normality has been hitherto defined as a matter of *not needing* the police or policelike detectives. The investigation repairs this normality not only by solving the crime, but also, far more important, by withdrawing from what had been, for an aberrant moment, its "scene"' (3). In these academic women detective novels, however, the amateur sleuths do not withdraw; they stay and do what good professors are always doing – questioning rather than repairing normality, deliberately *not* policing 'abnormal' roles and desires but giving them free play. As Martha Nussbaum observes in her elegant argument against the conservative assault on gay studies, 'History and philosophy [and literature, law, psychology, and all manner of other academic pursuits] are, in their very nature, forms of inquiry into the strange and unsettling' (35). Again, then, we note the consanguinity of the detecting and scholarly enterprises and suggest that while the 'classic' detective novel may restore and so reinscribe old hierarchies, the academic detective novel's native bent, like that of the academic herself, is to goad, gently if possible, readers/students into the exploration of the strange and unsettling.

NOTES

1 Maureen T. Reddy says that 'the only female academics/detectives I have found who are *not* English teachers are not professors at all, but students' (43); she misses classics professor Antonia Nielson in Carol Clemeau's *The Ariadne Clue*. And I would include law professor Hilary Tamar in Sarah Caudwell's novels – though whether Hilary qualifies as a *female* detective is happily unclear. See below.

2 Professor Austin decides inexplicably, without knowing the student, that said student plagiarized a prizewinning essay. And Austin takes as supporting evidence the fact that the student expertly wields Freudian jargon (which Austin proclaims 'extraordinarily silly' [116]) yet had never taken a psychology course. No self-respecting English professor would, I hope, act and think so rashly. Who among us learned our Freud in Psych I? But perhaps I'm just annoyed at the novel's anti-feminism, theory bashing, and predictable romance.

3 Even when the biographical enterprise is not so integral to the plot as it is in these novels, there are clear biographical elements in all the Cross fictions. Kate is always trying to 'get in' the life stories of the suspects and/or the victims – Janet Mandelbaum, for example, in *Death in a Tenured Position* and Beatrice Sterling in 'Murder without a Text.' Kate asks one of the teachers in *The Theban Mysteries* to tell her 'a bit ... about the five ... girls in the seminar' (147), all suspects. What she wants are not really 'bits' but histories and psychologies.

4 Steven R. Carter notes and delineates some of the changes: 'Shifting away from a defense of institutions and a mild contempt for homosexuals and the opinions of the young, she has more recently displayed a forthrightness and a desire for social justice that are matched by few other mystery writers' (270). While the 'she' is Amanda Cross rather than Kate Fansler, it is, of course Kate who demonstrates the evolution. And the changes have been, I would argue, even more dramatic since Carter's piece appeared in 1981, not

the least of which is Kate's increasing interest in and emphasis on women writers.

5 Kathleen Gregory Klein, for example, claims that 'the feminist detective winds up supporting the existing system which oppresses women when she re-establishes the ordered status quo ... No woman detective escapes the prospect of assisting in her own or other women's oppression whether women characters are the criminals, victims, or merely bystanders. Adopting the formula traps their authors' (201). Klein does, however, admit that one can alter the formula to feminist purposes and the 'foregrounding gender leads to questioning patriarchist assumptions through creating an interrogative text which urges readers to solve not only the problem of crime but also the problems of the social system' (227). She specifically cites two Cross novels which 'challenge the generic restrictions' (229), but since in this study Klein discusses only novels with professional private investigations, she does not elaborate.

6 For examples of the numerous novels with female (though not feminist) detectives which, far from transforming the genre, seem to try hard to reinscribe traditional assumptions about gender, see those by Lillian O'Donnell, Veronica Black, and (painful to mention because she's such a fine writer) P.D. James.

7 While the treatment is brief, B. Ruby Rich's comments on these novels and on many others are the most suggestive and exciting I've read on this topic. Klein also has an interesting section on *Angel Dance* (216–20).

8 Rich argues this in a wonderfully sophisticated, witty, and suggestive piece that appeared in the *Village Voice*: 'In an era insistently claimed for postmodernism, these girl-detective books are the real postfeminist texts, marking a shift from the engaged politics of the 70s in the *more* mainstream modes of entertainment, romance, and upscale empowerment typical of the 80s. They've finessed this shift via the sly appropriation of an overdetermined genre, one simultaneously embedded in the popular imagination and literary history. As fashion's rediscovery of the past has made clear, there's nothing like an overstated style to lend definition to the vagaries of the present. Voilà, the detective. What once was transparent and taken for granted becomes, second time around, a self-conscious set of choices, a strategy, a masquerade' (24).

9 An interesting challenge to the formula is Joan Smith's *Why Aren't They Screaming?*, in which English professor Loretta Lawson finds out that MP Colin Kendall-Cole is the murderer but, because he has destroyed the evidence, cannot convince the police that he and not the working-class, ex-con-

vict battered wife whom they accuse is the real killer. The novels ends with this failure.

10 A similarly disconcerting – though certainly not as radically disruptive – ambiguity occurs in Valerie Miner's *Murder in the English Department*, in which Nan Weaver's sexual orientation is unclear. The teasing clues culminate in an equally teasing conclusion that seems to me especially manufactured for a mainstream publisher. 'Coming out, thought Nan. Perhaps it was time for that. If they had stood by her at the murder trial, maybe she could tell them about ... who knew what would come out next?' (199). For a sympathetic (and Marxist) reading of this novel against *Death in a Tenured Position* see Anne Cranny-Francis, who finds Kate Fansler offensive – 'the kind of woman, perhaps the only kind of woman, of whom the academy might possibly approve. She's not black, poor, Asian, lesbian, militant, left-wing, ugly, working-class' (72).

11 Kate Fansler makes a similar point in *A Trap for Fools*: 'He thought to provide a diversion, but lit crit teaches you to be on the watch for exactly that. We deal in subtexts, in the hidden story' (210).

12 Caudwell also told that audience that the early reviewers who assumed Professor Tamar was male described him as witty and wise, while the ones who assumed Tamar was a woman called her obnoxious.

13 Julia describes herself by way of numerous hefty letters written to her colleagues, letters that add another narrative and thus contribute to the 'heteroglossia' of the narrative, already characterized by extensive dialogue.

14 This reversal of masculine/feminine stereotypes is one of the running jokes of the series. Selena continues it in *The Sirens Sang of Murder*: 'The trouble is that you and I, Julia, have been brought up in an era of emancipation and enlightenment, and we have got into the habit of treating men as if they were normal, responsible, grown-up people. We engage them in discussion; we treat their opinions as worthy of quite serious consideration; we seek to influence their behavior by rational argument rather than by some simple system of rewards and punishments. It's all a great mistake, of course, and only makes them confused and miserable – especially men like the Colonel, who have grown up with the idea that women will tell them what they ought to do without having to think about it for themselves' (77).

WORKS CITED

Bargainnier, Earl F., ed. *10 Women of Mystery.* Bowling Green, Ohio: Bowling Green University Popular Press, 1981.

Carr, Helen, ed. *From My Guy to Sci-Fi: Genre and Women's Writing in the Postmodern World*. London: Pandora, 1989.

Carter, Steven R. 'Amanda Cross.' In Bargainnier 269–96.

Caudwell, Sarah. *The Shortest Way to Hades*. 1984. New York: Penguin, 1986.

– *The Sirens Sang of Murder*. New York: Delacorte, 1989.

– *Thus Was Adonis Murdered*. New York: Penguin, 1982.

Clarke, Anna. *The Mystery Lady*. New York: Doubleday, 1986.

Clemeau, Carol. *The Ariadne Clue*. New York: Ballantine, 1982.

Coward, Rosalind, and Linda Semple. 'Tracking Down the Past: Women and Detective Fiction.' In Carr 39–57.

Cranny-Francis, Anne. *Feminist Fiction*. New York: St Martin's, 1990.

Cross, Amanda. *Death in a Tenured Position*. New York: Ballantine, 1981.

– *In the Last Analysis*. New York: Macmillan, 1964.

– *The James Joyce Murder*. New York: Macmillan, 1967.

– 'Murder without a Text.' *A Woman's Eye*. Ed. Sara Paretsky. New York: Delacorte, 1991. 81–96.

– *No Word from Winifred*. New York: Dutton, 1986.

– *The Players Come Again*. New York: Random House, 1990.

– *Poetic Justice*. New York: Knopf, 1970.

– *Sweet Death, Kind Death*. 1984. New York: Ballantine, 1985.

– *A Trap for Fools*. 1989. New York: Ballantine, 1990.

– *The Theban Mysteries*. 1971. New York: Avon, 1979.

– *The Question of Max*. New York: Knopf, 1976.

Heilbrun, Carolyn G. 'Gender and Detective Fiction.' *The Sleuth and the Scholar: Origins, Evolution, and Current Trends in Detective Fiction*. Ed. Barbara A. Rader and Howard G. Zettler. Westport, Conn.: Greenwood, 1988. 1–8.

– *Writing a Woman's Life*. New York: Norton, 1988.

Kaplan, Cora, and David Glover. 'Guns in the House of Culture? Crime Fiction and the Politics of the Popular.' *Cultural Studies*. Ed. Lawrence Grossberg, Cary Nelson, and Paula Treichler. New York: Routledge, 1992. 213–26.

Klein, Kathleen Gregory. *The Woman Detective: Gender and Genre*. Urbana and Chicago: University of Illinois Press, 1988.

Marchino, Lois A. 'The Female Sleuth in Academe.' *Journal of Popular Culture* 23 (Winter 1989): 89–100.

Miller, D.A. *The Novel and the Police*. Berkeley: University of California Press, 1988.

Miner, Valerie. *Murder in the English Department*. New York: St Martin's, 1983.

Nussbaum, Martha. 'The Softness of Reason.' *New Republic*, 13 and 20 July 1992. 26–35.

Reddy, Maureen T. *Sisters in Crime: Feminism and the Crime Novel*. New York: Continuum, 1988.

Rich, B. Ruby. 'The Lady Dicks: Genre Benders Take the Case.' *Village Voice Literary Supplement* 75 (June 1989). 24–7.

Skom, Edith. *The Mark Twain Murders*. New York: Dell, 1989.

Smith, Joan. *Why Aren't They Screaming?* New York: Fawcett, 1988.

Wender, Theodora. *Knight Must Fall*. New York: Avon, 1985.

9. Talkin' Trash and Kickin' Butt: Sue Grafton's Hard-boiled Feminism

Scott Christianson

Sue Grafton's series of hard-boiled mystery novels, featuring the female private investigator Kinsey Millhone, challenges patriarchy and asserts feminine autonomy.[1] As the narrator of Grafton's stories, Millhone talks tough and cracks wise – and occasionally cracks skulls and other parts of her antagonists' anatomies in the true tradition of hard-boiled detective fiction. Like her many male counterparts – Sam Spade, Philip Marlowe, Lew Archer, and Spenser – Millhone attempts to order her chaotic and violent experience in a careful narrative which, above all, tries to remain true to her experience even when she cannot make sense of what exactly is happening to her. She talks dirty, she talks tough, and she talks smart as she moves through a diverse cultural milieu in which she – a working-class woman – figures all too often as an outsider, an 'other.' Unlike her male counterparts, however, Kinsey Millhone seldom relies on a dominant rhetorical device in hard-boiled narrative: the 'hard-boiled conceit,' the kind of poignant metaphor or simile which peppers the writings of Raymond Chandler, Ross Macdonald, and Robert B. Parker as frequently as bullets and shots of booze. Millhone nevertheless reveals a similar 'complex sensibility' which is at once hard-boiled, feminist, and working class. Unlike several contemporary women (and men) detective novelists, Grafton is not an academic slumming in the streets of popular culture and social activism, and her detective Millhone is neither a pampered amateur solving crimes for fun nor a fantasized idealist saving the world through political correctness. Millhone is a flawed realist: joyfully single and lonely at times, sexually active in between long spells of celibacy, a liar by choice and habit who struggles to tell the truth about herself and her experience. Sue Grafton uses language to gain a little power within a patriarchal culture which still denies it to women, minorities, and members of the working class.

As hundreds of books and articles testify, the study of 'popular' as distinct from 'serious' fiction requires no defence – which is not to deny the historical and theoretical significance of the marginalization of popular fiction, which over the centuries has been written overwhelmingly by women. What deserves mention, however, is that popular fiction is definitively *generic*. Formerly an indictment of all popular fiction, the title 'generic,' or 'genre fiction,' can actually be seen as one of its more critically valuable features. Contrary to 'popular' belief – in this case, the belief of critics preferring 'high' or 'serious' culture – readers of popular fiction are critically comparative readers. For whatever reasons and with whatever outcomes, readers of popular fiction are highly cognizant of the forms and conventions of the genres they read. Far from the limited view that such readers will tolerate only those works which 'correctly' conform to the rules of formation of their favoured genres, the proliferation and development of popular fictional genres suggests that playing off and even violating norms of genres are essential aspects of reader enjoyment. The popularity of Sue Grafton, as well as of Sara Paretsky, Marcia Muller, and other women writing within the specific genre of hard-boiled detective fiction, suggests that much of the pleasure derived from such works by women writers arises from comparisons made with traditional (and male) norms. Thus, what some feminist critics have often demanded but seldom got, a 'radical comparativism, in which texts by male and female authors working within the same historical conditions and genres are set against each other' (Showalter 5), has been a consistent feature in the writing and reading of women's hard-boiled detective fiction.[2]

TOUGH TALK AND WISECRACKS

In an *Armchair Detective* interview from 1989, Sue Grafton says, 'When I decided to do mysteries, I chose the classic private eye genre because I like playing hardball with the boys' (Taylor 12). I will be ranging over all nine Kinsey Millhone novels published to date (1992) and attempting to let Grafton teach me to read as a feminist, to see the world of her novels through her feminist perspective.[3] For as she affirms in the 1989 interview, 'I am a feminist from way back' (11). Grafton plays hardball with the boys through her appropriation of hard-boiled language – her use of tough talk and wisecracks – and in the process transforms the classic private eye genre into a place from which a woman can exercise language as power.

The distinguishing feature of the hard-boiled detective genre of fiction since its inception has been its language. As Dennis Porter observes, 'The language chosen is a mode of address, a style of self-presentation, and an affirmation of American manliness' (139). Porter is writing about Dashiell Hammett and Raymond Chandler and does not discuss women hard-boiled writers, of whom there were not many in 1981, and who obviously are not concerned with affirming 'American manliness'; but his focus on language as mode of address – how and to whom one is speaking – and style of self-presentation – who is speaking, the kind of person narrating – is important. With few exceptions, hard-boiled detective stories – novels and short stories – speak in the first person. The narrator is the hard-boiled detective him/herself, who talks all the time to the reader in direct, evocative, colloquial language that represents the hard-boiled hallmark of the genre. Hard-boiled language or style is a generically distinctive combination of active verbs and fast-moving prose, of tough talk, wisecracks, and the often crude vernacular or colloquial idiom familiar to readers of the hard-boiled tradition, who will recognize its deployment in Grafton's novels.

Through Kinsey Millhone, Grafton comments self-referentially on a mode of address and exhibits in microcosm her hard-boiled style of self-presentation. In *'B' Is for Burglar*, the second novel in the alphabetical series, Kinsey Millhone writes, 'I start by asserting who I am and what I do, as though by stating the same few basic facts I can make sense out of everything that comes afterward' (1). In *'A' Is for Alibi*, at the outset of the series, we learn that who she is is a private investigator who has recently killed somebody, and that the subsequent narrative is her attempt to sort through that experience since the official reports don't say 'quite enough' (1). Seven of the nine novels begin in the same way, and all tell us early on who Kinsey Millhone is and what she does. Interestingly, in only the first three novels does Grafton have Millhone comment directly on why she is writing her narrative: in the first two, as we have seen, to make sense of her experience; in the third, *'C' Is for Corpse*, for that reason and as a memorial and final full report to her dead client, Bobby Callahan. We are apparently supposed to read the novels as elaborated case reports, suspending our disbelief that so long a narrative should be written to serve that professional purpose. Subsequent novels do not try to maintain this 'fiction,' and like most hard-boiled detective novels they assume that readers do not need a firmer anchor in 'reality' for such long-winded 'reports.' The important point is that these long first-person narratives have been 'written' by Kinsey Millhone as an attempt to make sense of her experience, and that the first three novels self-consciously and self-referentially acknowledge that fact.

Overwhelmingly in hard-boiled narratives, the style of self-presentation and language is tough – tough-talking and tough-minded. A character in Hammett's *Red Harvest* describes the Continental Op: 'You're a great talker ... A two-fisted, you-be-damned man with your words. But have you got anything else? Have you got the guts to match your gall? Or is it just the language you've got?' (Hammett 9).[4] The hard-boiled detective/narrator *always* has the guts to match his or her gall, as readers familiar with the genre know. He or she talks tough, talks smart, and talks all the time to the reader in an attempt to assert personal autonomy, to make sense of experience, and to exercise language as power. Tough talk is a prominent feature of the hard-boiled style and is an important, character-defining element in Grafton's narratives. Like her male counterparts, Kinsey Millhone talks tough as an exercise of power – the power to express her emotions and sensibilities, and power over situations and circumstances.

Kinsey Millhone talks tough, and occasionally she backs up the tough talk with violence or the promise of violence – a promise, we are made aware, she is able to keep.[5] A vivid example is found in *'H' Is for Homicide*, when Kinsey – after chasing down a violent criminal who has essentially held her hostage for days and just shot her close friend from childhood – lands with her knees on his back, gun drawn: 'He turned over as I raised the barrel of the gun and placed it between his eyes. Raymond had his hands up, inching away from me. For ten cents I would have blown that motherfucker away. My rage was white hot and I was out of control, screaming *"I'll kill your ass! I'll kill your ass, you son of a bitch!"'* (285). This is literally tough talk with a vengeance, the link between the talk and the violence, in Kinsey's word, 'white hot' and apparent. Similarly, in *'G' Is for Gumshoe*, Kinsey has been toyed with and threatened by a hit man contracted to kill her; although seriously afraid for her life – and not afraid to admit she needs the protection of the (male) bodyguard she has not-quite-hired to protect her – she tells him: 'Lighten up and let's figure out some way to kill his ass. I hate chickenshit guys trying to shoot me. Let's get him first' (211). The tough talk here shows toughness to be a combination of tough-mindedness in the face of physical danger, a willingness to exercise violence if necessary, and both vulgarity and a sense of humour. 'Lighten up,' she tells her bodyguard, not exactly in a situation which calls for that laid-back phrase. 'I hate chickenshit guys trying to shoot me,' she says with humorous vulgarity and matter-of-factness, as if it happens all the time and is merely annoying. The blend of vulgarity, humour, and toughness is characteristic of hard-boiled language or tough talk.

As noted earlier, we know from the outset of the series that Kinsey's tough talk is ultimately backed up by the promise of violence: she announces in the third sentence of '*A*' *Is for Alibi* that she killed someone, and in typically hard-boiled style she is matter-of-fact about it, bringing into the same first paragraph details about who, how, and where she lives. That novel closes, prior to the epilogue, with Kinsey killing the murderer from a garbage can in which she is hiding from him; as he lifts the lid, peering down at her, she sees a butcher knife in his hand and writes, 'I blew him away' (214). In the most recent instalment, '*I*' *Is for Innocent*, Kinsey is shot by the murderer near the end of the novel yet bravely talks to her would-be killer about his crimes as she tries to figure out how to kill him first; as the killer discovers her hiding place in the deserted office, he says, clowningly, 'Are you prepared to die?' – to which she responds, in characteristic hard-boiled style, 'I wouldn't say prepared exactly, but I wouldn't be surprised.' 'How about you?' she asks, 'Surprised?' With that, Kinsey writes, 'I fired at him point-blank and then studied the effect' (282). My point is that the 'posture promising violence' is established from the outset and figures throughout the series. Kinsey Millhone's 'tough talk' is 'of the kind' of hard-boiled language found throughout the genre.

If talking tough is one way of exercising 'language as power' – over one's self in violent situations, and over one's antagonist as the threat or overture to violence – the hard-boiled detective has also invariably talked smart through glibness, humour, and wisecracks. Again, Kinsey Millhone is no exception. In '*I*' *Is for Innocent*, as just discussed, Kinsey keeps up a patter of glib talk, along with the tough talk, with her would-be killer, and at one point she cracks wise in response to his philosophizing about killing people, who, he claims, are no more than ants: 'Jesus,' Kinsey says, 'This is really profound. I'm taking notes over here' (279). Similarly, albeit in a non-violent situation in the first novel, Kinsey wisecracks to an unresponsive witness, 'Try to keep your answers short so I can get 'em on one line' ('*A*' 107). A wisecrack is a characteristic remark from a 'wise guy' – as Dennis Porter says, 'someone who is no respecter of authority, wealth, power, social standing, or institutions' (166). A fundamental feature in Chandler's style, according to Porter, the wisecrack is also 'an ideal form of the vernacular characterized by its tough mindedness and its terseness' which figures throughout the hard-boiled genre (166). It is usually reserved, in hard-boiled fiction, for dialogue, for presentation to an audience who will fail to appreciate it. But it is linked with vulgar language and humour generally, as aspects of hard-boiled language which reveal the narrator's complex sensibility and attitude towards experience.

Porter calls the wisecrack, specifically, 'the maxim of the American working classes' which 'combines at its level the quintessence of style with the body of wisdom' (144), but I think wisecracks join vulgar language and humour to provide that function in hard-boiled fiction. It's all humorous smart talk from a 'smart alec' who doesn't respect convention or authority. Kinsey Millhone cracks wise, from time to time, as we have seen. She also makes humorous observations about things which, though not technically wisecracks, contribute to the hard-boiled style of her language in similar ways. In *'D' Is for Deadbeat*, Kinsey writes, 'Even with low-heeled pumps, my feet hurt and my pantyhose made me feel like I was walking around with a hot, moist hand in my crotch' (138). Remembering summer camp as a child – a less than positive experience – Kinsey details: 'The horses were big and covered with flies, hot straw baseballs coming out their butts at intervals ... Nature turned out to be straight uphill, dusty and hot and itchy. The part that wasn't dry and tiresome was even worse' ('H' 240). Apparently horses made a big impression on Kinsey, for in the next novel she comments, about the stable she is in, 'The air smelled faintly musty, a blend of straw, dampness, and the various by-products of horse butts' ('I' 153). Like the wisecrack proper, such remarks are maxim-like, relying for their effects, in Porter's words, on 'the shock of the vernacular' (but not, as he claims, on 'cynical irreverence,' though irreverent they certainly are) (144). They reveal a sensibility that is not only irreverent but humorously thoughtful – which insists that thoughtfulness is not monopolized by the higher classes or their more highfalutin, proper language. About the inadequacy of her report to the attorney employing her to prove his case in *'I' Is for Innocent*, Kinsey reflects philosophically, 'Small comfort to an attorney who could end up in court with nothing in his hand but his dick' (98). The remark not only conveys knowledge of what lawyers need in court but offers an oblique and vulgar comment on what they usually rely on.

The wisecrack and related humorous, maxim-like remarks help reveal the hard-boiled narrator's complex sensibility – a streetwise knowledge-ability about the world and its workings combined with the verbal facility to encapsulate that knowledge in pithy, humorous utterances. In other words, we are talking about language as a form of power to articulate a complex understanding about and attitude towards experience. The wisecrack and related forms are similar to but definitely not synonymous with another rhetorical device, one which, as I have claimed elsewhere, is the feature of hard-boiled language which becomes a structuring device of great importance in much hard-boiled fiction. That device I call the 'hard-boiled conceit,' a particularly pointed or extended metaphor or simile which is usually serious, and which is spoken to the reader directly to convey the detective/narrator's complex sensibility. On this functioning of the hard-boiled conceit, I disagree with Porter, who conflates it with the wisecrack and, while acknowledging that it structures the hard-boiled detective novel (144), limits its significance to a 'digressive effect,' an example of Barthes's 'playful excess' enjoyed only at 'the level of pure language.'[6] I contend that the hard-boiled conceit is a more serious and evocative device used by the narrator to communicate his complex sensibility directly to the reader.

First, some examples from the male tradition. From Chandler alone, Porter provides a lengthy list: 'nasty meaty leaves and stalks like the newly washed fingers of dead men' (64); hair 'like wild flowers fighting for life on a bare rock'; 'lower than a badger's balls'; 'smart as a hole through nothing'; 'a face like a collapsed lung'; 'a mouth like a wilted lettuce' (66). Not found in Chandler alone, the hard-boiled conceit appears throughout the tradition. In Robert B. Parker's latest novel, *Double Deuce*, Parker has Spenser 'set up' a hard-boiled conceit describing a housing project through a parody of the smart talk of a different – and 'higher' – class of people: 'The urban planners who had built it to rescue the poor from the consequences of their indolence had fashioned it of materials calculated to endure the known propensity of the poor to ungraciously damage the abodes so generously provided them' (24). Hard-boiled PI Spenser then offers the hard-boiled conceit describing the housing project: 'Everything was brick and cement and cinderblock and asphalt and metal. Except the windows. The place had all the warmth of a cyanide factory' (245). The final line is delivered like a punch-line for the reader alone, carefully prepared for first by the highfalutin language parody, then by the terse descriptive language also characteristic of the hard-boiled style.

In Sue Grafton's novels, we find metaphors and similes – often, I have noticed, animal-related – but only occasionally a full-blown hard-boiled conceit. In *'C' Is for Corpse*, Kinsey describes the hospital morgue: 'The temperature was cool and the air was scented with formaldehyde, that acrid deodorant for the deceased' (71). The closing metaphor has the vivid, maxim-like quality of the hard-boiled conceit. Locating an aged missing person in a nursing home in 'G' Is for Gumshoe, Kinsey observes that 'the truncated shape of her skull gave her the look of some long-legged, gangly bird with a gaping beak. She was squawking like an ostrich, her bright, black eyes snapping from point to point' (60). Here we have the extended metaphor, another version of the hard-boiled conceit, which links with a briefer version on the following page. When the commotion in the ward finally awakens two other elderly patients, Kinsey notes that they 'woke up and began to make quacking sounds' (61). Later in the same novel, Kinsey compares herself to the attractive ex-wife of the hitman contracted to kill Kinsey: 'In her presence, I felt as dainty and feminine as a side of beef. When I opened my mouth, I was worried I would moo' (290). Humorously, Kinsey here worries that the hard-boiled conceit – the simile comparing her to a side of beef – will become literal reality. As these few examples show, Grafton appropriates an important feature of hard-boiled language style, though generally the hard-boiled conceit figures much less prominently in her hard-boiled style than it does in that of male practitioners of the genre (especially Chandler, Macdonald, and Parker). Nevertheless, this feature of Grafton's style demonstrates – as do the examples of tough talk and wisecracks – that she is aware of the linguistic conventions of the genre, and more important, that she adopts the hard-boiled style in order to accomplish what she has affirmed is her goal in writing mystery novels: 'What I hope to do is engage in a kind of truth-telling about what I see' (Taylor 12). Such truth-telling, of course, represents an important use of language as power in Grafton's novels, and throughout hard-boiled detective fiction.

The desire or intent to 'engage in a kind of truth-telling' about what one sees accounts in Grafton's novels for a final kind of hard-boiled 'smart' talk found throughout the genre. Grafton herself has observed, 'I view the mystery novel as a vantage point from which to observe the world we live in' (Taylor 12). An integral part of Grafton's use of language, found throughout the hard-boiled genre, is a form of philosophical commentary that counterpoints the tough talk, wisecracks, humour, and vulgarity. In 'C' Is for Corpse, we can see the counterpoint in action. Following the death (later revealed to be murder) of her client, Kinsey expresses her grief in a quick sequence that constitutes a hard-boiled conceit: 'Something in her face spilled over me like light through a swinging door. Sorrow shot through the gap, catching me off-guard, and I burst into tears' (88). That comment ends a chapter, and the first sentence of the next chapter reads, 'Everything happens for a reason, but that doesn't mean there's a point' (89). The sentence is clearly a maxim, and the two contractions enhance the colloquial style; it is direct and poignant, especially following immediately the more emotional and verbally evocative hard-boiled conceit.

One other example must suffice to detail this stylistic feature found throughout Grafton's novels. In *'I' Is for Innocent*, Kinsey writes something like a hard-boiled conceit but, I think, discernibly different – perhaps more philosophical than hard-boiled. She is describing a woman she has just arrived to interview, and the description leads purposefully up to the philosophical comment:

Francesca was tall, very slender, with short-cropped brown hair and a chiselled face. She had high cheekbones, a strong jawline, a long straight nose, and a pouting mouth with a pronounced upper lip. She wore loose white pants of some beautifully draped material, with a long peach tunic top that she had belted in heavy leather. Her hands were slender, her fingers long, her nails tapered and polished. She wore a series of heavy silver bracelets that clanked together on her wrists like chains, confirming my suspicion that glamour is a burden only beautiful women are strong enough to bear. She looked like she would smell of lilac or newly peeled oranges. (154)

The description of Francesca is subtly elaborate, like Francesca's carefully constructed appearance, and leads to the punch-line, which, I think, is not as 'punchy' as such lines can often be in hard-boiled narrative. The maxim is neither cynical nor resentful but conveys a matter-of-fact truthfulness. Only a page later, the 'strong enough to bear' is recast in more powerful terms: Francesca explains that she got into designing headwear for cancer patients – the activity she engages in while talking to Kinsey – during her own battle with breast cancer two years previously. Francesca reveals her own brand of toughness: 'One morning in the shower, all my hair fell out in clumps. I had a lunch date in an hour and there I was, bald as an egg. I improvised one of these from a scarf I had on hand, but it was not a great success. Synthetics don't adhere well to skulls as smooth as glass' (155). Commenting on how this got her started in business, Francesca delivers a maxim of her own: 'Tragedy can turn your life around if you're open to it.' She then asks Kinsey, 'Have you ever been seriously ill?' to which Kinsey (sort of) wisecracks: 'I've been beaten up. Does that count?' Kinsey observes: 'She didn't respond with the usual exclamations of surprise or distaste. Given what she'd been through, merely being punched out must have been an easy fix' (155).

VOICE AND AUTONOMY

I have discussed the foregoing scene at length because it offers, in microcosm, the distinctive and original quality of Grafton's hard-boiled style, and I will return to this scene shortly. To this point in my analysis of that style, I have pointedly not referred to Grafton's 'feminism.' I have tried to show that Grafton's style is 'of the kind' of hard-boiled language found in the male-dominated portion of the tradition. My position differs from that of other critics, who feel that Grafton's style or voice is unlike 'the cynical, detached one typical of male creators of hard-boiled novels,' that the similarities are superficial, or that any similarity of language is merely a 'digressive effect' which does not offset the basic ideological difference between Grafton's hard-boiled novels and the male-dominated genre of hard-boiled detective fiction (Reddy *Sisters* 120).[7] Generally, the view seems to be either that Grafton essentially transforms the hard-boiled style or genre for her feminist purposes, or that her feminism is vitiated by her appropriation of generic characteristics inherently marked by the male gender and its hard-boiled ideology. In my view, Grafton appropriates hard-boiled language for feminist purposes as an exercise of language as power; in Foucauldian terms, she seizes the 'rules of formation' for the 'discourse' of hard-boiled fiction, thereby occupying a space or 'subject position,' formerly reserved for men only, from which she may speak with power as a woman. In plainer terms – offered by Grafton herself – she plays hardball with the boys, on what had been their own turf. To claim otherwise, I believe, is to deny Grafton her sense of what she is doing in her novels, and to enforce a narrowly 'essentialist' notion of feminism as the only feminism that really counts.[8]

To return to the scene between Kinsey and Francesca: without making Francesca hard-boiled – I have already demonstrated the difference in style between the two women – Grafton reveals her to be as tough in her own way as Kinsey is in hers. As a perceptive feminist observed to me, 'Toughness is being willing to do the hard stuff no matter how hard it is to do' (Huber). We have seen Kinsey humorously remark, 'Glamour is a burden only beautiful women are strong enough to bear.' As the scene unfolds, we learn that glamour had indeed been a burden Francesca had had to bear – her identity had been almost exclusively defined by her beauty, and by her need to use it to attract a husband who remained infatuated with his previous wife. Facing the assault on life – as well as beauty – of breast cancer, Francesca made the symbolic gesture of designing a turban to cover her bald head, fighting first for beauty but turning that fight into self-actualization. She tells Kinsey she will probably leave her husband: 'Now I realize my happiness has nothing to do with him ... I woke up one morning and realized I was out of control' (157). She says a page later, about her whole life, 'I woke up one day and thought, What am I doing?' (158). Now she has begun to see with 'great clarity': 'It's like being nearsighted and suddenly getting prescription lenses. It's all so much clearer it's astonishing' (160).

Waking up and seeing more clearly, I think Grafton is saying, is possible for women in the world *now*. Doing the hard stuff no matter how hard it is to do is the real measure of toughness, not just macho posturing, backing up the tough talk with a posture promising violence. Grafton *problematizes* hard-boiled toughness throughout her novels – which is not to say that she radically transforms male hard-boiled attitudes and languages or manages to avoid them altogether. She appropriates hard-boiled style and works through it to articulate her own brand of feminism. Throughout her narratives, Kinsey Millhone reflects on what it means to be tough. In *'A' Is for Alibi*, as we have seen, she voices her struggle with having killed a man. In *'B' Is for Burglar*, she discusses that killing briefly with her octogenarian landlord, Henry Pitts, and tries out the self-justifying posture of someone unwilling to be a victim any more; but as Henry points out to her, and as she agrees, trying to turn the killing into a philosophical statement just doesn't ring true, and Kinsey notes the surprising unsureness in her voice as she asks, 'I'm still a good person, aren't I?' (77). The point isn't that Kinsey denies that there are victims, and that they are often women victimized by men, but that she is willing to explore what it means to be tough and hard-boiled. In *'E' Is for Evidence*, her integrity as an investigator is being challenged by an accusation of her complicity in insurance fraud; the people she must investigate – and with whom she is implicated – are of a much higher class, and her dealings with them leave her disconcerted; she is caught in a power game in which she doesn't know the rules, and which causes her to question her strength and integrity – all exacerbated by her solitary personal life, which has left her completely alone at the holidays. She soliloquizes: 'It's not my style to be lonely or to lament, even for a moment, my independent state. I like being single. I like being by myself. I find solitude healing and I have a dozen ways to feel amused. The problem was I couldn't think of one. I won't admit to depression, but I was in bed by 8:00 p.m. ... not cool for a hardassed private eye waging a one-woman war against the bad guys everywhere' (63). Or as she writes in 'I' Is for Innocence, 'I wanted to feel like the old Kinsey again ... talkin' trash and kickin' butt. Being cowed and uncertain was really for the birds' (221). She *is* a hard-assed private eye, she is tough – tough-talking, tough-minded, willing to do the hard stuff – but she is also willing to explore her toughness as she explores, generally, her autonomy, her existence as a woman in a male-dominated profession in a male-dominated world.

Hard-boiled language is a matter of *voice*, and Grafton makes the hard-boiled voice her own. Grafton acknowledges: 'Voice is a big issue. Until I found the right voice for Kinsey Millhone, I wasn't in business. Voice is about gettin' connected to your stuff. A sense of authenticity or truth. A writer's voice is that unique blend of viewpoint and language that echoes a writer's soul, if that doesn't sound too lofty or pretentious' (Taylor 10). Kinsey Millhone's voice, talking non-stop through nine novels, represents 'a blend of viewpoint and language' which is discernibly 'hard-boiled' at the same time it is individual; in other words, it is 'of the kind' of voice or language found throughout the hard-boiled genre even as it is distinctive, original.

According to Porter, the language style of the genre allows for 'a perfect match between language and behavior, speech and ethics' (138), and he claims further that it represents what V.N. Voloshinov calls 'behavioral ideology,' which, in the case of hard-boiled detective fiction, Porter interprets as 'an affirmation of American manliness' against – specifically – English gentility, formality, and high culture (139). As Porter says in relation to hard-boiled fiction, 'In a novel, speech makes the man who is offered up for the reader's evaluation' (138–9). Seemingly contradicting Grafton's claim that 'voice' is a matter of finding a style to match the writer's soul, Porter – through Voloshinov – asserts that speech or voice 'makes the man' in hard-boiled detective fiction.

Obviously problematical here is Porter's assumption that the hard-boiled style is definitively male. In fairness to Porter, he does not discuss women writers within the genre, and he is writing specifically about its originators, Hammett and Chandler. But his close linking of 'voice' or speech with 'behavioral ideology' – 'that atmosphere of unsystematized and unfixed inner and outer speech which endows every instance of behavior and action and our every conscious state with meaning' (139)[9] – must give us pause as we analyse the voice of a hard-boiled narrator whose speech does not, literally, 'make the man.' The implication of Porter's formulation, his linkage of voice and ideology, must be either that adoption of the hard-boiled voice makes the female detective/narrator a man, or that a female narrator is proscribed from adopting such a voice, such a gender-marked style of language and self-presentation. In short, with the female hard-boiled narrator we have either a case of cross-dressing or a style which cannot, by definition, be hard-boiled. In my view, neither implication or conclusion is applicable to the novels of Sue Grafton.

Let me return briefly to Voloshinov, whose 'constructionist' position – that individual consciousness is a social structure, rather than innate – is close to the poststructuralist view that consciousness is structured like and by language.[10] Writers, it seems to me, are generally pretty resistant to such a formulation, and Grafton seems to be no exception when she claims that 'voice' is 'that unique blend of viewpoint and language that echoes a writer's soul.' Voloshinov actually writes that 'it is a matter *not so much of expression accommodating itself to our inner world but rather of our inner world accommodating itself to the potentialities of our expression, its possible routes and directions*' (91; italics in original). For my purposes, I am going to seize on the equivocal nature of Voloshinov's statement: 'it is a matter not so much of.' While asserting that we accommodate our inner world to 'the potentialities of our expression' – to a style of self-presentation through language – Voloshinov's equivocation indicates that we do not exclusively do so. In plainer terms, we not only form ourselves according to the forms of expression available to us but, reciprocally, form our expression according to who we are. That my own formulation is in keeping with Voloshinov's is seen in his affirmation that individual consciousness which has entered 'into the power system of science, art, ethics, or law' becomes 'a real force' for change in the world. In Grafton's fiction, her adoption of the hard-boiled style allows her to pursue 'possible routes and directions' in the production of a distinctive 'voice' that, in turn, transforms the style into something unique and feminist.

This first-person exercise of language as power, I contend, works in a way described by the anti-essentialist feminist Monique Wittig. At this point I want to address how, in theoretical terms, Sue Grafton teaches me to read as a feminist.

For when one becomes a locutor, when one says 'I' and, in so doing, reappropriates language as a whole, proceeding from oneself alone, with the tremendous power to use all language, it is then and there, according to linguists and philosophers, that the supreme act of subjectivity, the advent of subjectivity into consciousness, occurs. It is when starting to speak that one becomes 'I.' This act – the becoming of the subject through the exercise of language and through locution – in order to be real, implies that the locutor be an absolute subject ... I mean that in spite of the harsh law of gender and its enforcement upon women, no woman can say 'I' without being for herself a total subject – that is, ungendered, universal, whole. (Wittig 80)

Against 'essentialist' theories that predicate distinctive 'women's ways of knowing,' Wittig insists, with Simone de Beauvoir, that 'one is not born a woman' (9 ff.). Yet, while 'language as a whole gives everyone the same power of becoming an absolute subject through its exercise,' gender works 'to annul it as far as women are concerned and corresponds to a constant attempt to strip them of the most precious thing for a human being – subjectivity ... The result of the imposition of gender, acting as a denial at the very moment when one speaks, is to deprive women of the authority of speech' (80–1). Wittig's conclusion: 'Gender then must be destroyed. The possibility of its destruction is given through the very exercise of language. For each time I say 'I,' I reorganize the world from my point of view and through abstraction I lay claim to universality. This fact holds true for every locutor' (81).

Glenwood Irons has described Sue Grafton's hard-boiled fiction as 'gender-bending' and has claimed that 'Grafton actually reinvents the "rugged individual" – as woman' ('New Women Detectives' 135).[11] If we follow Wittig's formulation, I think we must perceive Grafton's hard-boiled feminism as 'gender-busting.' Through the hard-boiled voice of her narrator, Grafton inserts Kinsey Millhone into the position of locutor who, through her point of view and through abstraction, can lay claim to universality and can become 'a total subject – that is, ungendered, universal, whole.' However much this is a 'fiction,' and however challenged 'universal subjectivity' has been by poststructuralist thinking, I respond to Kinsey Millhone as if this is what happens in her narratives. To conflate my terms with Wittig's, Grafton – through Kinsey Millhone – exercises hard-boiled language as power in order to become an absolute subject; it is through speaking non-stop to the reader in hard-boiled language that Kinsey Millhone becomes an 'I.' She attains, in Wittig's terms, the 'most precious thing for a human being – subjectivity.' Grafton accomplishes what Carolyn G. Heilbrun demanded of women writers over twelve years ago: 'We must ask women writers to give us, finally, female characters who are complex, whole, and independent – fully human' (Heilbrun 34).[12] Significantly, as I have shown, she accomplishes this on the turf of hard-boiled detective fiction, playing hardball with the boys.

Heilbrun contends: 'Woman has too long been content to accept as fundamental the dependent condition of her sex. We avoid aggressive behavior, fear autonomy, feel incomplete without the social status only a man can bestow' (29). The result has been a relative handful of successful women who have actually been 'honorary men,' who have succeeded by 'preserving the socially required "femininity," but sacrificing their womanhood' (29). As my discussion of her hard-boiled voice has shown, Kinsey Millhone does not avoid aggressive behaviour (though she problematizes, not celebrates, it); she explores autonomy; and she does not feel incomplete without a man (though she is not averse to having a good one around, like the bodyguard Robert Dietz in 'G' Is for Gumshoe). Most important, Kinsey Millhone is not an 'honorary man' in Heilbrun's terms. Finally, Grafton teaches me to read as a feminist by having Kinsey Millhone explore what it means to be a woman with the emphasis on a woman, who happens to be a hard-boiled private detective.

In Reinventing Womanhood, Heilbrun observes that she learned from her mother 'the importance of autonomy for women,' and she goes on to describe her mother's 'lasting gift' and 'remarkably clear' message: 'Be independent, make your own way, do not pay with your selfhood for male admiration and approval: the price is too high' (16–17). In 'D' Is for Deadbeat, Kinsey describes what she learned from the aunt who raised her after her parents died in a car crash: 'Rule Number One, first and foremost, above and beyond all else, was financial independence. A woman should never, never, never be financially dependent on anyone, especially a man, because the minute you were dependent, you could be abused ... Any feminine pursuit that did not have as its ultimate goal increased self-sufficiency could be disregarded. "How to Get Your Man" didn't even appear on the list' (107–8). The similarities between the advice given Heilbrun by her mother and the advice given Kinsey by her aunt are unmistakable. Grafton echoes Heilbrun, which should not be surprising from a self-proclaimed feminist who has probably read this feminist scholar who is also the detective novelist Amanda Cross. Grafton, in short, accomplishes Heilbrun's dictum 'Womanhood must be reinvented.' Grafton approaches the writing of detective fiction as an opportunity to reinvent herself; as she says in the *Armchair Detective* interview: 'I don't just make this stuff up, you know. Because of Kinsey, I get to lead two lives – hers and mine. Sometimes I'm not sure which I prefer' (Taylor 10). If, as Grafton says, Kinsey Millhone is a 'stripped down version' of Grafton herself (Taylor 10), Kinsey also comments throughout the series on inventing and reinventing herself. In *'A' Is for Alibi*, Kinsey reflects that she knows more about other people's lives than her own, and speculates, 'Perhaps, in poring over the facts about other people, I could discover something about myself' (132). In *'F' Is for Fugitive*, Kinsey is hired to prove the innocence of murder of a man who walked away from prison seventeen years ago: 'Curious, I thought, that a man can reinvent himself. There was something enormously appealing in the idea of setting one persona aside and constructing a second to take its place' (11). And in *'H' Is for Homicide* Kinsey gets an actual opportunity to reinvent herself as an unwilling undercover agent in an insurance fraud gang: about her assumed identity as 'Hannah' Kinsey writes, 'I was making up Hannah's character as I went along, and it was liberating as hell. She was short-tempered, sarcastic, out-spoken, and crude. I could get used to this. License to misbehave' (142). A 'license to misbehave' is as good an expression as any to describe Grafton's hard-boiled feminism throughout the Kinsey Millhone series. Grafton invents and reinvents herself and Kinsey Millhone in an attempt to exercise hard-boiled language as power.

NOTES

I must acknowledge the invaluable assistance throughout my work on this project (and in pretty nearly everything else I do) of one of the most astute feminist thinkers I know: Randee Huber, my wife. I have benefited greatly from her knowledge of feminist criticism, her perceptive readings of Grafton's fiction, and her sage advice on this paper.

1 See especially Faludi. Faludi's hard-boiled journalism is a lot like Grafton's hard-boiled feminism, and reading Faludi's thoroughly researched book was important in my thinking about Grafton's fiction.
2 For a man to 'do' feminist criticism requires a critical tiptoeing through a theoretical minefield. Showalter in 'Introduction: The Rise of Gender' (Showalter 6–7) uses the memorable phrase 'Some "male feminism" looked a lot like the old misogyny dressed up in Wolf's clothing,' illustrating that such

male feminism is not 'genuine self-transformation' but an 'intellectual appropriation' involving 'the mastery of the feminine' which 'has long been a stance of masculine authority.' Men's enthusiasm for 'essentialist' feminism – theories that assert essentially feminine or female qualities of women, women's distinctive ways of knowing and being – seems too much like the long-standing habit of thinking through 'sexual analogy,' described and denounced by Ellmann (2–26) twenty-five years ago. Moi's discussion of Ellmann underscores, I believe, the continued relevance of Ellmann's early and ground-breaking study; see Moi 31–41.

That kind of thinking has dichotomized the sexes and resulted in the egregious sex and gender stereotypes that have sustained (if not necessarily caused) women's subjugation. But men adhering to a poststructuralist mistrust of all essentialism (an *essential* mistrust of essentialism, it should be noted) have tended to ignore the gendered nature of human experience; in their deconstructions of binary oppositions – including 'male/female' and 'man/woman' – male poststructuralists have effaced women's experiences and reduced *différance* to a textual effect which can be 'deconstructed' but which leaves women's oppression in the world intact. For discussions of feminists' problems with poststructuralist theories, especially 'anti-essentialism,' see Fuss 6–18 (on the essentialism/anti-essentialism controversy) and 23–37 ('Reading like a Feminist'). Balbus specifically discusses the problems of applying Foucault to feminism. Sawicki's response to Balbus ('Feminism') underscores the problems of male feminists appropriating essentialist feminism and argues strongly in favour of a Foucauldian feminism. Sawicki includes this response in her book on Foucault and feminism (*Disciplining Foucault*), which presents a sound case for an 'anti-essentialist,' poststructuralist, Foucauldian feminism, and the ideas of which have profoundly informed this paper.

As the feminist psychoanalyst and critical theorist Flax notes, 'Male scholars tend not to read feminist theories or to think about possible implications for their own work' (24). Important as it has become, as Showalter has noted (1–11, quoting Flax 2), to think and talk about gender, it has still been left largely to women critics and theorists to do the thinking and talking – often at the risk of having this important work 'devalued or segregated from the "mainstream" of intellectual life' (Flax 24). While having benefited greatly from the diversity of feminist criticism as well as from the controversies within feminism, I am less interested in taking a position on those controversies than in making use of insights wherever I can find them. Accordingly, I have brought to bear feminist theories which help illuminate what is 'there' in the text.

3 See Reddy 'The Feminist Counter-Tradition' 176. Reddy writes about Grafton and three other writers, 'By writing as feminists and by creating feminist detectives, all four novelists teach their readers to read as feminists, to look on the world – at least temporarily – from a feminist perspective.' As I will explore later in this chapter, the problem with Reddy's analysis is the singular designation in '*a* feminist perspective.' Grafton's feminist perspective shares features with other feminisms but her individual working through of her perspective deserves specific attention.

4 My brief discussion here of tough talk and wisecracks in the male branch of the genre of hard-boiled detective fiction derives from my longer treatment of the topic in 'Tough Talk and Wisecracks.'

5 From this point on, I will usually refer to Kinsey Millhone by her first name, as Grafton does in the Taylor interview. (As noted in one of the novels, 'Kinsey' is the detective's mother's 'maiden' name.) I found that the impersonal reference 'Millhone' simply did not suit a narrator who reveals herself so personally – and who usually introduces herself as 'Kinsey' and never refers to herself as 'Millhone.'

6 See Porter's discussion, 53–6, and my response, 'Tough Talk' 156–9 and Irons *Gender* 147–51. I have discussed the relation of the hard-boiled conceit to the larger project of literary modernism in 'A Heap of Broken Images,' where I also discuss the ideology of hard-boiled detective fiction and its appropriation by the popular audience.

7 See also Reddy 'The Feminist Counter-Tradition' 174–6. As noted, Porter finds the language to be a digressive effect in hard-boiled fiction, and discusses the ideology of the genre generally (115–29) and the language and ideology of hard-boiled detective fiction specifically (133–45). Klein concludes that being a hard-boiled private investigator is 'an unsuitable job for a feminist,' and that the feminism of writers like Grafton is severely compromised by their adoption of the hard-boiled genre – that their novels 'demonstrate a triumph of the genre over feminist ideology' (200–21). Ogdon goes so far as to say that 'there is a hard-boiled ideology' that is white, heterosexual, and male, and that 'describes a specific way of speaking and seeing' which is different in kind from that employed by 'detectives from the margins' (those who are not white, male, and heterosexual) (71). Klein and Ogdon seem to read novels like catalogues of ideological markers or effects, and with Humm, Stigant, and Widdowson I think we must 'avoid a functionalist sociology which insists upon mechanically reading off ideological effects from the formulae ossified in a "lesser tradition" of popular fiction' (10). Palmer's recent analysis of gender, genre, and ideology is more thorough and less categorical than the studies mentioned but still suggests that 'the elements of

thriller structure ... make central female roles within this genre difficult to sustain' (14g). See also my discussion on the relation of ideology and reader response to hard-boiled detective fiction in 'A Heap of Broken Images.'

8 Works by Foucault which inform my approach include *The Archaeology of Knowledge; Politics, Philosophy, Culture;* and, in particular, two essays/interviews, 'Truth and Power' and 'The Subject and Power.' Although I favour feminisms which align themselves with Foucault and other poststructuralist 'anti-essentialist' theories, I am not indicting 'essentialist' feminisms put forward, for example, by Reddy in her book and article and represented, variously, by Carol Gilligan, Nancy Chodorow, and others. As I have noted, however, I am leery of any 'essentialist' feminism put forward by male critics and do not want to make pronouncements about 'the nature of women' as it might appear in Grafton's fiction.

9 Porter cites Voloshinov's discussion (Voloshinov 91), to which I will turn shortly.

10 See Fuss xi–xii, 1–6.

11 Irons usefully describes the problematic nature of 'toughness' for women writing in the hard-boiled genre, and I would be one of those that *would* argue, as he says one *could*, 'that Kinsey Millhone's narrative space in the discourse of feminism may be less problematical than that of the more consciously feminist V.I. Warshawski' (135). I think, however, that Grafton 'busts' rather than 'bends' gender, and that she reinvents woman as rugged individual rather than reinventing the rugged individual as woman – but there I may be splitting hairs.

12 For a discussion of how well Heilbrun in her Amanda Cross novels fulfils her own requirements for creating women characters and writing feminist fiction, see Roberts, reprinted and extended in this volume.

WORKS CITED

Arac, Jonathan, ed. *After Foucault: Humanistic Knowledge, Postmodern Challenges.* New Brunswick, N.J.: Rutgers University Press, 1988.

Balbus, Isaac. 'Disciplining Women: Michel Foucault and the Power of Feminist Discourse.' *Praxis International* 5.4 (1985): 466–83. Revised in *Feminism as Critique.* Ed. Seyla Benhabib and Drucilla Cornell. Minneapolis: University of Minnesota Press, 1987. 110–27. And in Arac 138–60.

Christianson, Scott. 'A Heap of Broken Images: Hard-boiled Detective Fiction and the Discourse(s) of Modernity.' In Walker and Frazer 235–48.

– 'Tough Talk and Wisecracks: Language as Power in American Detective Fiction.' *Journal of Popular Culture* 23.2 (1989): 151–62. Rpt. in Irons *Gender* 142–55.

Ellmann, Mary. *Thinking about Women*. San Diego: Harvest/HBJ, 1968.

Faludi, Susan. *Backlash: The Undeclared War against American Women*. New York: Crown, 1991.

Flax, Jane. *Thinking Fragments: Psychoanalysis, Feminism, and Postmodernism in the Contemporary West*. Berkeley: University of California Press, 1990.

Foucault, Michel. *The Archaeology of Knowledge and the Discourse on Language*. New York: Pantheon, 1972.

– *Politics, Philosophy, Culture: Interviews and Other Writings, 1977–1984*. Ed. Lawrence D. Kritzman. New York: Routledge, 1988.

– 'The Subject and Power.' *Michel Foucault: Beyond Structuralism and Hermeneutics*. By Hubert L. Dreyfus and Paul Rabinow. 1982. 2d ed. Chicago: University of Chicago Press, 1983. 208–26.

– 'Truth and Power.' *Power/Knowledge: Selected Interviews and Other Writings, 1972–1977*. By Foucault. Ed. Colin Gordon. New York: Pantheon, 1980. 109–33.

Fuss, Diana. *Essentially Speaking: Feminism, Nature, and Difference*. New York: Routledge, 1989.

Grafton, Sue. *'A' Is for Alibi*. 1982. New York: Bantam, 1987.

– *'B' Is for Burglar*. 1985. New York: Bantam, 1986.

– *'C' Is for Corpse*. 1986. New York: Bantam, 1987.

– *'D' Is for Deadbeat*. 1987. New York: Bantam, 1988.

– *'E' Is for Evidence*. Book Club ed. New York: Henry Holt, 1988.

– *'F' Is for Fugitive*. Book Club ed. New York: Henry Holt, 1989.

– *'G' Is for Gumshoe*. 1990. New York: Ballantine, 1991.

– *'H' Is for Homicide*. 1991. New York: Ballantine, 1992.

– *'I' Is for Innocent*. New York: Henry Holt, 1992.

Hammett, Dashiell. *The Novels of Dashiell Hammett*. New York: Knopf, 1965.

Heilbrun, Carolyn G. *Reinventing Womanhood*. New York: Norton, 1979.

Huber, Randee. Conversation. 8 July 1992.

Humm, Peter, Paul Stigant, and Peter Widdowson, eds. *Popular Fictions: Essays in Literature and History*. London: Methuen, 1986.

Irons, Glenwood. 'New Women Detectives: G Is for Gender-Bending.' In Irons *Gender* 127–41.

– , ed. *Gender, Language, and Myth: Essays on Popular Narrative*. Toronto: University of Toronto Press, 1992.

Klein, Kathleen Gregory. *The Woman Detective: Gender and Genre*. Urbana and Chicago: University of Illinois Press, 1988.

Moi, Toril. *Sexual/Textual Politics: Feminist Literacy Theory*. London and New York: Methuen, 1985.

Ogdon, Bethany. 'Hard-Boiled Ideology.' *Critical Quarterly* 34.1 (Spring 1992): 75–87.

Palmer, Jerry. *Potboilers: Methods, Concepts, and Case Studies in Popular Fiction.* London: Routledge, 1991.

Parker, Robert B. *Double Deuce.* New York: G.P. Putnam's Sons, 1992.

Porter, Dennis. *The Pursuit of Crime: Art and Ideology in Detective Fiction.* New Haven: Yale University Press, 1981.

Reddy, Maureen T. 'The Feminist Counter-Tradition in Crime: Cross, Grafton, Paretsky, and Wilson.' In Walker and Frazer 174–87.

– *Sisters in Crime: Feminism and the Crime Novel.* New York: Continuum, 1988.

Roberts, Jeanne Addison. 'Feminist Murder: Amanda Cross Reinvents Womanhood.' *Clues: A Journal of Detection* 6.1 (1985): 3–13.

Sawicki, Jana. *Disciplining Foucault: Feminism, Power, and the Body.* New York: Routledge, 1991.

– 'Feminism and the Power of Foucauldian Discourse.' In Arac 161–78 and Sawicki *Disciplining* 49–66.

Showalter, Elaine, ed. *Speaking of Gender.* New York: Routledge, 1989.

Taylor, Bruce. 'G Is for (Sue) Grafton.' Interview. *Armchair Detective* 22.1 (Winter 1989): 4–13.

Voloshinov, V.N. *Marxism and the Philosophy of Language.* Trans. Ladislav Matejka and I.R. Titunik. Cambridge: Harvard University Press, 1973.

Walker, Ronald G., and June M. Frazer, eds. *The Cunning Craft: Original Essays on Detective Fiction and Contemporary Literary Theory.* Macomb: Western Illinois University Press, 1990.

Wittig, Monique. *The Straight Mind and Other Essays.* Boston: Beacon, 1992.

10. The Female Dick and the Crisis of Heterosexuality

Ann Wilson

In recent years, critics have hailed the work of three American writers – Sue Grafton, Marcia Muller, and Sara Paretsky – as revising, perhaps even renewing, the tradition of the hard-boiled detective novel.[1] Each of the writers has created a detective who is a single woman in her mid-thirties, and who works as a licensed private investigator. Physically and mentally tough, willing to take tremendous personal risks as she negotiates the treacherous underworld of urban America, each of these detectives recalls the tradition of Sam Spade more than that of Miss Marple. For these authors, the problem is one of having the heroine occupy a male subject position – the role of hard-boiled detective – without making her seem as if she is a man in drag. The negotiations of gender and sexuality in Grafton, Muller, and Paretsky are deft attempts to remain faithful to the tradition of tough-guy detective fiction while disrupting its gender codes. The three novelists retain for these heterosexual women detectives the traditional self-sufficient individualism of the private investigator even though they are writing within a genre which has always defined women in relation to male loners.

The hard-boiled detective is a familiar figure in the novels best exemplified by those of Raymond Chandler and Dashiell Hammet and in the cinematic adaptations of those works. Worldly-wise, and cynical because he has stared corruption dead in the face, the hard-boiled detective has nevertheless adopted only a veneer of inaccessibility. Despite appearing to be immune to the contagion of the world, he is vulnerable underneath and capable of falling in love with a pretty girl – who often turns out to be treacherous, a femme fatale, an agent of evil. The attractive woman is duplicitous, her physical beauty working a deadly web in concert with her depraved spirit. This scheme of gender relations gives hard-boiled fiction a decidedly male, even misogynistic, quality.

Another feature contributing to the genre's tough-guy masculinity is the gritty, unrefined language, evoking a 'realistic' sense of place, even when that place is ugly. Critics have suggested that the willingness to describe reality as the hard-boiled gumshoe sees it, neither flinching when faced with corruption nor softening his description to spare the sensibility of the audience, points to Ernest Hemingway's influence (Hart 310; 'Hard-Boiled' 416). That hard-boiled detective fiction seems to be a hyper-masculine form gives rise to the question, Why are so many women writers and readers interested in this kind of novel?

The primary appeal is readily evident: a heroine modelled on a hard-boiled detective is a woman who is self-reliant and independent, a prototype of a feminist ideal. Each of the three authors under discussion has created a detective who is university educated, her trained intellect finding a corollary in a trained body maintained through rigorous physical exercise. In top shape both mentally and physically, Kinsey Millhone, Sharon McCone, and V.I. Warshawski are capable of meeting the challenges of the world – or perhaps more accurately, the threats of the underworld. The conventional representation of the female body as weaker than a man's and therefore less effective in situations which require physical power is exposed by Grafton, Muller, and Paretsky as a ruse: each author puts her heroine in situations which require agility of mind and body. For example, in Paretsky's *Burn Marks*, Warshawski is abducted by the villain and taken by him to a construction site, where they meet three of his accomplices, who are holding Warshawski's elderly, alcoholic aunt. The captors take their two hostages to the top of an unfinished building. Although Warshawski's hands are bound, she cleverly devises a way to retrieve her gun from the waistband of her jeans. She shoots one of her abductors in the shoulder blade, and when another is about to shove her aunt over the ledge of the building to her death, she kills him.

The incident is typical of these novels inasmuch as the heroines never initiate the violence, and respond violently only when it is clear that inaction on their part would result in death either for themselves or for someone who is defenceless. Their violent actions, cast as the only possible actions if the lives of the innocent are to be preserved, seem to involve an almost maternal instinct to protect those incapable of protecting themselves.[2] The novels affirm that when faced with threatening situations, women are fully capable of taking care not only of themselves but of others. This is probably a good thing given that, like the tough guys of the 1930s, Grafton's, Muller's, and Paretsky's detectives all have problematic relationships with the local police forces and cannot necessarily count on them for protection.

The antagonistic relationship between the woman PI and the local police force reflects the difficulties women face in dealing with institutions dominated by men. The tough-gal investigators are like many women in Western culture, who lack access to the power and prerogatives of masculinity. Moreover, if the police could effectively control criminal activity – particularly against women – the female private investigator would have a much less prominent role to play in the mystery genre.

In the work of the three novelists, the problematic relationship between the woman PI and the police extends into her private life: each of the three detectives has had a love affair with a policeman. Grafton's Kinsey Millhone, who in *'E' Is for Evidence* is thirty-two and describes herself as 'twice divorced, no kids, and no close family ties' (3), is having an affair with Jonah Robb of Missing Persons, Santa Teresa Police Department. Millhone recalls the beginning of the affair:

He's thirty-nine, blunt, nurturing, funny, confused, a tormented man with blue eyes, black hair, and a wife named Camilla who stalks out intermittently with his two little girls, whose names I repress. I had ignored the chemistry between us for as long as I could ... And then one rainy night, I'd run into him on my way home ... Jonah and I started drinking margaritas in a bar near the beach. We danced to old Johnny Mathis tunes, talked, danced again, and ordered more drinks. Somewhere around 'The Twelfth of Never,' I lost track of my resolve and took him home with me. I never could resist the lyrics on that one. (31–2)

This love affair is initiated because the normally rational Millhone surrenders logic for the lure of romance. But taking leave of her senses renders her emotionally vulnerable, as with many of her male counterparts in the novels of the genre written in earlier decades. When Millhone needs information to which the police have access, she calls her lover at work only to find that, without telling her, he has taken his family away on a Christmas skiing holiday. In a twist on the figure of the duplicitous woman who betrays the male detective, Millhone the woman detective is betrayed by a man, but with the further ironic complication that he returns to his wife and children, thereby implicitly affirming the value of the stable family, which Millhone, as the other woman, threatened to disrupt. The woman detective in this case becomes the femme fatale.

Like Grafton's Millhone, Muller's Sharon McCone has an affair with a police detective, Greg Marcus of the San Francisco Police, Homicide Division. Even when she has extricated herself from this relationship, McCone maintains professional respect for Marcus. Nevertheless, a tension remains. In *There's Nothing to Be Afraid Of*, McCone investigates the harassment of Vietnamese refugees living in a tenement hotel. During the course of her investigation, she calls Marcus to discuss a murder. After a second murder, Marcus asks to interrogate McCone, but she resists. He insists that she 'go into it now' (129), causing her to bridle 'at the order' (130). This response is symptomatic of the clash of wills which characterized her affair with him. That relationship now over, she rationalizes that the feeling of irritation 'belonged to another time, when I had a right to take offense' (310). The tension in her relationship with Marcus was initially a consequence of his demeaning her. Aside from his relentlessly insinuating that she was ineffective at her job, he insisted on calling her 'Papoose,' a nickname which patronizingly referred to her Native heritage and doubly insulted her, on the basis of both her race and her gender. The use of the name marks a structure of power within the relationship which positions Marcus, the figure of the law, as a dominating father rather than a sympathetic lover.

McCone's tempestuous relationship with Marcus has been replaced by an easier one with her current boyfriend, Don del Boccio, a disc jockey for a rock and roll station who, in contrast to the forceful, occasionally abrasive Marcus, is sensitive, 'a quiet man, a classical pianist' (50). Nevertheless, despite her more equitable and indeed happier relationship with del Boccio, McCone discovers that her attraction to Marcus is still strong. She invites him in for wine after he drives her home. As he prepares to leave, she feels the urge to invite him to stay but musters the strength to resist the impulse. She tidies up and readies herself for bed, only to discover that, unbeknown to her, del Boccio has been lying in her bed waiting. Without rancour, he comments, 'For a while there, I thought the three of us were going to end up in bed together' (142).

McCone and Millhone have relationships with the police which complicate both their personal and their professional lives. Not only is Millhone involved in a problematic relationship with Robb, but she is herself an ex-cop who left the force because the role given a woman officer did not allow her the autonomy she enjoys as a self-employed private detective. In *'E' Is for Evidence*, she allegedly has falsified an arson report to make it look legitimate, and her arrest on charges of fraud seems imminent. In *There's Nothing to Be Afraid Of*, McCone is warned off the case by Marcus, who claims that her investigation 'may not be to the Department's advantage' (140). McCone and Millhone are attracted to police officers, because the men's positions as enforcers of the law make them seem particularly masculine; at the same time, the heroines are repulsed, because the power and authority over others which these men enjoy makes them unable to respect women as professional and personal equals.

The inequity between the police and the private detective, between men and women, is at the core of Sara Paretsky's novels featuring V.I. Warshawski. Like the other women detectives, Warshawski is single and, as the only child of parents who are now dead, has no close family ties. Her father, a beloved detective on the Chicago police force, had a protegé named Bobby Mallory, who is now a senior detective. Mallory fulfils his filial obligations to his dead mentor by assuming the role of surrogate father to Warshawski, advising her on her love life and attempting to protect her from the perils of her job, perils he views as unsuitable for a woman. His disapproval is marked by his belittling of Warshawksi's professionalism. He insists that by 'playing police' she resists the grown-up responsibility of a woman – selfless devotion of herself to marriage and motherhood: 'Maybe true love will get her mind off wanting to be a boy and play boys' games with baseballs and guns' (134). Mallory himself now has a protegé on the police force and believes that this man would be the ideal mate for Warshawski. The two dated, but by the beginning of *Burn Marks* Warshawski has ended the relationship because 'Michael hangs out with a crowd where the wife is the little woman who stays home and has kiddies ... It's not my style, never has been and never will be' (134). 'Michael,' as it turns out, is Michael Furey, the villain of *Burn Marks*, who as the action unfolds turns out to be a corrupt cop. As his name suggests, he is consumed by rage, which he turns on Warshawski when she realizes that he is involved in a complicated scheme of fraud. When Furey abducts Warshawski and takes her to the construction site where he intends to finish her off, he says: 'I'm not taking any chances with you ... You're not interested in the things a normal girl is – you just play the odds and wait your chance to sit on a guy's balls' (316).

In the novels of Grafton and Muller, the female private investigator poses a threat to male police officers – their heterosexual manhood is threatened by the mere existence of the female dick. The responses to that threat are explored in *Burn Marks* when Furey responds to War-shawski with a violence fuelled by misogynistic logic that his masculin-ity is threatened by Warshawski's refusal to conform to his ideal of woman. The inability of these police officers to accept women as profes-sionally equal and to resist asking them to conform to a male-generated image of woman is not simply a matter of benign misunderstanding; women detectives constitute a profound threat to the officers' masculin-ity, which realizes its full potential in physical violence – one of the few areas in which the male character has the potential to better the woman detective. It is not difficult to understand why there is little possibility of a satisfying romantic relationship with a man.

Even the apparently contented relationship which McCone enjoys with del Boccio suggests a problematic sexual connection. Del Boccio's sexual orientation may be somewhat fluid. There is a radical discrep-ancy between his public persona as the fast-talking dee jay for a com-mercial rock and roll station and his private self as a soft-spoken man who takes pleasure in good conversation and classical music. While this discrepancy does not, in and of itself, suggest that del Boccio is gay, there is an analogy between the duality of his life and that of a closeted gay man who presents himself to the world as straight. This duality, which is fundamental to the construction of woman in patriarchy, has the effect of equating a gay man with a woman. In patriarchy, woman is presented as having a split nature, the façade of the nurturer masking her dangerous sexuality, which destroys men. Similarly, in the early part of the twenti-eth century, sexologists understood the homosexual to have a nature split between a feminine spirit and a masculine body. This split nature, like that of a woman, is represented within patriarchal (and hence, het-erosexist) perspectives as dangerous to dominant, masculine order because appearance is a façade under which the 'true' nature or spirit of a woman or a homosexual is hidden.

The discrepancy is important in the context of two incidents in *There's Nothing to Be Afraid Of*. As I have noted, del Boccio is waiting in McCone's bed, listening to her conversation with Marcus, her former lover. Del Boccio's response to the incident is to muse that the three might have found themselves in bed together. Later in the novel, looking for comfort after having discovered another murder, McCone goes to del Boccio's loft. She expects that he will be out at first because this is the evening that he broadcasts his show, after which he usually goes to his favourite bar, the Blue Lagoon, which 'had been a gay bathhouse before the AIDS epidemic; now it was converted into a bar with a tropical theme and a heated courtyard with wrought-iron tables surround[ing] the Olympic-sized swimming pool' (65). While waiting for del Boccio, McCone nestles into the pillows, which 'smelled of Don, his talcum powder, the spray he used in an unsuccessful attempt to control his thick black hair' (65). The next morning, del Boccio explains his late return by telling McCone that he had been at the bar with his producer, Tony, and the members of a rock band, when one of the band members jumped into the pool and the others followed until 'twenty people were in the pool and the cops were arriving' (67). Everyone mentioned is male, leaving the impression that the Blue Lagoon may no longer be a bathhouse but has kept its clientele, including del Boccio.

In 'E' Is for Evidence, Kinsey Millhone's second husband, a jazz musician named Daniel Wade, who has a history of heroin use, arrives at her doorstep having lost touch with her for eight years. Even after the years of separation, Millhone notes: 'Daniel Wade is quite possibly the most beautiful man I've ever seen – a bad sign. Beautiful men are usually either gay or impossibly narcissistic' (90). Wade explains his sudden reappearance by saying that his therapist has told him that if he is to come to terms with his addiction, he must resolve his feelings about the dissolution of his marriage to Millhone. But she is reluctant to allow Wade back into her life for fear that she will be caught in the old patterns of a relationship which left her feeling alone and dissatisfied. When Millhone is injured in an explosion, Wade is able to enter her life because he alone seems available and willing to nurse her through her convalescence. The injured Millhone, who feels vulnerable not just because of her physical condition but because of her rekindled desire for Wade, asks him why he left her. 'It wasn't you, babe. It wasn't anything personal' (143). When she presses him whether there was someone else, he avoids answering. Soon enough, Millhone discovers that Wade's reappearance, the murders she is investigating, and the attendant allegations of fraud are all connected. Like her hard-boiled male counterparts, the woman detective has fallen for the villain, but in this case the betrayal consequent upon her love is more than the discovery that the beloved is an agent of the criminal underworld. The evidence which finally reveals Wade as an accomplice in the network of fraud also reveals him as gay and thereby uncovers a complex betrayal of her affections, not just in the immediate situation but in their former marriage. As in There's Nothing to Be Afraid Of, in 'E' Is for Evidence the homosexual man has a double nature. The depiction of homosexuality as betrayal in 'E' Is for Evidence is troubling inasmuch as it suggests a degree of homophobia: the misogynistic depiction of woman as the femme fatale in male hard-boiled fiction here has been replaced by the depiction of a 'beautiful' man as the duplicitous traitor who turns out to be gay.

The doomed romantic relationship is, of course, part of the tradition of detective novels, not just hard-boiled fiction, because detective fiction tends to celebrate the individual: one person uncovers the truth. However, the female dick's transgression of gender codes is represented as her personal refusal of these codes; her selection of a lover is similarly a matter of her personal choice. The convention of the hard-boiled novel precludes seeing the female detective as breaking through socially produced codes, so that even as she becomes something of a role model – the independent, self-reliant woman – she remains an anomaly – an individual and something of an outsider, both conventional characteristics of the detective in hard-boiled fiction. The failure of her romantic relationships seems to be a matter of personal incompatibility rather than a symptom of larger social issues of gender and sexuality. Her inability to find a lover with whom she can sustain a relationship is a consequence of her personal psychology and not of the constraints imposed on both men and women by socially produced gender roles. Whatever impulse these novelists have to disrupt social codes, the constraints of form prevent a radical analysis of gender and sexuality. Female hard-boiled fiction offers a mild challenge to the dominant social order but not a radical assault on it.

NOTES

A version of this paper was presented at the conference of the Association of Canadian College and University Teachers of English held at Queen's University, Kingston, Ontario, in 1991.

1 An article in *Newsweek* proclaimed: 'Call her Samantha Spade or Philipa Marlowe and she would deck you. A tough new breed of detectives is reforming the American mystery novel: smart, self-sufficient, principled, funny – and female. For decades, the male hard-boiled private investigator dominated and defined the genre ... Not anymore' (Ames 66). Credit for initiating this revision of the tradition is given to Marcia Muller, who in 1977 'shattered the hard-boiled P.I. barrier, introducing Sharon McCone of the All Souls Legal Cooperative in San Francisco. That helped break the ice for Grafton and Paretsky, who each kicked off her series in 1982' (Ames 67).

2 In a sense, the protection of the defenceless innocent is a rehearsal of what is paradigmatically a maternal role. But there is another explanation of the impulse. Ames notes that 'Paretsky, Grafton and many of their colleagues came of age in a period of political activism; their books tend to reflect their experiences' (66). That is, the political ideology of these novels tends towards a liberal humanism that is deeply concerned with the plight of the socially disenfranchised.

WORKS CITED

Ames, Katrine. 'Murder Most Foul and Fair.' *Newsweek.* 14 May 1990. 66, 67.
Grafton, Sue. *'E' Is for Evidence.* 1988. New York: Bantam, 1989.
'Hard-Boiled Fiction.' *Benet's Reader's Encyclopedia of American Literature.* Ed. George Perkins, Barbara Perkins, and Phillip Leininger. New York: Harper and Row, 1987. 416.
Hart, James. 'Hammett, Dashiell.' *The Oxford Companion to American Literature.* New York: Oxford University Press, 1983. 310.
Muller, Marcia. *There's Nothing to Be Afraid Of.* New York: Warner 1990.
Paretsky, Sara. *Burn Marks.* 1990. New York: Dell, 1991.

11. 'Friends Is a Weak Word for It': Female Friendship and the Spectre of Lesbianism in Sara Paretsky

Rebecca A. Pope

The opening chapter of Sara Paretsky's seventh V.I. Warshawski novel, *Guardian Angel*, is titled 'Sex and the Single Girl.' Here is the first paragraph: 'Hot kisses covered my face, dragging me from deep sleep to the rim of consciousness. I groaned and slid deeper under the covers, hoping to sink back into the well of dreams. My companion wasn't in the humor for rest; she burrowed under the blankets and continued to lavish urgent affection on me' (1). Experienced readers of Paretsky, those who know that the series is narrated by the detective herself, may stumble on the 'she,' conjuring as it does a picture of the heretofore heterosexual Vic in bed with another woman. Experienced readers of Paretsky who are lesbians – many of whom, if my own unscientific polling can be trusted, have never quite understood how Vic can fight the patriarchy all day and sleep with it at night – may applaud what appears to be Vic's change of erotic practice.

Some readers, then, may be relieved and others disappointed when Vic reveals that her bedmate, and the single girl whose sexual activity is under scrutiny in the chapter, is her dog, Peppy. I suppose, further, that whether or not one finds funny what appears to be a little joke depends on whether or not one's reaction to the novel's reassertion of Vic's heterosexual credentials is relief or disappointment. What I want to argue here is that this little joke, with its mild flirtation with the theme of lesbianism, is more than a joke, that the entire series of novels, like this passage, has an approach/withdraw orientation towards lesbianism. Much of the series' exploration of (and anxiety over) the possible kinds of intimacies between women centres on Vic's relations with her closest friend Dr Lotty Herschel. A scene in *Bitter Medicine*, for example, calls up and defends against lesbianism when Lotty loses a special patient and, grief-stricken, turns up at Vic's apartment: 'I took her with me to the living room, away from the unmade bed, to the big chair like the one Gabriella [Vic's deceased mother] used to hold me in when I was a child. Lotty sat with me a long while, her head pushing into the soft flesh of my breast, the ultimate comfort, spreading through giver and receiver both' (26). As Vic turns herself and Lotty away from the unmade bed, conventional image of sexuality, so she turns to a model for the intimacy of their friendship and the pleasure of their physical contact which convention-ally assumes/requires a turning away from sexuality, the mother-child relation.

I am not convinced that Vic's invocation of the mother-daughter bond accomplishes what she hopes it will – the complete separation of her relations with Lotty from the erotic – and will return to that question. But first I want to take a wider look at Paretsky's exploration of female friendship in the V.I. Warshawski series and place that enterprise in the tradition of literary representations of female friendship. As Janet Todd's study of female friendship in eighteenth-century fiction, *Women's Friend-ship in Literature*, and Tess Coslett's *Woman to Woman: Female Friendship in Victorian Fiction* show, the mother/daughter model for female friendship has a long history. Vic's repeated use of that model to capture the warmth, support, and nurturance of her relations with Lotty looks back to this tradition, but also departs from it, and from many contemporary theories of female development. In traditional literary and cultural dis-courses on the mother-daughter relation and the female friendships which replicate it, these bonds are vehicles for patriarchal interests. Mothers pass down traditional familial/patriarchal values to their daughters; close female friendships school women in intimacy and car-ing and help to usher them into heterosexual romantic relations. In Paretsky's novels, however, female friendship is explicitly opposed to patriarchal values and institutions.

An earlier generation of women detective novelists provides Paretsky with precedents for what one critic has called the novels' emphasis on V.I.'s 'special links with women' (Klein 214). Rosalind Coward and Linda Semple observe that this earlier generation produced 'a number of notable detective novels,' Dorothy L. Sayers's *Gaudy Night* and Jose-phine Tey's *Miss Pym Disposes* for example, 'concentrating on a closed community of women' (52). The device of the closed female community, they argue, yielded sympathetic and deep portrayals of the relations between women which caught the richness and complexity of women's bonds in ways that few other novels of the period achieved (53). Isolated from the male world, although not free from the pressures of its power and values, female communities like women's colleges provide a site for the exploration of women's bonds outside the romance plot. Paretsky reinserts representations of rich, complex, and at times conflicted women's bonds into the wider, masculine world while keeping them separate from the heterosexual romance plot. In this, Vic and Lotty are prefigured by those famous (and oft-cited in critical writing on women's friendship in literature) friends, Chloe and Olivia, the women in Virginia Woolf's *A Room of One's Own*, who, surprisingly and unconventionally, like each other. Neither romantic rivals nor confidantes whose exchanges serve one or the other's progress towards marriage, they enjoy a relationship that escapes traditional plots, literary and otherwise, for women's lives and relations. Mary Carmichael's rejection of the conventional heterosexual romance for these women, Woolf argues, provides a new model and opens new ways of thinking and writing about women's relations to other women. Chloe and Olivia share a laboratory in London; they have in common not a man but a profession; they share the experience of making their independent ways in a male world.

Paretsky takes up these themes – deep and affectionate female bonds outside the confines of the romance plot, the experience of women professionals in traditionally male fields, and the dangers and opportunities that urban spaces present to women who leave (or are pushed out of) domestic spaces – and inserts them into an unlikely context, the hard-boiled detective novel. Much of the pleasure of reading Paretsky is watching how she reworks so conservative and masculine, even misogynist, a genre to address women's experience and aspirations, and we miss an important feature of this project if we neglect the relations between V.I. and Lotty. Vic's romantic objects change from novel to novel, but Lotty appears in every one, her most important connection. As a guilty Vic reminds herself in *Guardian Angel* after having stupidly put Lotty in danger: 'I loved Lotty. More than any other person I could think of' (181).

Explaining to a man she is dating that her marriage failed because she was too independent, Vic observes: 'I have some close women friends, because I don't feel they're trying to take over my turf. But with men it always seems, or often seems, as though I am having to fight to maintain who I am' (*Indemnity Only* 141). It is hardly surprising, then, that while Vic's romantic involvements change from novel to novel, Lotty appears in every one, a constant in Vic's life and her most important attachment.

'[Lotty's] the one person I never lie to,' she says, 'not my conscience – the person who helps me to see who I really am' (*Blood Shot* 251). She helps Vic see past her frustrations with a case and ahead to constructive action (*Deadlock* 121); she pays her the compliment of respecting her professional judgment and the courtesy of ignoring her inadequate housekeeping (*Killing Orders* 67, 55). When, in *Burn Marks*, Vic's attempts to help a wayward aunt endanger Vic's own life, Lotty gives her friend permission not to sacrifice herself on the altar of family duty. After days of dealing with male crooks, male clients who question her judgment, and male cops who never tire of telling her that detecting is not women's work, a few hours with Lotty are clarifying and restorative. They provide each other with psychological nourishment: the novels are filled with scenes in which Lotty and Vic have dinner together after a long day's work. Whereas in earlier fiction female friendship sometimes served as a refuge from the 'strenuous demands of romantic love' (Todd 2), in Paretsky's novels it functions as a counter to the oppressive assaults – here physical and psychological – of urban patriarchy.

This is not to say that Lotty is an ideal of uncritical and unlimited acceptance and support. She points out when Vic is being stubborn or taking too many risks, and dismisses her when she is self-pitying. 'Lotty is sometimes about as pleasant as a can-opener, but she braces me. I know myself better when I talk to Lotty,' Vic acknowledges (*Killing Orders* 56). While relations with men are turf battles that threaten, even deny, selfhood – with men she feels that she has to fight to maintain who she is – female friendship enhances her sense of herself, helps her know better who she is. All self-knowledge may indeed be relational, but Vic sees that what men would have her learn is that she is 'other,' that she is not a man and cannot share the same turf with them. The self-knowledge she obtains through her relations with Lotty, by contrast, is a kind of self-understanding. For example, Lotty knows Vic well enough to point out when she is behaving in uncharacteristic ways, and her observations encourage Vic to analyse her motivations and circumstances more fully (*Deadlock* 19–20). Although I'm not altogether comfortable with the rhetoric of 'identity' she employs, Elizabeth Abel makes an observation about Lily and Mrs Ramsay in Woolf's *To the Lighthouse* that applies as well to V. I. and Lotty: 'Friendship becomes a vehicle for self definition for women, clarifying identity through relation to an other who embodies and reflects an essential aspect of the self' (416).

Similarities of gender, temperament, and professional experience highlight their commonalities and throw their differences into relief, thus enhancing self-understanding. Significantly, Vic and Lotty's friendship has its origin in a context which is political, professional, and gendered – they met while working for an abortion underground. Given this context, the novels constitute a study of the issues called up within friendships between independent professional women who see themselves and the world from a feminist perspective: the competing claims of affectional and professional responsibilities, for example, and the way the independence and autonomy necessary for women to function professionally affects their non-professional relations with other women and their need and capacity for nurturance.

The line between the professional and the personal is not as rigid for working women as for men in Paretsky's fiction. Vic's uncle Peter, for whom taking a job in Kansas City is also divorcing himself from troublesome and needy relatives, can maintain rigid boundaries, but Vic cannot. Deeply, often reluctantly, embedded within a network of friends and family, Vic is far from the socially isolated (male) private eye of traditional hard-boiled detective fiction. Only in the first of the novels does she pursue a case that has no connection with family, friends, or neighbours. Aunts in trouble, a cousin suspiciously dead, a childhood friend, and in *Bitter Medicine* Lotty herself get Vic started on the trail.

This blurring of boundaries between the personal and the professional reappears in the novels' portrayal of Vic's relations with Lotty. They are friends, patient and physician, and in *Bitter Medicine* and 'The Case of the Pietro Andromache,' a short story in which Lotty is accused of murder and Vic tracks down the real killers, something like detective and client. A scene in *Burn Marks* suggests the tensions that result. Angry and anxious after treating Vic for yet another serious injury, Lotty asks: 'Do you know how I feel every time I see your body come in on a stretcher not knowing if you're dead or alive ...? Do you think you could manage your affairs so that you stopped a *few feet short* of the point of death, maybe even ask the police to take *some* of those risks?' (205; emphasis added). Weary and defensive, Vic recognizes Lotty's fear of losing her but sees her request as a threat to her professionalism: 'Sometimes I have to fight a hundred people just to be able to do my job. When you're the hundred and first I feel like all I want to do is lie down and die.' Lotty's response doesn't so much resolve the conflict as suspend it: 'So to help you I have to do things that are a torment to me? I'll have to think about that one Victoria ...' (205).

The ellipses are in the text. Lotty drops the topic without arriving at a resolution or issuing an ultimatum. It will be taken up again, no doubt, the next time Vic is injured. Supporting V.I. in her work may mean being often worried and anxious. When the men Vic dates become similarly worried, they encourage her to turn everything over to the police, to not do her job at all. Lotty is upset and frustrated but asks only that Vic take more care on the job and fewer risks with her life. To ask more is to deny Vic the independence and autonomy she needs to do her job at all. The conflict is suspended because they know that as long as they both care for each other and respect each other as professionals, it can never be fully resolved. Competing claims can only be subject to regular and ongoing negotiation and compromise.

In the fourth novel of the series, *Bitter Medicine*, Peter Burgoyne com-plainingly, whiningly, asks Vic to show as much concern about his prob-lems as she does about Lotty's. Vic replies: 'I've known Lotty for close to twenty years. First she filled in for my mother, and then we became – friends is a weak word for it. Close any way. So when she has problems, they trouble me, too' (142). V.I.'s sense of linguistic poverty is revelatory. What vocabulary and what models to use to talk about close relations between independent adult women? Like the other men Vic becomes involved with, Burgoyne is not fully comfortable with her profession, and Vic's response in such situations is to rebel against what she sees is an attempt to reinscribe her in the role of the traditional female who needs protection. This may be why she backs away from the mother/ daughter model, with its suggestions of dependence, at this moment but is willing to embrace it, in one form or another, elsewhere. (In the latest novel, *Guardian Angel*, Lotty and Gabriella keep transmuting into each other in Vic's dreams.) But Vic may have ambivalent feelings about the model for other reasons, perhaps in part because it is so tempting: Vic lost her mother, Gabriella, at fifteen. Lotty is significantly older than Vic. Both Lotty and Gabriella are strong-willed and independent women who came to the United States to escape fascism. They both deeply love and support Vic. 'Be careful: You have no mother, but you are a daughter of my spirit,' Lotty says in the first novel (*Indemnity Only* 193), and, in the third, 'You have been the daughter I never had, V.I. As well as one of the best friends a woman could ever desire' (*Killing Orders* 276).

In the passage I quoted earlier from *Bitter Medicine*, Vic reverses their roles. The reversal, in which the younger Vic nurtures and comforts Lotty in a classic pose of mother/daughter love, can be read as an attempt to recoup the pleasure and nourishing love of this bond without calling up the dependence and blurring of ego boundaries that psycho-analysis has accustomed us to associate with it. From this vantage point, we see the attraction, perhaps the threat, but also the final inappropriateness of the model for friendship between mature professional women. But there is something else going on here as well. Coslett argues that the mother/daughter model for female friendship is so attractive because it 'allows for physical closeness and emotional intensity' (7). Indeed, it is perhaps the only model for 'permissible' loving physical contact between women still available in our culture. After sexology and psychoanalysis began to recognize, in the late nineteenth and early twentieth century, that close affectional bonds between women could be erotic ones as well, the possibilities for affectional bonds between women were reduced, and female friendships were increasingly represented as pernicious rather than wholesome and ideal.[1] Thus, when Vic searches for another way of describing her loving bond with Lotty but can't find one – 'friends is a weak word for it. Close any way' – we see clearly that there isn't another word for it because only the mother-daughter relation recoups loving physical contact between women for patriarchy. When Vic reverses the mother/daughter roles and directs Lotty away from the unmade bed, she signals her frustration with the two traditional models – one celebrated, the other condemned – for close emotional and physical relations between women. Neither the lover nor the mother/daughter model is finally accurate and emotionally comfortable enough to figure her love for Lotty. 'Friends' is too weak a word for the relationship, both bracing and embracing, that they construct together. It doesn't capture the nurturance we have traditionally equated solely with the maternal or allow for the pleasure of physical contact between women so long taboo outside the mother-daughter bond. Nor does it suggest that aspect of their bond which is shared experience as feminist professional women in a city that is, as Paretsky represents it, run by men and full of dangers for women. What the friendship between V.I. and Lotty shows is not only that women can like each other very much, but that we need a new vocabulary and set of models to talk about it.

But that is not the entire story. As I observed earlier, when Vic describes herself steering Lotty away from the unmade bed and to the living-room chair, she calls up and moves away from the possibility of erotic relations between herself and Lotty. Significantly, *Killing Orders*, the novel that most features lesbianism – the victim, Agnes Paciorek, is a lesbian stockbroker with whom Vic did feminist political work when both were students at the University of Chicago – is also the novel in which V.I. and Lotty have one of their two most serious and lengthy estrangements. The other deep estrangement – indeed, the novel closes without a reconciliation – occurs in the novel I began with, *Guardian Angel*. That novel opens with a bedroom scene which suggests and then rejects the possibility of lesbian relations for Vic. It closes with a bedroom scene as well; while in bed with her lover, Conrad, Vic dreams that Gabriella and Lotty abandon her.

Early in *Killing Orders*, when Lotty behaves in an uncharacteristically suspicious and defensive manner, Vic wonders, 'Could a friendship evaporate in the same mist as a marriage?' (57). Vic's comparison of her friendship to marriage suggests, at the very least, both its closeness and its importance in her life; her worry over the vulnerability of their hitherto solid bond, moreover, foreshadows greater difficulties between them. Lotty's Uncle Stefan dreams up a scheme to flush out the murderers, Vic goes along with it, and when Stefan is seriously, almost fatally, injured, Lotty blames an already guilt-ridden Vic. During much of the second half of the novel they rarely speak, except to trade accusations: Lotty accuses Vic of an egotistical single-mindedness that makes her too willing to sacrifice others in pursuit of her goals. Bolstered by Stefan's contention that Lotty herself is stubborn and hot-tempered, Vic accuses Lotty of unreasonableness and a tendency to martyrdom.

Meanwhile, Vic is not only tracking down Agnes's killer but constantly reasserting her own heterosexual credentials while battling with Agnes's homophobic mother, who wrongly blames V.I. for having 'converted' her daughter to lesbianism. Mrs Paciorek brings that accusation to the police lieutenant on the case, an old colleague of Vic's dead father, Lieutenant Bobby Mallory. He is perfectly happy to believe it – lesbianism provides a handy explanation for what Bobby sees as Vic's 'unnatural' desire to do the man's work of detection and to forego a woman's work of marriage and motherhood. This conjunction of Vic's estrangement from Lotty, the person she loves most in the world, and the appearance of the spectre of lesbianism in her own life is telling. Lesbianism, it appears, is too charged a subject for her to deal with while she is feeling her customary deep love and affection for Lotty. And it is a charged topic for Vic. Throughout the novel, she gallantly defends the right of Agnes and her lover, Phyllis, to live and love as they choose. But when she responds to charges that *she* might be a lesbian, her vocabulary is less measured, careful, and supportive. She hotly accuses Bobby of unfairly believing Mrs Paciorek's 'shopping list of calumny' against her (86) and calls his accusations 'really disgusting' (156). Only after the mystery of Agnes's murder is solved – the man responsible is an eminently patriarchal and crooked archbishop – do V.I. and Lotty make peace. 'I want your forgiveness,' says Lotty, 'I want to – not go back to where we were. We can't. I want to continue our friendship from here' (276).

As Vic seems, almost in spite of herself, defensive about the subject of lesbianism, so the novel, despite the important work it does to fight homophobia, employs defensive strategies within its representation of lesbianism to neutralize and diminish it. For example, Vic is uncertain about the reasons for Agnes's behaviour and can think of her friend's sexuality only in terms of political choice. 'I don't know why Agnes chose lesbian relations. But she loved Phyllis Lording and Phyllis loved her,' she tells Catherine Paciorek (137). She tells Lieutenant Mallory, 'When our rap group followed the national trend and split between radical lesbians and, well, straights, she became a lesbian and I didn't' (87–8). Casting lesbianism as a political act that threatens patriarchy underscores the lesson of the plot, which casts the lesbian murder victim as a victim of patriarchy because her erotic practice is, from the perspective of male interests, criminal. But Vic's reluctance to figure lesbianism in terms of desire as well as political choice elides complications and has the effect of narrowing women's desire for other women into something that must be seen in terms of patriarchy. Vic's construction sets up lesbianism as a reaction against patriarchy rather than as a practice that privileges women and female desire. In other words, by figuring lesbianism solely in terms of the politics of gender relations, the novel's representation of it does just what its representations of female friendship don't do. We value the way Paretsky represents Vic's special relations with women because they explore women's bonds without reference to men. But while, as I have shown, female friendship in the novels is not structured and mediated by relations to men, lesbianism is.

A similar defend–get defensive logic is at work in the characterizations of Agnes and her lover, Phyllis. Agnes and Phyllis are sane, mature, and untroubled by their lesbianism. How good it is to see lesbians represented in a way that doesn't reinscribe phobic stereotypes of them as sick, suicidal, masculinized, and man-hating. The representation of Agnes and Phyllis as a couple, however, depends on oppositions, and the binary structure is, of course, the foundation of heterosexuality.[2] Phyllis, for example, is a retiring scholar, and Agnes is an aggressive stockbroker. Indeed, when Vic concludes that the police are working on the assumption that Agnes was 'sweet and impressionable,' she warns them not to view Agnes in such stereotypically feminine terms: 'Keep in mind that sweet impressionable people don't build up the kind of brokerage business that Agnes did' (87). These complementary differences in temperament and profession, as well as those in age (Phyllis is significantly older), reinscribe binary difference within the threatening same that is lesbianism. Such representational strategies tend to imply that lesbian relations are structured like heterosexual ones, and they privilege and reassert heterosexuality as the standard, the norm, against which all other relations are to be understood and judged. In other words, to reinscribe complementary difference within the lesbian couple is to figure lesbianism not as fundamentally different from heterosexuality but rather as a variation, as it were, on it.

I am not arguing here that Vic is, despite her uniformly heterosexual practice, a 'latent lesbian' (if there can be such a thing). I do feel secure in claiming, however, that the novels leave open the possibility that Vic's desire is more various and fluid than her practice. And I am not just thinking here of Vic's deep love for Lotty and the pleasure Vic finds in physical contact with her. As Richard E. Goodkin has correctly argued, Agnes and V.I. are double figures whose beliefs and behaviour undermine the familial/patriarchal order (94). Given that *Killing Orders* casts desire for another woman as one form of resistance to patriarchy, it is difficult to see why the logic of their doubleness should not extend to the issue of V.I.'s desire. Indeed, Vic's most explicit statement about her own orientation and practice – 'while I love many women dearly, I've never had women lovers' – is nicely ambiguous and open to a variety of readings (139).

But while the novels intuit that Vic's desire might extend beyond the narrow confines of the heterosexual, they show as well how hard, and on how many levels, patriarchal culture works to diminish this threat to its primacy and interests. Agnes dies not merely because what she knows threatens the success of the archbishop's financial schemes, but because, as her patriarchal mother complains, what she does threatens patriarchy on other levels as well: 'It was enough for Agnes to know I believed in something for her to believe the opposite. Abortion. The war in Viet Nam. Worst of all, the Church. I thought I had seen my family name degraded in every possible way. I didn't realize how much I could have forgiven until she announced in public that she was homosexual' (136). Heterosexuality, the passage makes clear, is a patriarchal institution. Thus, lesbianism gets the death penalty in *Killing Orders*, and a death threat is a powerful incentive to repress desire and conform. In other words, the novel shows why the possibility of a lesbian erotic practice doesn't even come up for most women – including, perhaps, Vic – regardless of their desire.

Phyllis Lording, Agnes's lover, is the author of a scholarly book called *Sappho Underground*. The title invites us to see it as a *mise-en-abyme* and to ask whether there is a Sapphic subtext in Paretsky's fiction. Judith Roof provides support for this move: 'But just as humans rarely exhibit purely heterosexual or homosexual desires, so narratives might inscribe conflicting and inconstant desires. The mixture of heterosexual and lesbian desire in many novels by women may account in part for the kind of undecidable tension in women's writing that prevents it from easily adhering to oedipal expectations [the drive towards closure, completeness, mastery, and the unification of opposites]' (118). Although Roof does not discuss Paretsky in her study, her analysis gives us a way of capturing the tensions I have been trying to isolate here. Significantly for our purposes, Roof's reading of the lesbian subtexts of so many women's fictions and so much feminist theory is grounded in an alternative reading of the mother-daughter relation which refuses to diminish or evade – as, Roof argues, so many theorists who plot out a heterosexual trajectory for female development do – the erotic implications of the fact that an infant daughter's primary, original, love object is her mother.

Through a complicated argument too long and sophisticated to summarize here, Roof shows how even in theories like Nancy Chodorow's and Julia Kristeva's, which assume/set a heterosexual trajectory for the infant girl's development, 'the memory of the mother stands in the place of desire' (108). Turning from theory to fiction, Roof finds lesbian narratives filled with absent mothers and 'already differentiated and very independent protagonist daughter[s for whom] the lack represented by the absent mother is displaced into the lack constituting desire itself' (116). The 'lesbian omission of the mother removes the threat of mother/daughter incest' and the possibility of pre-Oedipal fusion, Roof argues, and 'perceives woman-to-woman relations as relations between two individuals' (117).

This is certainly the case in *Killing Orders*. Agnes and Phyllis are not, as is traditional in heterocentrist theories and representations, bad cases of arrested development but mature, differentiated, and independent women. But these adjectives apply equally to Vic, and it is Vic whose mother, every novel in the series repeats, is absent and mourned. Heterocentrist narratives and theories cast relations with the mother in nostalgic terms and focus on a lost primal plenitude; lesbian narratives, Roof claims, 'privilege the moment of separation from the mother [in other words, the moment of individuation] rather than the time of [pre-

Oedipal] unity with her' (114). And it is surely the moment of loss and separation from Gabriella that the novels privilege again and again. At the close of *Killing Orders*, just after she is reconciled with Lotty, Vic recounts a dream and the story of her name, Victoria Iphigenia: '"Do you know what my middle name is, Lotty?" I burst out. "Do you know the myth of Iphigenia? How Agamemnon sacrificed her to get a fair wind to sail for Troy? Since that terrible day at the priory [when her angry aunt Rosa tells Vic that she threw the young Gabriella out on the streets because her husband had fallen in love with her], I can't stop dreaming about it. Only in my dreams it's Gabriella. She keeps laying me on the pyre and setting the torch to it and weeping for me. Oh, Lotty! Why didn't she tell me? Why did she make me give her that terrible promise [to help Rosa if she is ever in trouble]?"' (277). While the dream narrative dramatizes Vic's death and figures it, like Agnes's death, as a sacrifice to the patriarchal order, the dream also marks the death of some of Vic's beliefs about Gabriella and enacts Vic's separation not just from her but from the patriarchal family order to which Gabriella is here tied and to which she appears to abandon Vic. Lotty holds Vic and encourages her to grieve, but despite all the mother/daughter modelling in the novels, does not offer herself as a substitute Gabriella: 'Yes, my darling, yes, cry, yes, that's right. They named you well, Victoria Iphigenia. For don't you know that in Greek legend Iphigenia was also Artemis the huntress?' (277).

The close of *Guardian Angel*, the latest novel, brings together, once again, Lotty, Gabriella, and dreams of loss and separation. Asleep with Conrad Rawlings and still estranged from Lotty, Vic wakes from yet another of a series of nightmares about her mother's death, 'dreams in which Lotty and Gabriella were inextricably entangled' (369). Vic reads the dream as a symptom of her fear of being abandoned, especially by Lotty, as she had been by her mother. This is certainly true, but Vic's reading doesn't go far enough. The explicitly erotic and heterosexual scenario dissolves and uncovers the mother-daughter relation that heterosexual relations have displaced. A memory of the lost mother underpins heterosexual desire, is posited as the origin of desire. And given the eroticized scene, the mother-daughter bond and the female-female relations it makes possible are eroticized as well. Beneath the heterosexual surface is a subtext that isolates women's desire for women as the origin of desire. Faithful to the law of the repressed, what the opening of the novel jokingly banishes, the possibility of erotic relations between women, returns in displaced form at the end. But perhaps Paretsky knows this, and perhaps it is this knowledge that allows Vic in *Guardian Angel* to respond to the accusation that she is a lesbian in an entirely different fashion than she did in *Killing Orders*. Only a few pages before a close that brings male lover, mother, and female friend together at the scene of desire, Vic is accused of being a 'dyke.' Her response to what she calls 'such a feeble insult' is to laugh (347). But then again, laughter is often, and might be here, a defence.

NOTES

1 For an excellent analysis of these changes and their effects, see Faderman, especially 1–61.
2 I am indebted in this section to Roof's analysis of the way heterosexist representations tend to represent lesbian relations in terms of binary oppositions that reinscribe the structure of heterosexuality; see especially 2–5.

WORKS CITED

Abel, Elizabeth. '(E)Merging Identities: The Dynamics of Female Friendship in Contemporary Fiction by Women.' *Signs* 6 (1981): 413–35.
Coslett, Tess. *Woman to Woman: Female Friendship in Victorian Fiction*. Brighton: Harvester, 1988.
Coward, Rosalind, and Linda Semple. 'Tracking Down the Past: Women and Detective Fiction.' *From My Guy to Sci-Fi: Genre and Women's Writing in the Postmodern World*. Ed. Helen Carr. London: Pandora, 1989. 39–57.
Faderman, Lillian. *Odd Girls and Twilight Lovers: A History of Lesbian Life in Twentieth Century America*. 1991. New York: Penguin, 1992.
Goodkin, Richard E. '*Killing Order(s)*: Iphigenia and the Detection of Tragic Intertextuality.' *Yale French Studies* 76 (1989): 81–107.
Klein, Kathleen Gregory. *The Woman Detective: Gender and Genre*. Urbana and Chicago: University of Illinois Press, 1988.
Paretsky, Sara. *Bitter Medicine*. 1987. New York: Ballantine, 1988.
– *Blood Shot*. New York: Delacorte, 1988.
– *Burn Marks*. New York: Delacorte, 1990.
– 'The Case of the Pietro Andromache.' *Sisters in Crime*. Ed. Marilyn Wallace. New York: Berkley 1989. 113–35.
– *Deadlock*. 1984. New York: Ballantine, 1985.
– *Guardian Angel*. New York: Delacorte, 1992.
– *Indemnity Only*. 1982. New York: Ballantine, 1983.

– *Killing Orders*. 1985. New York: Ballantine, 1986.

Roof, Judith. *A Lure of Knowledge: Lesbian Sexuality and Theory.* New York: Columbia University Press, 1991.

Todd, Janet. *Women's Friendship in Literature.* New York: Columbia University Press, 1980.

12. *Habeas Corpus*:
Feminism and Detective Fiction

Kathleen Gregory Klein

Having reached for the compact OED to insert a brief definition of the term *habeas corpus* at the beginning of this essay, I was amazed to discover that it does not mean what I had thought. Associating the phrase with detective fiction, corpses, and legal procedures, I was no doubt influenced by Dorothy L. Sayers into mentally translating the phrase as 'have his carcase.' In the opening chapter of *Have His Carcase*, Harriet Vane not only inspects the body of Paul Alexis carefully, detailing his possessions and inspecting his wounds, but also takes a photograph of the body so that her discovery will be believed in even though the corpse has been washed out to sea. Readers familiar with tabloid accounts of the Loch Ness monster, aliens, and UFOs supported by numerous photographs, or well versed in the more imaginative possibilities of contemporary photography, might well laugh at the naïveté of police, press, and Harriet, but the novel expects its readers to take her two-dimensional image of proof for granted; and it expects us to connect that proof with the demand called forth in its title – produce a corpse in order to claim that death (never mind murder) has occurred.[1] So Harriet has her photo, and I have my mis-definition. The OED actually says: 'A writ issuing out of a court of justice, or awarded by a judge in vacation, requiring the body of a person to be brought before the judge or into the court for the purpose specified in the writ' (1235). Instead of the law requiring that the corpse be produced, it calls forth the suspect. *Black's Law Dictionary* lists nine varieties of *habeas corpus*, none bearing any relation to the meaning I inferred from Sayers's title.[2] The most important form of the writ, acclaimed as the cornerstone of individual liberty, is *habeas corpus ad subjiciendum*: 'A writ directed to the person detaining another, and commanding him to produce the body of the prisoner, or person detained. This is the most common form of *habeas corpus* writ, the purpose of which is to test the legality of the detention or imprisonment; not whether he is guilty or innocent' (Black 638). Due process is a subject hardly ever addressed in detective fiction. Instead, guilt and innocence are paramount no matter how they are determined. In detective fiction, the ultimate verification of the crime, the absolute indicator of the crime, is the detective. For what is the penultimate chapter of a detective novel except the secularized 'witnessing' to Truth, from Genesis to Revelations, chapter and verse, unarguably the word/law of the father? In the conclusion of a detective novel, a version of the truth becomes the only truth; the detective's authority is unassailable; the suspect is transformed into the criminal.[3]

As I read the definitions of *habeas corpus* in Black's or the OED, I am struck by the masculine pronouns; like Sara Paretsky's V.I. Warshawski, I am a child of the sixties doing my affirmative-action headcount. In England, the *habeas corpus* act dates from the reign of Charles II, 1679; in the United States, it is part of the first amendment to the Constitution, 1791. So of course the pronouns are masculine; in the seventeenth, eighteenth, and nineteenth centuries, women had virtually no standing in law. Well, they could be victims of crimes (the dead body I initially went searching for) or criminals; but they could not be detectives or judges or juries or witnesses. Women, you remember, were classified with idiots and children, not capable of swearing, giving evidence, or being trusted.

But if in the mind/body split women's minds were dismissible, society has always known what to do with women's bodies. As Gayle Rubin has so aptly demonstrated, unindustrialized societies used women's bodies as the most convenient and most successful medium of exchange. In what amounted to commercial transactions, sisters and daughters were bartered as brides out of their own communities in exchange for the trading rights, power connections, or tangible commodities which their fathers and brothers valued. Although Rubin does not extend her argument to industrialized societies like England or the United States, others might easily demonstrate the economic exchange which women's bodies signal even in the ... nineteenth century. The individual women involved were stripped of their uniqueness in being coined for exchange. Representation, as theorists now describe it, can be seen in the transformation of those women into a category – Woman. Mail order brides, prostitutes, 'my girl,' 'the little woman' – exchangeable commodities in the social and fiscal economy.

The Cartesian binaries inherent in the mind/body division and male/ female opposition should remind us of two important truisms about these pairings. First, they come in twos like the animals parading into Noah's ark; there is no room for shades of difference, degrees of intensity, or hybrid varieties. There is the A term and the B term; no Cs allowed. Second, they are ranked: the first term, the A term, the alpha term, is superior; B is definitely a lesser quantity, a Johnny-come-lately, a subordinate. As the mind controls the body, so too the man controls the woman. Detective fiction also has its binaries – criminal/victim and detective/criminal. The former is illustrated in the narrative of the crime, the latter in the narrative of detection. In the battle for position, the criminal moves from alpha to beta, from superior to inferior status, a kind of criminal cross-dresser.[4] The detective, whose existence is called into being by the criminal (for to speak of the criminal's action in this context is tautological; without the action he is not criminal), is always superior or controlling, just as the victim is always controlled, subordinate. Additionally, as the narrative of investigation supersedes the narrative of crime, the victim gradually becomes less visible, fading almost into irrelevance. Just as the discovery of the victim dominates the opening of the novel, the discovery of the criminal dominates its closing. The gradual descent of the victim is matched by the growing ascent of the criminal; the 'invisibility' of the victim gives way to the visibility of the criminal, the one out of many suspects who can lay claim to the title. The criminal/victim pairing succumbs to the detective/criminal binary. In this vein, I would argue that the victim – or to return to my earlier terminology, 'the body' in the library – is, despite biology, always female.

Moving the argument from pop culture to high theory, Luce Irigaray claims that women constitute the silent ground on which the patriarchal thinker erects his discursive constructs (Moi 131). Or to paraphrase back into pop culture, the Woman is the body in the library on whom the criminal writes his narrative of murder. On top of that narrative, the detective inscribes his narrative of investigation. The resulting palimpsest foregrounds process and text, taking for granted the materials required for composition. Like the Vicomte de Valmont in *Les Liaisons dangereuses* penning a love letter to Madame de Tourvel on the naked backside of the courtesan Emilie, the detective – and before him the criminal – writes his story on the ever available body of the victim.[5]

Following this train of thought, it is apparent that the detective is always male, always in the dominant position in the pairing. Consequently, we see the dilemma writers have faced in using a biological female in a definitionally male space. The result has been to call into question at least one side of the phrase 'woman detective,' rendering it an oxymoron. If female, then not detective; if detective, then not really female. Or perhaps I should say she either is or is not Woman. After all, the definition of that representation allows for no deviations; Woman is the patriarchal construction which women refuse to honour at considerable risk of erasure, of silencing.

But what would happen if this dualistic universe were suddenly and unceremoniously dismantled by the insistent presence of a C term? How do the relationships between the two terms shift when a third is posited; what happens to detective fiction when its organizing structures are challenged? Suppose that Man/Woman gave way to Man/Woman/not-Woman?[6]

In her 1981 article 'One Is Not Born a Woman,' Monique Wittig echoes Simone de Beauvoir's famous dictum in *The Second Sex* 'One is not born a woman, but rather *becomes* one.' But Wittig is not merely redundant. Extending de Beauvoir, she insists on the following: First, the purportedly natural categorization by sex functions politically to serve the economic needs of heterosexuality – that is, reproduction. Because feminists have argued against the false-natural claims for gendering and emphasized the political and economic purposes served therein, it is Wittig's second claim which opens new grounds for consideration: A lesbian is not a woman. A lesbian is, in fact, a third sex, a C term. Wittig's argument goes like this: 'Woman' is a term which exists only as the subordinate, B term in a binary and oppositional relationship to 'man.' The relationship is implicitly heterosexual and constructs the patriarchy (and is constructed by it) as heterosexual. In refusing heterosexuality, a lesbian is outside that binary and by her very presence destabilizes the heterosexual contract and imperative.[7] If 'man' calls forth 'woman' but does not call forth 'lesbian,' then there are forces outside patriarchal control which implicitly challenge its institutionalization and, by extension, must be eliminated.[8] In a system whose continuing existence and success relies on binary opposition, the duality cannot tolerate any attempts to transform it into a triad.

Initially, it may seem that the lesbian is identified by what she is not or what she does not do. Not a part of the heterosexual contract, the lesbian is not an available means of production; she is not a bartering tool. The lesbian withdraws her body – and its reproductive capacity – from the power structure. In a system where 'have the body' is a legal as well as social right, her body is not available. In the legal meaning of *habeas cor-*

pus, illegal confinement is prohibited; remedies against it are specified. But as any feminist historian can verify, custom and the law have turned a blind eye to the religious and familial control of women – wives, sisters, daughters. And to go beyond the Anglo-Saxon concept of *habeas corpus* only brings us back to Rubin's analysis of women as items of exchange in preindustrialized societies. No escape, it would seem. But the lesbian escapes, though she inevitably pays a heavy price; and, I would argue, she is more accurately identified by what she is than what she is not. The lesbian is a disruption, a wild card ... a joker. Her existence is a challenge.

The emphasis on *corpus* in the term *habeas corpus* – whether the actual legal sense of the term or my misplaced reading of corpse – focuses attention on the body as the carrier of identity of a person. Yet to return to the mind/body split reminds us that Western culture has always acknowledged the thinking process as the measure of a person: I think, therefore I am. But if to think is to be rational, in Western culture, to be rational is to be male. And so to be defined by the not-mind is to be categorized by the body, and that is to be seen as not male. In such a not-male over-characterization, lesbians too are 'of the body,' as are heterosexual women who reproduce. But the not-male, not-female lesbian of Wittig is also not-body, because she opts out of the reproductive treadmill. Not-mind, not-body, not-male, not-female: lesbian subjectivity.

But what, you ask, of feminism and detective fiction? If the binary of gender – male/female – can be thrown off track by the introduction of a third term – lesbian – then so too can the apparently unchanging pairs of criminal/victim and detective/criminal. If the non-negotiably male space of the detective is invaded by a lesbian detective, then arguably the fiction in which she operates could be a very different narrative. Such a disruption of the traditional, masculinist, linear, rational, or active formula could transform detective fiction in ways which I call feminist.[9] If detective, criminal, victim are not either-or identities but fluctuating subjectivities, if crime is both criminal and legal, if detection is both discovery and concealment, what then is detective fiction?

One of the most successful sub-genres of detective fiction since the late 1970s has been predicated on detectives who are not-Woman; and the category, once familiar only to a group of self-selected readers, has entered the mainstream. Now, not only Naiad, Daughters, Spinsters–Aunt Lutie, and Seal but also St Martin's publish lesbian detective fiction. But as one of my students plaintively asked, 'Is this really detective fiction?' Yes, Virginia ... and no. To answer that question, I want to consider Barbara Wilson's three novels about Pam Nilsen: *Murder in the Collective*, *Sisters of the Road*, and *The Dog Collar Murders*.[10] Bonnie Zimmerman notes that detective fiction has been the most popular lesbian adventure genre since the earliest publications in 1977, replacing the science fiction or utopian novel as the quintessential lesbian genre. She sees that the association between danger or evil and the heterosexual, male-dominated world fits the expectations of both lesbian and detective fiction readers. Zimmerman's reservations about the sub-genre are that the characters and landscape are seldom believable, and that the formula forestalls surprise or inventive endings (210–11). However, I would argue that in Barbara Wilson's novels neither of these caveats applies, and furthermore that Wilson's artful manipulation of the conventions of detective fiction, which challenges the genre at both its surface and its core, are a direct result of the lesbian detective and lesbian fiction.[11]

Although it is entirely artificial to do so, I want to separate – for the purpose of argument only – the detective from the fiction, the character from the narrative. A crucial element in Wilson's successful creation of a new kind of feminist detective fiction is her capacity to blend the two; other examples of lesbian detective fiction tend to focus more on the protagonist and the motives of the crime without challenging the formula and its conservative message.[12] Wilson's fiction gives readers a model so distinctive that some may be inclined to reject it – 'not detective fiction.'

In each of the novels, Pam Nilsen grapples with her sexuality and with criminality; neither issue is resolved conventionally. From the outset, Nilsen is defined as a character whose contradictions undermine the anticipated roles of lesbian and detective. Although an amateur detective who investigates murders in all three novels, Pam learns that pinpointing the killers does not necessarily mean solving the crimes. Wilson insists vigorously that there can be no return to social innocence through the detective's efforts. Thinking of herself as a temporarily unattached heterosexual, Pam 'comes out' to herself and others in the first novel; but there is never the happy ending of a conventional romance. Numerous critics have pointed out the liminal position which the detective occupies in the novel's society; operating between the innocent and the guilty, the detective becomes society's surrogate in dealing with the criminal.[13] His willingness to move closer to evil allows others to keep their distance. But in this position the detective becomes more like his prey than like those whom he protects; the detective parallels the criminal. When the detective is female, the criminality takes on an aura of inevitability; descendants of Eve, all women are wrongdoers, lawbreakers. Furthermore, in breaking social taboos by attempting to take over male position and prerogatives, women detectives emphasize their deviancy, their distance from the proper role of Woman. When the female detective is also a lesbian, her transgressive behaviour multiplies exponentially. By religious dictates, her sexual behaviour and orientation are sinful; according to laws in many countries, her actions are illegal. If closeted, she risks exposure and punishment; if out, she faces homophobic discrimination. In her essence and merely by her existence, the detective who is lesbian approaches the positionality of a criminal to an extent which a heterosexual male detective can reach only if his actions are truly beyond the law.

In the first novel, *Murder in the Collective*, Pam explicitly decides to work against the sanctioned legal establishment. When the collective's cameraman, Jeremy, is killed in their darkroom, the most likely suspects are either other collective members or the lesbians of B. Violet Typesetting, which had been proposing a merger with Best Printing. Pam's detection is motivated by concern for both groups, but her investigation of B. Violet is also connected with her growing interest in lesbians. She hides a frightened suspect in her attic although sure that Zee would not have committed murder; later, when she learns that Zee is the killer, Pam and the other women decide to shield Zee. From Zee, the others learn that Jeremy had probably been a CIA agent who infiltrated the Philippine anti-Marcos movement; certainly he had married Zee, a Filipina, to obtain access to some of the rebels in the United States. But Jeremy was killed for more than betraying his friends and the freedom movement: Zee shot him to prevent his abusing one of the collective members, whom he was blackmailing. She explains: 'He was saying he had asked Elena to bring him a hundred dollars, but maybe he wouldn't make her pay. He said he would tell her that if she fucked with him that he would forget it. He had never fucked with a lesbian before, he said. He was telling me the things he would like to do with her' (178). Without reservation, the three women who hear Zee's story agree to protect her. She is not the criminal. From their refusal to provide fingerprint samples to the investigating police through their attempts to hide prime suspects to their decision to stonewall the investigation, Pam and her friends recognize implicitly that there is no innocent society, no safe legal system, and no benevolent government on which to depend. The victim, with his CIA and Marcos-army connections, was more evil than the woman who killed him. But the so-called justice system would have disagreed. So they bypass the system; they do not kill in retribution (one kind of eye-for-eye justice), but they safeguard the truly not-guilty.

In the second and third novels, Wilson increases the difficulty of deciding right from wrong by intensifying the ambiguity; Pam finds herself in the middle of arguments with no easy answers. In *Sisters of the Road*, a young black prostitute is murdered – by her pimp, as we discover – and her friend, another prostitute who has witnessed the murder, is in danger. Pam's search for the still living fifteen-year-old eventually nets her the murderer as well, but solving that crime is clearly not her priority. In searching for Trish, Pam encounters child abuse and neglect, which she and the novel unequivocally condemn. But Trish has escaped from home into prostitution, which is not so easily pigeon-holed. Pam finds that women she respects do not share a single position on prostitution: a lawyer who supports decriminalization leaves her 'trying to grab hold of an argument and feeling almost defeated before I began by her energy' (132); a satisfied prostitute 'could have been the loquacious lady at my dry cleaner's' (144). But the lawyer hedges – 'Sometimes I'm as full of bullshit as my clients' (148) – and the prostitute has an investment in what she does. So Pam feels 'like I've just had a shock treatment ... What kind of theoretical arguments can you put up against the reality of someone's life?' (147).

The stakes in heteroglossic arguments come closer to home when an anti-pornography, lesbian activist is murdered during a conference on women and sexuality in *The Dog Collar Murders*. Pam listens to all sides of a debate which includes feminists against pornography, feminists against censorship, lesbian sado-masochists, Christian fundamentalists, legalistic moderates, and more. What is pornographic and what erotic? For Pam, personal and political collide when she discovers herself both aroused and outraged. Suddenly, it is not merely the role of the detective which is liminal but also that of the woman, that of the not-Woman lesbian, which is equally suspended between conflicting versions of the world; if the fictional detective often has to do wrong to achieve right, where then is Pam, who sees beyond the oppositional discourse of right and wrong?

Unlike the conventional detectives – both amateur and hard-boiled – Pam does not have a 'code' which provides comforting answers. The isolation which male detectives seem unable to escape because of their liminal position is rejected by lesbian detectives, who find or create a small but safe community for themselves.[14] Consequently, they are, in Carol Gilligan's terms, operating in the area not of rights but of responsibilities. For Pam, the impact of her actions on others dominates her *modus operandi*. From the opening page of *Murder in the Collective*, Pam's style is made clear: she is the meeting's facilitator – 'It was something I was usually good at: understanding what people meant even when they were floundering' (7). But in the last pages of *The Dog Collar Murders*, the limits of her style for detecting are also clarified: 'It's my old problem of making the final argument I suppose. I can't summarize and resolve things. The nearest I seem to get is making everyone so nervous with my questions that I precipitate events' (202). Surrounded by her extended family and friends at that moment, Pam is the antithesis of the lone-knight or the gentleman detective. She is as far from Sam Spade or Sherlock Holmes as her lesbian house-warming is from her heterosexual sister's wedding – 'a little bit like' and 'the nearest *we'll* get' (202).

The references to house-warmings and weddings bring us to the heart of the lesbian detective's transgressive behaviour. Virtually every series in which the sleuth is a lesbian includes her 'coming out' story.[15] Often the novels blend, as does *Murder in the Collective*, the character's investigation of crime and her discovery of her sexuality in parallel and intersecting narratives. Frequently, the 'coming out' is the detective's discovery of her own lesbianism; often it includes acknowledging her sexuality to friends and family. Such a statement brings cultural norms and expectations into the open; the character forces others to acknowledge their sexual positions and their attitudes towards difference. But it can also bring fear of unwanted exposure.[16] Just as identity politics requires self-disclosure, detective investigations reveal what would be kept secret: detecting is like 'outing.' Does this provide contradictory or logical connections between 'lesbian' and 'detective'?

The plot of *The Dog Collar Murders* hinges on multiple varieties of outing. The characters' motives are varied, but all believe that their acceptance in the specific communities they prefer will be undercut if their 'deviance' is revealed; some are willing to kill to maintain their secrets. But what they are anxious to hide is surprising and ironic: lesbianism, sado-masochism, acting in pornographic films, and heterosexual marriage. Pam's contrasting openness is offered as a model of alternative behaviour for which she is rewarded. Her lesbian identity is public knowledge; her investigation of pornography is tolerant and relatively non-judgmental; she works to keep her jealousy – both of her lover's friends and of her sister's marriage – under control. In a detective narrative, secrets exist to be uncovered: those which have been motives for crime are revealed in the process of identifying the criminal; but often those which are merely embarrasing are also disclosed by the investigation. As Wilson's narrative of investigation gradually unfolds the secrets of the characters, her lesbian narrative rewards Pam's self-disclosures and disinterested curiosity by bringing her romance to a satisfying – if non-traditional – closure.[17]

What is perhaps the most shocking moment in the series comes towards the end of *Sisters of the Road*, when Pam is raped by the pimp-and-murderer she had been looking for.[18] In the tradition of amateur detectives, violence against the detective is typically minimal and off-stage. In hard-boiled fiction, the detective is frequently beaten up and sometimes shot; although sexually harassed as a matter of course, none of the new women detectives faces rape.[19] Victims in village novels are sometimes 'interfered with'; in the newer explorations of child abuse and incest, suspects (who often prove to be murderers) have been victimized. Rape or the threat of it is sometimes used by criminals to control witnesses who might otherwise assist the detective. But raped detective is, understandably, an oxymoron. If, in the binary division of detective/criminal, the placement of the terms is paralleled with the gender binary of male/female, then the rape to be inferred is male rape. The necessary circumlocution of 'male rape' versus simply 'rape' indicates how far from the norm the former is, both in reality and in cultural perception. Rape transforms the detective into a victim, moves him from the dominant position to the subordinate one in the power struggle and the linguistic configuration (criminal/victim). Consequently, Pam's rape violates the normative standards for the narrative of investigation. Unfortunately, it is a classic feature of the female narrative, whether lesbian or heterosexual. Wilson underscores both the power and the homophobia of the rapist: '"Bitch, cunt lezzie, pervert, whore, how do you like this, you fucking dyke." The cocaine and his fury made him demonic; he slapped my face over and over and thrust into me again and again. It seemed endless; a world of pain spread through my back, down my legs. I felt that whatever made Pam a person, whatever I knew or had known about myself was being crushed out of me, was spinning into fragments like a planet smashed by meteors' (194). The violence to a woman's essence as well as to her body which rape represents would destroy the heroic position of a detective in his narrative. The authority and control which, despite setbacks, detectives exercise are called into question here.[20] This moment encapsulates but does not delimit the challenge which Barbara Wilson's Pam Nilsen series offers to the detective genre.

Wilson's reconfiguration of the detective genre can be found in both terms of that phrase; her 'detective,' as I have just demonstrated, is a challenge to the formulation represented in either the classic or the hard-boiled modes. Her re-visioning of the genre – that is, of the narrative conventions – is equally striking. The risks which Wilson is willing to take need to be matched by openness from readers and critics; it is time, perhaps past time, to reconsider how rigidly the conventions control the genre. If the Pam Nilsen novels are read as 'not really detective fiction,' then the opportunity for re-examining assumptions about readers' expectations is lost or abandoned. Wilson's intertextual references, both explicit and implicit, to the range of detective fiction from Poe to Christie to Chandler to Wilson make clear her grounding in the genre and her willingness to depart from it. Some might argue that what she produces is a detective who is not quite a detective (certainly not a conventionally successful one), criminals who might be victims, crimes which are as much a function of society's structuring as of the criminals' malfeasance, and a solution which does not resolve the problems. Is it detective fiction? Well, yes and no. And that's what makes these novels interesting, provocative, surprising (*pace* Zimmerman), and feminist.

The satisfaction of the classic detective novel with solutions to criminal behaviour which depended on the security of police action, legal systems, and judicial disinterestedness to produce a return to the edenic world that had been disrupted by crime was rightly critiqued by the hard-boiled initiators. Perhaps in making their point, Raymond Chandler and his cronies overstated the cosiness of the house-party mysteries of their competition and similarly overstated their own gritty realism. But the optimistic kind of conclusion to detective novels, singling out the criminal and reifying the innocent, has not disappeared but merely changed configuration. The detectives of such hard-boiled authors as Robert B. Parker or Andrew Vachss recognize that the world is corrupt in ways they cannot hope to change; they settle for intervention on a small scale. They kill a few bad guys, save an innocent or two, lose an innocent or two, scare almost everyone in their path, and conclude that they've done their best, lived up to their code. Wilson's novels situate the battleground in an altogether different locale. Pam Nilsen investigates the old-fashioned, unaffiliated criminal: a blackmailer, a pimp, murderers who kill from greed or to protect their secrets. With the exception of Jeremy Plaice in *Murder in the Collective*, who is killed because of his blackmailing, none has an organization or even a few homeboys on his or her side. In the great American tradition, they apparently act as individuals. But Wilson's revisionistic narratives short-circuit that assumption; these criminals and their crimes are woven more deeply into the fabric of American culture than organized crime or street gangs or chain letters. They *are* the culture, not some malevolent force which has wormed its way into society and taken over; they represent and are represented by the cornerstones of American life and institutions. The crimes which Pam solves are ancillary to the hidden crimes which underpin them and which are protected from solution: imperialism, racism, homophobia, misogyny, sexism, sadism, incest, self-righteousness, religiosity. The laws against rape, pornography, prostitution, blackmail, and even murder have little effect against the cultural behaviour which engenders them. The crimes which exist before the crimes which are committed are not resolved in the simplistic solutions of the latter; but perhaps even those solutions are not resolutions. In terms of conventional detective fiction, order cannot be restored because it has not existed; the status quo is preserved, but the novels explicitly call into question whether or not it is worth saving. At the conclusion of *Sisters of the Road*, Pam tackles her fears and goes skydiving; in order to return to the world, she must escape – however temporarily – the world. Only in the dimension of space can she be free; but this momentary solution is an individual one. All three of the novels are as open-ended as Pam's free fall.

Wilson's indictment of conventional detective fiction is also clear in each of the three novels. In *Sisters of the Road*, Pam's rape is halted by the arrival of her friend June and several state troopers. June attacks the rapist while the police – guardians of law and order – stop her from killing him. And one of them, Pam is sure, 'was turned on' by seeing her 'degraded and exposed.' She says, 'I remember the secret glint in the officer's eyes; I can't seem to forget it' (195). And the rape's aftermath is not so quickly dismissed as the beatings and woundings of the hard-boiled detectives: in *The Dog Collar Murders*, Pam speaks of her time in therapy, learning to deal with the violation. Genre fiction's inadequate narrative conventions are first underscored in *Murder in the Collective*: teamed with her new lover, Hadley, Pam urges the most likely suspect to get out of town and hides the next likely one in her attic. But she discovers with some pain that crime solving doesn't take place in a vacuum; instead, the two suspects confront and comfort each other. Pam feels excluded: 'June's sense of direction had been as keen or keener than ours, but she hadn't pursued Zee like a detective, she'd confronted her like a woman and stayed to comfort her like a friend' (179). The model of Holmes and Watson, a.k.a. Pam and Hadley, is an empty, hierarchical, masculinist void. When Pam and her infant niece are almost drowned by the two-time killer in *The Dog Collar Murders*, Pam justifies her inappropriate gather-the-suspects scenario unconvincingly: '"The police had their suspect," I said. "I didn't think I'd convince you unless I had a confession that had been witnessed by a whole group of people. And anyway," I said, "Hercule Poirot did it. Lots of times"' (199). Wilson has not published a Pam Nilsen detective adventure since *The Dog Collar Murders*; but she has written another so-called detective novel, which is more like a romp through Barcelona on a search for missing persons in plain sight, and a similar adventure set in Transylvania.

Structurally, Wilson deliberately undercuts the narrative fluidity of the genre. Since the early examples of Edgar Allan Poe and Arthur Conan Doyle, the detective's investigation has led inexorably through red herrings to the single, unchallenged explanation of the crime and positive identification of the murderer. The convention was so strong that in 1913 in *Trent's Last Case*, E.C. Bentley could mock the form by making his detective – gasp! – wrong before finally allowing him to succeed. Consequently, readers perceive what the dust cover on Sue Grafton's *'I' Is for Innocent* calls seamless fiction. One authoritative voice and one infallible solution are required; the detective alone holds the alpha position as the binaries of crime solving are unfolded. Borrowing what Joanna S. Frye calls a 'community of voices' and M.M. Bakhtin has labelled 'heteroglossia,' Wilson refuses to allow Pam to speak unassailably. Instead, a multitude of voices discuss, argue, and debate the U.S. presence in the Philippines, the decriminalization of prostitution, and lesbian sadomasochism; and the multiplicity of irreducible positions increases as the series progresses. *Murder in the Collective* ends with a bibliography 'For Further Information on the Philippines, on Filipinos in America, and on the Role of Women in Developing Countries' (182–3). By *The Dog Collar Murders*, the references are scattered throughout, beginning with a quotation from Foucault's *The History of Sexuality* whose opening phrase announces Wilson's enterprise: 'But more important was the multiplication of discourses concerning sex in the field of exercise of power itself: an institutional incitement to speak about it, and to do so more and more; a determination on the part of the agencies of power to hear it spoken about, and to cause *it* to speak through explicit articulation and endlessly accumulated detail' (2). In typical feminist fashion, Wilson blows the power structure of detective fiction wide open. Nobody controls the centre of discourse; discourse becomes discourses.

Not all Wilson's critics have been sympathetic to this de-centring effort. Although Lyn Pykett recognizes Wilson's role in revamping the detective novel, she levels the charge of 'a slight preachiness' at *The Dog Collar Murders*, concluding that the epigraph from Foucault suggests that Wilson is 'more interested in polemics than in mystery plotting' (1098). Maureen T. Reddy echoes Pykett when she writes, 'Both the author and her character seem much more interested in exploring the various feminist positions in the pornography debate than they are in investigating the murder of anti-porn activist Loie Marsh, resulting in a lack of plot balance that seriously undermines the novel' (177). After a longer critique of the novel's lack of seamless attention to crime solving, Reddy does acknowledge the possibility that Wilson's strategy is deliberate, an attempt to reflect women's realities. One element of that strategy is posited by Maggie Humm; writing of the disruption of diachronic thinking and linear chronology, she notes that Wilson's books 'are structured by the progress of character development and character relationships, not by a single-minded progress to the crime solution' (246). This, she concludes, represents resistance to both social power and a major aspect of the generic form. The theories of reader-response criticism offer a different perspective for assessing Wilson's challenge to the conventional formula.

Despite the popularity of detective fiction, no serious and extended study of readers comparable to Janice Radway's feminist ethnography of romance readers in *Reading the Romance* has been done. In Ronald G. Walker and June M. Frazer's *The Cunning Craft*, which is subtitled *Original Essays on Detective Fiction and Contemporary Literary Theory*, only one of the fourteen essays is based on reader-response approaches. Yet there is virtually no such thing as a totally inexperienced Anglo-American reader of detective fiction; television, movies, and cultural references all borrow from the conventions – which is how my students, who solemnly assure me they don't read detective fiction, can announce that *Sisters of the Road* isn't really a detective novel. Knowing what to expect of the genre but not finding it in a novel marketed as detective fiction makes an unusual set of demands on the readers. In fact, what might be called the 'rough join' of Wilson's multiple narratives in all three novels offers an explicit invitation to readers. In the theories of Wolfgang Iser, the novel and the reader come together to form a reading, creating this full-fledged composition as the reader fills in what Pierre Macherey would call 'gaps' in the text. The spaces or ellipses which Wilson consciously creates are found around the debates, lectures, and bibliography which are so unexpected in detective fiction; the gaps she less blatantly leaves centre around sexism, homophobia, law-and-order, imperialism, and racism. The openings she unconsciously leaves depend on the readers' expectations of the genre; their experiences, biases, preferences, and pleasures help them to create a text which satisfies (even if negatively) their desires. The ties between feminist criticism and reader-response theory are obvious: both acknowledge and empower the reader equally with the author, the text, and the critics. And in so doing they destroy another conventional binary: text/reader (sometimes perceived as writer/reader or critic/reader).

I want to conclude by looking at Wilson's handling of what psychologists insist is the most central human binary: self/other. In *The Reproduction of Mothering*, Nancy Chodorow distinguishes between girls' and boys' discovery of self in recognizing their distance from the mother: girls, she says, because they are not 'different' from the women who first nurture them (typically mothers), separate more slowly and never as completely as boys. Pam Nilsen is a twenty-nine-year-old orphan; her relationship with her mother will continue one-sided. But Pam is also a twin, merged in the womb with her identically initialled sister, Penny Nilsen. In the years immediately after their parents' death, the two share a business, a house, and (consecutively) a lover as they had earlier shared childhood. The three novels chart the individuation of the sisters through a range of experiences and politics but particularly through their sexuality; by the end of the series, Penny has had a child and married the shared lover while Pam has reunited with her first lesbian lover and bought a shared house. But the bond of twinning means that there will always be a 'Pam and Penny' as well as 'Pam' and 'Penny': individual yet merged, separate as well as joined, self *and* other.

There are numerous arguments to make for the feminism of Barbara Wilson's detective fiction series; other critics have made them elsewhere, as have I. But in challenging the simplistic and limiting practice of dichotomizing culture, she strikes at the root of patriarchy and its institutions (which include conventional detective fiction). By exposing the narrative practices of the genre, she undercuts its power to define itself. Wilson could have chosen to write a feminist novel, a lesbian novel, a coming out story without also writing a detective novel; but she chose not to abandon the most popular fictional ground. Instead, she wrote her own strategy, unwrote the existing customs, and established the prospect of an exciting and challenging new game.

NOTES

I want to thank the numerous students with whom I read *Sisters of the Road* for their insights, especially Tammy Aiello, Tracey Bloom, Jane Moore, Susan Norris, and Kathleen Oser.

1 To be fair, Sayers never uses *habeas corpus,* although she does have Lord Peter Wimsey refer to 'have his carcase' and the 'Have-His-Carcase Act.'

2 I surveyed ten college-educated friends, to find that none knew the official definition of *habeas corpus;* seven mis-defined it as I had.

3 See Klein and Keller on the contradictions between the conventions and the actual fiction.

4 The link between the criminal and the detective is discussed in Klein and Keller ii.

5 Before I had seen either the Broadway production or the Hollywood film, Nancy K. Miller had pointed to the importance of this scene in a presentation; unfortunately, I cannot now locate the exact reference.

6 Farwell's discussion of Marion Zimmer Bradley's *The Mists of Avalon* helped me to conceptualize some of the issues in lesbian fiction.

7 Findlay and deLauretis rightly emphasize that just as there are many feminisms, so there are many varieties of lesbianism.

8 See Butler 112 ff.

9 Even Roger Bromley's essay on Joseph Hansen's gay male detective Dave Brandstetter shows the influence of disruptive feminist examinations of gender naturalization.

10 See Glover and Kaplan's discussion in *Cultural Studies* as well as Glover's earlier contrast between *Sisters of the Road* and Robert B. Parker's *Ceremony.*

11 Wilson has emphasized the difficulty of publishing lesbian-feminist work: 'It's important to remember how very little lesbian literature was available up until the late seventies, and how little has been published by mainstream New York houses. Homophobia still plays a great role in suppressing the work of lesbian writers' (Letter).

12 See Cranny-Francis 176 for a discussion of the failure of hard-boiled detective fiction to encompass difference.

13 See Rabinowitz 20 for a discussion of the detective's position, albeit it in a different context.

14 For example, as in the novels of Nikki Baker, M.F. Beal (*Angel Dance*), Lauren Wright Douglas, Sara Dreher, Katherine V. Forrest, Claire McNabb, Valerie Miner (*Murder in the English Department*), Mary Morrel (*Final Session*), Maria-Antonia Oliver, and J.M. Redmann.

15 See Reddy ch. 6 on coming out stories.

16 This is especially true for the police detectives created by Claire McNabb and Katherine V. Forrest.

17 The 'non-traditional' ending here is not the lesbian commitment but the clever device of two homes in one house.

18 Glover notes that 'the all-pervasive presence of male violence acts as a brake upon the narrative, a limit upon movement and access, threatening to hold the investigation back by transforming the heroine into a victim, interrogating the meaning of suspense in the process' (80).

19 The only detectives I've encountered who were actually raped are Angela Harpe, the black protagonist of James D. Lawrence's four 1970s soft-porn novels, and Julie Hayes, in Dorothy Salisbury Davis's series. Elizabeth Bowers's Meg Lacy and Sandra Scoppettone's Lauren Laurano were raped before their careers as private eyes started. However, there may be characters and novels which I do not know.

20 Kathleen Oser's pointed questions about rape's undermining the woman detective's apparent competence helped me to rethink this segment of the novel.

WORKS CITED

Bakhtin, M.M. *The Dialogic Imagination: Four Essays*. Trans. Carl Emerson and Michael Holquist. Ed. Michael Holquist. Austin: University of Texas Press, 1982.

Black, Henry C. *Black's Law Dictionary*. St Paul, Minn.: West, 1979.

Bromley, Roger. 'Rewriting the Masculine Script: The Novels of Joseph Hansen.' *Gender, Genre, and Narrative Pleasure*. Ed. Derek Longhurst. London: Unwin Hyman, 1989. 102–17.

Butler, Judith. *Gender Trouble: Feminism and the Subversion of Identity*. New York: Routledge, 1990.

Chodorow, Nancy. *The Reproduction of Mothering*. Berkeley: University of California Press, 1978.

Cranny-Francis, Anne. *Feminist Fiction*. New York: St Martin's, 1990.

De Beauvoir, Simone. *The Second Sex*. Trans. H.M. Parshley. New York: Bantam, 1961.

deLauretis, Teresa. 'Sexual Indifference and Lesbian Representation.' *Theatre Journal* 40.2 (May 1988): 155–77.

Farwell, Marilyn R. 'Heterosexual Plots and Lesbian Subtexts: Toward a Theory of Lesbian Narrative Space.' *Lesbian Texts and Contexts: Radical Revisions*. Ed. Karla Jay and Joanne Glasgow. New York: New York University Press, 1990. 91–103.

Findlay, Heather. 'Is There a Lesbian in This Text? Derrida, Wittig, and the Politics of the Three Women.' *Coming to Terms: Feminism, Theory, Politics*. Ed. Elizabeth Weed. New York: Routledge, 1989. 59–69.

Frye, Joanne S. *Living Stories, Telling Lives: Women and the Novel in Contemporary Experience*. Ann Arbor: University of Michigan Press, 1986.

Gilligan, Carol. *In a Different Voice*. Cambridge: Harvard University Press, 1982.

Glover, David. 'The Stuff That Dreams Are Made Of: Masculinity, Femininity, and the Thriller.' *Gender, Genre, and Narrative Pleasure*. Ed. Derek Longhurst. London: Unwin Hyman, 1989. 67–83.

– , and Cora Kaplan. 'Guns in the House of Culture? Crime Fiction and the Politics of the Popular.' *Cultural Studies*. Ed. Lawrence Grossberg, Cary Nelson, and Paula Treichler. New York: Routledge, 1992. 213–26.

Humm, Maggie. 'Feminist Detective Fiction.' *Twentieth Century Suspense*. Ed. Clive Bloom. London: Macmillan, 1990. 237–54.

Iser, Wolfgang. 'The Reading Process: A Phenomenological Approach.' *Reader Response Criticism*. Ed. Jane P. Tomkins. Baltimore: Johns Hopkins University Press, 1980. 50–69.

Klein, Kathleen Gregory. *The Woman Detective: Gender and Genre*. Urbana and Chicago: University of Illinois Press, 1988.

– , and Joseph Keller. 'Deductive Detective Fiction: The Self-Destructive Genre.' *Genre* 19.2: 155–72.

Macherey, Pierre. *A Theory of Literary Production*. London: Routledge and Kegan Paul, 1978.

Moi, Toril. *Sexual/Textual Politics: Feminist Literary Theory*. London and New York: Methuen, 1985.

Oxford English Dictionary. Compact ed. Vol. 1. New York: Oxford University Press, 1971.

Porter, Dennis. *The Pursuit of Crime: Art and Ideology in Detective Fiction*. New Haven: Yale University Press, 1981.

Pykett, Lyn. 'Barbara Wilson.' *Twentieth Century Crime and Mystery Writers*. 3d ed. Ed. Lesley Henderson. London: St James, 1991. 1097–8.

Rabinowitz, Peter J. 'Chandler Comes to Harlem: Racial Politics in the Thrillers of Chester Himes.' *The Sleuth and the Scholar: Origins, Evolution, and Current Trends in Detective Fiction*. Ed. Barbara A. Rader and Howard G. Zettler. Westport, Conn.: Greenwood, 1988. 19–30.

Reddy, Maureen T. 'The Feminist Counter-Tradition in Crime: Cross, Grafton, Paretsky, and Wilson.' In Walker and Frazer 174–87.

– *Sisters in Crime: Feminism and the Crime Novel*. New York: Continuum, 1988.

Rubin, Gayle. 'The Traffic in Women: Notes on the 'Political Economy of Sex.' *Towards an Anthropology of Women*. Ed. Rayna R. Reiter. New York: Monthly Review Press, 1975.

Sayers, Dorothy L. *Have His Carcase*. 1932. New York: Avon, 1968.

Walker, Ronald G., and June M. Frazer, eds. *The Cunning Craft: Original Essays on Detective Fiction and Contemporary Literary Theory.* Macomb: Western Illinois University Press, 1990.

Wilson, Barbara. *The Dog Collar Murders.* Seattle: Seal, 1989.

– Letter to Kathleen Gregory Klein. 15 April 1992.

– *Murder in the Collective.* Seattle: Seal, 1984.

– *Sisters of the Road.* Seattle: Seal, 1986.

Wittig, Monique. 'One Is Not Born a Woman.' *The Straight Mind and Other Essays.* By Wittig. Boston: Beacon, 1992. 9–20.

Zimmerman, Bonnie. *The Safe Sea of Women: Lesbian Fiction, 1969–1989.* Boston: Beacon, 1990.

Contributors

SueEllen Campbell is author of *The Enemy Opposite: The Outlaw Criticism of Wyndham Lewis*. She teaches twentieth-century literature, literary theory, and environmental literature at Colorado State University, Fort Collins, Colorado.

Scott Christianson has published a variety of essays on popular culture. He teaches English at Radford University, Radford, Virginia.

Glenwood Irons edited *Second Language Acquisition: Selected Readings in Theory and Practice* and *Gender, Language, and Myth: Essays on Popular Narrative* and is co-author of *La phonétique comparée du français et de l'anglais nord américain*. He teaches applied linguistics and communications studies at Brock University, St Catharines, Ontario.

Kathleen Gregory Klein is author of the award-winning book *The Woman Detective: Gender and Genre*. She is editor of *Great Women Mystery Writers: Classic to Contemporary* and *Women Times Three: Writers, Detectives, Readers*. She is a member of the advisory boards of *Twentieth Century Crime and Mystery Fiction*, the *Oxford Companion to Crime and Mystery Writing*, and *Clues: A Journal of Detection*. She teaches English and women's studies at Southern Connecticut State University, New Haven, Connecticut.

Susan J. Leonardi is author of *Dangerous by Degrees: Women at Oxford and the Somerville College Novelists*. She teaches English at the University of Maryland, College Park, Maryland.

Bobbie Ann Mason is author of numerous works of fiction and criticism.

Nicola Nixon has published essays on cyberpunk science fiction and on Jean Rhys. She is a SSHRC post-doctoral fellow in the English department at the University of Toronto.

Rebecca A. Pope is author of various articles on popular culture and literary theory. She teaches English at Georgetown University, Washington, D.C.

Jeanne Addison Roberts is author of numerous publications on Shakespeare and Milton, including *Shakespeare's English Comedy:* The Merry Wives of Windsor *in Context* and *The Shakespearean Wild: Geography, Genus, and Gender.* She is Professor of Literature at the American University, Washington, D.C.

Joan Warthling Roberts is author of *Sicily and Naples, or the Fatal Union: A Tragedy, by S. Harding.* She teaches English at SUNY College, Buffalo, New York.

Sandra Tomc has published a variety of essays on contemporary and nineteenth-century American culture and is currently at work on a study of the ethic of idleness among antebellum authors. She teaches English at the University of British Columbia, Vancouver, British Columbia.

Ann Wilson teaches in the Department of Drama at the University of Guelph, Guelph, Ontario. She has published works on contemporary Canadian, British, and American drama and recently edited *Howard Brenton: A Casebook.* She is co-editor, with Harry Lane, of *Essays in Theatre / Etudes Théâtrales.*